W9-AWR-040

Global Software Teams

Collaborating Across Borders and Time Zones

Erran Carmel

Prentice Hall PTR
Upper Saddle River, NJ 07458
http://www.phptr.com

ISBN 0-13-924218-X

9 780139 242182

90000

Library of Congress Cataloging-in-Publication Data

Carmel, Erran.
    Global software teams: collaborating across borders and time zones/Erran Carmel
      p. cm.
    Includes bibliographical references and index.
    ISBN 0-13-924218-X
    1. Computer software—Development. 2. Transborder data flow.
    I. Title.
    QA76.76.D47C38   1999
    005—dc21   98-53011
                                                  CIP

Editorial/production supervision: *Vincent J. Janoski*
Acquisitions editor: *Michael Meehan*
Marketing manager: *Kaylie Smith*
Manufacturing manager: *Pat Brown*
Cover design director: *Jayne Conte*
Display illustrations: *Don Martinetti*
Interior figures and exhibits: *Erran Carmel & Meg VanArsdale*

© 1999 by Erran Carmel

Published by Prentice Hall P T R
Prentice-Hall, Inc.
Upper Saddle River, NJ 07458

Prentice Hall books are widely used by corporations and government agencies
for training, marketing, and resale.

The publisher offers discounts on this book when ordered in bulk quantities.
For more information, contact: Corporate Sales Department, Phone: 800-382-3419;
Fax: 201-236-7141; E-mail: corpsales@prenhall.com; or write: Prentice Hall P T R,
Corp. Sales Dept., One Lake Street, Upper Saddle River, NJ 07458.

Exhibit 4–1 is reprinted with permission from *Managing the Flow of Technology* by Tom Allen. Cambridge, MA:
MIT Press, 1977. Exhibit 4–4 is reprinted with permission from "Verfone: The Transaction Automation Company
(A)," case 195-088 by Hossam Galal, Donna Stoddard, Richard Nolan, and John Kao. Boston: Harvard Business
School, © 1994 by the President and Fellows of Harvard College. Exhibit 5–3 and exhibit 5–4 are used with
permission from *The Seven Cultures of Capitalism* by Charles Hampden-Turner, © 1993 by Charles Hampden-
Turner. New York, NY: Doubleday, a division of Bantam Doubleday Publishing Company. Chapter 14, "Holiday
Inn's 'A Passage to India,'" is reprinted with permission of Kuldeep Kumar and Leslie P. Willcocks from their co-
authored manuscript entitled: "Offshore Outsourcing. A Country Too Far," Management report, no. 298.
Erasmus University, Rotterdam, Netherlands, November 1996.

All products or services mentioned in this book are the trademarks or service marks of their respective companies or organizations.

Printed in the United States of America
10 9 8 7 6 5 4 3 2 1

ISBN 0-13-924218-X

Prentice-Hall International (UK) Limited, London
Prentice-Hall of Australia Pty. Limited, Sydney
Prentice-Hall Canada Inc., Toronto
Prentice-Hall Hispanoamericana, S.A., Mexico
Prentice-Hall of India Private Limited, New Delhi
Prentice-Hall of Japan, Inc., Tokyo
Simon & Schuster Asia Pte. Ltd., Singapore
Editora Prentice-Hall do Brasil, Ltda., Rio de Janeiro

CONTENTS

ACKNOWLEDGMENTS

My thanks go first to the dozens of developers, managers, and executives interviewed over the course of the study who provided the critical foundation of this book. The interviews were conducted anonymously so I cannot name those involved, but this book represents the collective experiences and wisdom of them all.

At different stages of research and book preparation many colleagues, friends, family, students, and reviewers helped in various ways. My appreciation goes to: Debra Adair, Barbara Bird, Amy Chiu, Judy Cohen, Bill Delone, Frank DuBois, Igor Hawryszkiewycz, Quelina Jordan, Richard Linowes, James McKim, Marty McCaffrey, George Metes, Lore Neumann, Fred Niederman, Madhu Rao, Ed Roche, Steve Sawyer, Eli Shlifer, Varadharajan Sridhar, Juliana Tioanda, and Katherine Zettl-Schaffer.

A special thank you goes to Kuldeep Kumar and Leslie Willcocks for graciously permitting me to use their Holiday Inn case in Chapter 14. I am also grateful for the research support of American University.

. . . And finally, after questioning the routine acknowledgment of spouses that one finds in books, I question it no longer: Pam, thanks for being so patient and understanding.

Erran Carmel
Washington D.C.

The author can be contacted directly at:

Program in Management of Global Information Technology
Kogod College of Business Administration
American University
Washington DC 2001-8044
USA

ecarmel@american.edu

PREFACE

This book is intended for the software professional or software manager who either is about to embark on globalization or has already taken the plunge and is discovering some unforeseen problems. It is designed to help the software professional think about and find solutions for the range of issues specific to global software teams—managerial, behavioral, cultural, and technological.

The book is about global software teams of all kinds, but primarily about those organizations that make *packaged software,* also known as software products. These are software organizations like IBM, Microsoft, SAP, Baan and their thousands of smaller competitors. Parts 1, 2, 3 are written predominately with those organizations in mind. These are the organizations that have been going through a major globalization surge. These are the development organizations that I have been studying over several years. The specific issues of global Information Systems (IS) teams are covered in Part 4. Packaged and IS organizations both develop software, but differ in many key organizational respects. For example, a basic difference is that packaged software organizations develop a product for many customers, while IS units develop a system (not a product) for one customer (albeit very large on occasion). More on these differences appear in Appendix B.

Many of the observations and recommendations in this book are derived from the *Globally Dispersed Software Development* study ("GDSD study" from hereon) of software companies, which I conducted in recent years. The study's research methodology is covered in Appendix A.

It is also important for the reader to know what this book is *not*. There are hundreds of books about teams, from medical teams to government teams. Many of them take an advocacy approach of "teams are wonderful." This book is not about team hyperbole or global hyperbole. It takes a sober-minded look at what is known about teams, culture, and managing software development. Managing global software teams is difficult. The pioneers described in this book are mostly a self-selected group who have a strong interest in making these new ventures succeed. Once the novelty wears thin, many of the difficulties will remain.

This book is also not a primer on technical issues. It assumes some experience with software development, with various collaborative technologies, and with development methodologies. It takes more of a beginner's approach to cultural issues because my assumption is that this will be a first exposure for many readers to this subject.

How to Read this Book

The book is structured in such a way that it can be read in the old-fashioned linear fashion, or it can be used more like a reference book. The reader interested solely in the reference book components ("How to") should skip to Part 3 and Part 4.

Part 1 provides background to the global software team phenomena. Why are so many organizations creating these globally dispersed organizational units? More than a dozen reasons are presented with data in Chapter 1. The reader new to the topic may want to plunge quickly into Chapter 2, which describes three cases of global software teams. Chapter 3 takes the reader to the really difficult managerial question—are these new organizational units successful using measures such as cost and time-to-market?

The bulk of the book is structured using the model of Exhibit P–1. Software globalization is like a centrifugal force that propels things outwards from the center as it disperses developers to the far corners of the world. A centrifugal force must be balanced by centripetal force, a counter force, that is directed into the center. Centrifugal is derived from the Latin "to flee the center," and centripetal, from the Latin "to seek the center." If you take a stone, tie it to a string, and whirl it with your arm, the centrifugal force exerts force outward. The centripetal force, analogous to the string, keeps the team

The centrifugal forces of global software teams

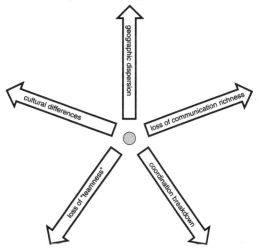

The centripetal forces of global software teams

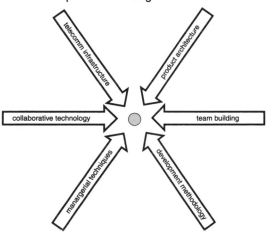

Exhibit P–1 The book's structure

from being launched into a state of disorder and exerts force inward. The centrifugal forces are the five problem areas presented in Part 2. The centripetal forces, the countervailing forces, are presented in Part 3.

Part 2 covers each of the five centrifugal forces—the problems—that pull the global software team apart and inhibit its performance. Chapter 4 includes the first four forces. The first of these is geographic dispersion. It highlights something we know intuitively, that it is harder to manage from a distance. This discussion is followed by two forces that build on the problem of distance. Teamwork depends on a process of coordination, much of it informal, a process that falls apart when teams are dispersed. Communication technology is but an alternative to the richness and satisfaction that comes from communicating face-to-face. With the loss of personal contact, team unity, in a team composed of multiple sites, is hard to achieve. Chapter 5 presents a lengthy treatment of cultural differences and cultural breakdowns. It includes ten important dimensions of national cultural differences as well as a specific focus on cultural differences of software developers in various nations.

Each of the six chapters of Part 3 covers one of the six centripetal forces—the solutions—that pull the global software team together and make it more effective. Chapter 6 discusses the telecommunications infrastructure—the foundation for all the other strategies, techniques, and solutions that come later. Chapter 7 introduces the cement that holds it all together, the collaborative technologies—from groupware, through e-mail, to the family of specialized collaborative technology tools for software engineering. Dispersion means that informal coordination cannot be done the way it used to be done. Coordination must be channeled through all forms of collaborative technologies. Some of the communication can remain informal, but much has to be formalized. Chapter 8 addresses another topic that requires some formalization: the systems development process itself. Ad hoc processes will not work in global teams. The organization needs to select and tailor a development framework and then have all sites subscribe to it. In Chapter 9, we come to the critical issue of product architecture and task allocation. The product architecture needs to be conceived carefully because it must correspond to the architecture of dispersed team sites. The team chapter, Chapter 10, brings human resources into the equation. After all, the software itself can be duplicated quickly. The company's primary competitive edge is its human capital. How do you glue together remote sites to bring them to their highest performance level? This is done by a combination of building trust, conducting kick-off meetings, fostering lateral communication among team members, traveling, and other means. Chapter 11 focuses on global managers and on a potpourri of managerial issues—from team structures, to special metrics measuring the unique characteristics of a global team.

Part 4 shifts to the particular issues of global Information systems (IS) teams. Global corporations are dealing with higher levels of IS cross-border, collaborative development because of increased cooperation between central and subsidiary IS units and the emergence of off-shore outsourcing. Chapter 12 addresses the question and implications of why companies globalize their IS functions. Chapter 13 presents a setp-by-step guide to the Process/System/Responsibility (PSR) methodology for global applications. This methodology helps corporate IS to design the global IS team, but only after comprehensively identifying the corporation's global processes and worldwide systems. Chapter 14, written by Professors Kumar and Willcocks, presents a colorful case study of IS global outsourcing at the US-headquartered hotel chain Holiday Inn. Holiday Inn began its outsourcing by insourcing—using contract software programmers that worked inhouse. At a later phase the contracting staff were moved to India. The different management issues of insourcing versus global outsourcing provide valuable lessons.

A note on convention used throughout the book: a (global software) *team* consists of two or more (geographically dispersed) *sites.*

What Is Unique About *Global* Software Teams?

Any software professional knows that even "normal"—much less "global"—software development is fraught with difficulties. Depending on whose estimates one subscribes to, perhaps half of all systems projects are failures. The entire field of software development, or software engineering, is still going through a maturation process. This book does not attempt to cover all the problems of software development, but rather to highlight the differences between "normal" software development projects (and those people who build them) and global software teams. The list of features that distinguish global software teams from normal (nonglobal) software teams is short and precise: distance (the distance of developers from each other and from their customers or end-users); time-zone differences; and national culture (including language, national traditions, customs, and norms of behavior).

What is unique about global software teams?

Distance

Time zone

National culture

Distance. Geographic distance (dispersion) between development sites has a direct impact on all forms of communication. Communication is less frequent and more constrained. Distance impacts the communication between designer and customer, the communication between two developers, and the communication between development teams and their remote managers. Communication constraints become increasingly significant for software development teams, whether the team's sites are in the same metropolitan area (e.g., Boston–Brookline), within the same country (e.g., Boston–Berkeley), or cross-ocean (e.g., Boston–Bangalore). (The problems of distance are expanded upon in Chapter 4).

Distance affects all manner of coordination and control. In general, managing a team of programmers and designers is dependent on rather minimal controls and commands, relying instead on informal coordination (such as socialization). This kind of coordination is very communication intensive. Of course, once the team is dispersed, this management style fails. Problem solving becomes more difficult. The socialization of teams becomes agonizing—teams do not develop cohesiveness when their members are many kilometers apart. Teams can only slowly come to share a common vision of their work and their products. Project managers become confused with distance: The instinctive mode of supervision by walking around and talking to team members is no longer available. Managers are reduced to managing through milestone charts and once-a-week conference calls and can slowly lose control over the development process. (Loss of "teamness" is explained in Chapter 4).

Distance forces most communication into electronic pipelines of various widths and colors. These pipelines (channels) are not as rich as face-to-face communication. In fact, not only are they not as rich in conveying the message that we wish to convey, but many are asynchronous (such as e-mail, or structured conversations in groupware). While some Western cultures may be somewhat comfortable forming relationships over electronic means such as e-mail, telephone, or video-conferencing, other cultures find these channels extremely uncomfortable unless solid personal relationships have already been formed. (Our desire for more "rich" media when we communicate is covered in Chapter 4).

Time zone differences exacerbate the communication problem. When developers in California and India have no natural overlap of working hours for voice or video conversations, then one side always has to compromise. More practically, almost all communication is channeled through various asynchronous technologies, such as e-mail, or formalized work flow arrangements. (Specific handling of time-zone differences appears in Chapter 10; collaborative technologies are presented in Chapter 7).

National Culture. Perhaps the most confusing intra-team feature is national culture. We use a broad definition of national culture in this book to encompass national and ethnic traditions, customs, norms of behavior, as well as language. Cross-cultural teams have more potential—more potential for productivity as well as more potential for problems—relative to that of more homogeneous cultural groups. Problems may stem from mistrust, miscommunications, and lack of cohesion. Global managers are faced with a balancing act: Foster a healthy conflict of ideas and opinions while controlling cultural differences among team members.

Software developers from different cultures exhibit different behaviors, norms, and assumptions even though the *lingua franca* of the computing world is unequivocally English. Most people are surprised when they learn that spoken words account for little of our total communication. The major part of communication, perhaps as high as 80%, consists of contextual information as well as nonverbal cues, such as greeting styles, gestures, and posture. Both verbal and nonverbal communication is awash with ambiguity. The nonverbal part is especially difficult because it relies much more on culture. Worse, the nonverbal cues are difficult to convey across ("nonrich") electronic communication channels.

One of managers' most important roles is to understand the sources of conflict within their team. National cultural differences make this task more complex. For example, an American software company acquired a British software company. The respective sites began collaborating and encountered a critical disagreement. Was this disagreement rooted in national culture differences, organizational cultural clashes, or professional differences? Unless one understands the root, the solution will be only superficial. (The problems of cultural differences are explored further in Chapter 5. Solutions appear in Chapters 10 and 11).

Cultural diversity also represents the tremendous potential of bringing in fresh ideas and perspectives. The cultural differences can be fused to create a cultural synergy: new ways to solve a problem, design a product, or think about the software production process itself. This is the primary energy that the global software team needs to harness.

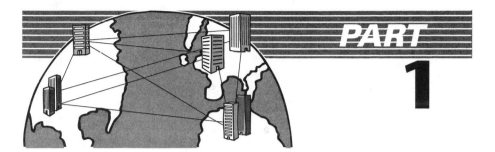

Why Global Software Teams?

WHY WE ARE SEEING MORE GLOBAL SOFTWARE TEAMS

Crossing Borders

Software development used to be the domain of engineers clad in white lab coats working inside air-conditioned data centers in a handful of advanced, industrialized countries. The PC revolution changed all that. In the 1990s, software development has become *global*.

There are two thrusts to software globalization. The first is the spread of development activities to newly industrialized, emerging, and developing nations—which until recently remained outside the software playing field.[1] In 1997, India and Israel exported $1 billion and $500 million, respectively, in software and software services.

The second thrust is the topic of this book—the transition of software development away from the traditional *centralized, co-located* form of development to a form in which global software teams collaborate across national borders, working on the same software project or product or system.

---

a **Global Software Team** is separated by a national boundary while actively collaborating on a common *software/systems project*

This new wave of globalization is inundated with tremendous optimism: Not only are the riches of high tech shared with developing nations, but these global software teams possess a utopian social organization. It is a social organization in which individuals communicate and collaborate over national boundaries, sending environmentally safe zeroes and ones across the information pipelines of the future. This futuristic organizational model is open to small start-ups in Moscow and Mexico City as well as large globally-competing firms headquartered in Los Angeles or London.

Why global software teams? There is no one reason that propels this phenomenon. Fifteen factors at different analysis levels are driving this new form of software development. Naturally, not all of these factors affect each global team and each company decision. The factors described in this chapter are divided into four categories: catalyst factors, sustaining factors, size factors, and vision factors.

Why global software teams? catalyst factors

The first six factors are labeled *catalysts,* factors that software executives cite as driving them to launch global software teams.[2]

Specialized talent.   Software companies want to deploy the best software designers and developers in the world regardless of their geographic location. For a variety of reasons, few firms can uproot programmers from their home country to work on a given project—be they inexpensive, but well-trained programmers from India or expensive, world-class programmers from Britain. For example, one joint venture that developed embedded software[3] was literally forced to find the few people on the planet who had the know-how to develop the project. Management had no choice but to mold together disparate sites—in the United States, United Kingdom, India, and Israel—some with only two to three developers, and make them into a productive team.

Programming "talent" is not a pretentious term. There are amazing differences in productivity between programmers. Watts Humphrey, one of the founders of the US-based Software Engineering Institute, conducted an experimental comparison of programmers. He gave 100 software engineers identical specifications for ten programs and measured the time it took them to develop the programs. The results were striking. In general the ratio between the fastest programmer and the slowest was between 1:15 and 1:30. That is, the fastest programmer was 30 times faster than the slowest[4] (while maintaining quality levels).

A related issue is scarcity of software professionals.[5] One of the primary reasons for the explosion in global software development teams is the acute *global labor shortage* in software professionals, now expected to last for some years to come. Silicon Valley openings for software positions remain unfilled. Due to this shortage, 40% of US IS shops are hiring immigrants and 16% are outsourcing abroad.[6] So great is the demand to import software professionals that in 1997 and 1998, the US immigration authorities reported that the quota for temporary work visas for technology workers (called H-1B visas) was filled well before the end of the fiscal year. Forty-four percent of the applicants were from India. Clearly this represents just part of the demand because so many firms are reluctant to go down the expensive and cumbersome path of securing H-1B work visas for employees. In early 1998 the US-based Information Technology Association of America[7] estimated the US software professional shortage at 346,000 jobs, representing a 10% gap between supply and demand. Industry researcher Howard Rubin[8] estimated that the US gap alone will grow to about one million by 2002. Meanwhile, US computer science departments have had declining enrollments. Successive rounds of new industry demand absorb any pockets of excess software labor: In the early 1990s it was new programming languages and environments such as C and object-oriented programming. In the mid to late 1990s it was Y2K, the euro, electronic commerce, and the mammoth enterprise software projects. One executive, who participated in building an Indian development center with hundreds of programmers, reported: "It would have been impossible to find so many programmers here [in Europe]."

Acquisitions.   Software companies are filling gaps and expanding product families through acquisitions. Flush with new wealth from the spectacular market appreciation of their stock, software firms have been much in the news with the volume of mergers and acquisition activity. In 1997, of the "Software 500" companies, 27% acquired a company, or a product line, or merged with another company.[9] This figure was up 30% from a year before. Overall, there were 678 transactions of private (usually smaller) software firms.

As with other maturing industries, the road to survival in software is growth. Smaller firms cannot survive against larger software conglomerates who possess marketing clout and diverse, ostensibly integrated, product offerings. We are now in the era of the global mega-mergers—in pharmaceuticals, chemicals, aerospace, telecommunications, and automobiles. Time will tell if this is necessarily healthy, but the mega-merger trend has been creeping into today's software powerhouses, who are increasing global software development in order to remain viable global players. Researchers de Meyer and Mizushima[10], who study global R&D management, have noted that "multinational corporations no longer compete primarily with numerous national companies—but with a handful of giants, who tend to be comparable in terms of size."

One global player is Netherlands-based Baan. Baan acquired Canadian Berclain and US-based Antalys in 1996, US-based Aurum in 1997, Spanish Meta4, and British Coda in 1998; they merged these distant sites into their preexisting development structure, while starting their own sites during this period in Hyderabad, India, and in several locations in the United States, Brazil, and Germany (see Exhibit 1–1). American firms have even raided Japan, buying dozens of software firms. As a result of this global acquisition binge, software teams thousands of miles apart are suddenly forced to collaborate and coordinate, sometimes rather reluctantly.

Reduction in development cost.   Software companies in high-wage nations are seeking low-cost programming. Just as many types of manufacturing shifted from high-wage countries, such as Japan and the United States, to low-wage countries, such as China and Mexico, so too is software. The giant of offshore programming is India, with programmers earning roughly ten to twenty percent of what their counterparts in the United States earn (more on relative costs appears in Chapter 3). Other emerging nations with low software labor costs that have become popular are the Philippines, Russia, China, as well as several nations in Central Europe and the Baltics. The low costs in emerging countries offer software companies more flexibility to "ramp" production up and down as their product cycles and customers demand.

Due to the hot employment markets, software professionals in advanced industrial countries are drawn to the more interesting and glamorous jobs, while developers in emerging countries are willing to do the less exciting tasks such as maintenance, porting, testing, and Y2K re-engineering.

Globalized presence.   Strategically, software executives need to position their organization as "a global firm," that is, to signal to the world, "we are a global player." They are selling products to two global constituencies: global businesses and global consumers. Global businesses seek large, established software suppliers for all their global subsidiaries rather than a hodgepodge of vendors in different countries. Individual software consumers have "global tastes" (the Coca-Cola phenomenon). Separately,

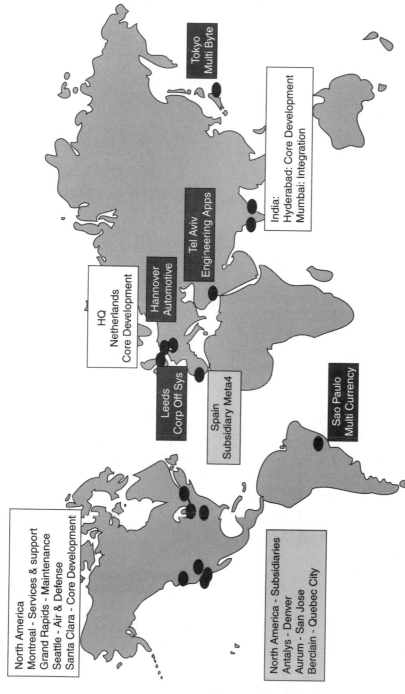

Exhibit 1-1 Baan's global software teams company-wide.

North America
Montreal - Services & support
Grand Rapids - Maintenance
Seattle - Air & Defense
Santa Clara - Core Development

HQ
Netherlands
Core Development

Leeds
Corp Off Sys

Spain
Subsidiary Meta4

Hannover
Automotive

Tel Aviv
Engineering Apps

Tokyo
Multi Byte

India:
Hyderabad: Core Development
Mumbai: Integration

Sao Paulo
Multi Currency

North America - Subsidiaries
Antalys - Denver
Aurum - San Jose
Berclain - Quebec City

Table 1–1 Global Software Teams

Company	Head-quarters	Remote Sites	Type
Baan	Netherlands	US, Canada, Germany, India, Japan, Israel, Brazil	packaged
Black Sun Interactive	Germany	US	packaged
Boeing Computer Services	USA	Ireland	IS
Chase Manhattan Bank	USA	India	IS
Citicorp.	USA	India	IS
Computer Associates	US	India	packaged
Deutsche Bank	Germany	India	IS
General Electric	USA	India	IS
General Motors	USA	Australia, France, Germany, Sweden	embedded
Holiday Inn	US	India	IS
IBM	USA	India, Latvia, China, Belarus	packaged
Lotus Development	USA	China	packaged
Magic	Israel	India	packaged
Microsoft	USA	Israel, India, UK	packaged
Oracle	USA	UK, Ireland, India	packaged
Shell Oil	UK/Neth	India	IS
Sidmar Steel	Belgium	Philippines	IS
Sun Microsystems	USA	Russia, China, India	packaged
Texas Instruments	USA	India, UK, Japan	IS, embedded
TSK	Japan	Israel	embedded
Verifone	USA	India	embedded

global presence means that large global companies need to foster relations with certain national governments by funneling high-profile investments (including R&D) to them.

Consequently, a software company with worldwide aspirations needs to attain the intangible of global legitimacy. While there are many ways to send this signal, increasingly it is done via bona fide product development centers in various significant countries. All these "positioning" issues are driving software development outside the company's home country.

Reduction in time-to-market. Given time zone differences, the ideal dispersed project can be productive around-the-clock, following the sun as the earth rotates. Follow-the-sun, or round-the-clock development as it is also known, has the potential to collapse time-to-market for project completion. Just as a factory can increase production speed by running the factory in 24-hour shifts, so can dispersed software teams.

The concept of follow-the-sun works as follows: When the team in San Jose, California finishes its work for the day, it sends its work, such as design modules or source code, to its sister team in Bangalore, India (10 1/2 time zones away). As members of this team finish their morning coffee, heavily fortified with milk and sugar, they read through the questions, summaries, and instructions written by their American colleagues and proceed to continue their work. As the sun sets in Bangalore, the local team finishes its day's tasks, reversing the information flow, together with its day's worth of added value.

Follow-the-sun development turns a disadvantage (geographical distance and time zones differences) into a competitive advantage. Several companies are experimenting with the allure of this approach (see Chapters 2 and 3), but it does not seem to be a primary factor in most companies decision to globalize.

Proximity to the customer. The maxim of the best corporations, the best salespeople, and the best designers is to stay close to the customer. Software is no different from other complex products. It requires a great deal of interaction—ideally face-to-face—between designer and customer. Hence software organizations need to set up sites near their customers, wherever they may be. Customer proximity is particularly important for requirements gathering and design, where rich communication and relationships are needed between customers and developers. Von Hippel's influential research conclusions interpret this maxim further: The best sources of innovation are the *lead customers*—those handful of customers who are particularly active and innovative in use of the firm's products.[11] For example, global automobile companies site their R&D centers in the global trendsetting locales of Los Angeles, Turin, and Stuttgart. For software firms, lead customers also seem to be concentrated. Customer proximity decisions were focused on only two nations: Germany and the United States.

Customer proximity was a primary catalyst factor for only a few of the global software teams in the GDSD study.[12] Why? Quite simply, because many of the global lead customers continue to be North American and most global software firms are American anyway. Second, software companies need proximity, not so much to their customers, but to hotbeds of new high-tech activity and innovation, such as Silicon Valley. Third, the software industry has created its own unique channel for "being close to the customer": the localization center. The software localization unit serves as a company beachhead in various nations. Generally, localization is not considered to be part of the core development activities.

Why global software teams? sustaining factors

We will shift from the catalyst factors which spurred the initial move to global software teams, to several additional *sustaining* factors for the existing global teams. Due to political and cultural distance as well as to objective problems, remote development sites are always candidates for the chopping block. It is natural for executives who wish to simplify, control, or retrench to look to exotic (e.g, cross-border) projects first. A number of sustaining factors were "discovered" by the software managers I spoke to after their global software teams were already running.

Development rigor.   Smaller, co-located software development teams rely on informal mechanisms and less on the discipline of formalized development methodologies and quality practices. In contrast, distance drives greater formalisms. For example, one global project manager recalled that the developers at three sites discovered that their collaborative documentation had improved significantly. Their explanation was: The improvement occurred in order to enhance communication between the development sites.

Internal freshness.   Diversity brings new creativity and inspiration to the software organization. The global software team creates a cultural synergy that finds new ways to solve a problem, design a product, or think about the software production process itself. Some of these synergies are drawn out and not immediately noticeable, while others come in surges of collaborative creativity. This synergy is illustrated by a global software manager who recounted with awe the recent product architectural review meeting that she had attended. The meeting participants were software product architects from the company's sites in six countries. The fresh perspectives and solutions that these varied people brought were destined to have a profound impact on the product.

Distance from distractions. Distant units are far from the numerous distractions of headquarters. One US development executive called his European site "Santa's little helpers." He saw them as very focused and industrious. The European site was not only far from the US headquarters, but they were far from the hustle and bustle of their own large cities. Most of the site's members grew up near their development offices (in a medium-sized European city). This proximity, in turn, resulted in higher levels of loyalty and lower turnover as compared with the company's other sites.

Professional cadre of software globalists. A new set of executives have established themselves at software companies. Their core business values include "global" ones. Many global software managers view themselves as pioneers in the software industry. One of them commented: "One of my goals here [at this software company] is to make them create global teams." These managers will set the tone for many years to come.

Experience. In most cases the remote sites have climbed up the experience curve and are performing well. Software managers often speak about the experience and specialized knowledge that have been built up within the distant site(s). The parent organization invested in training them in products and processes, and the remote sites developed genuine competencies not available at the headquarters site. Furthermore, the working relationships with the remote sites, while tenuous at first, have begun to mature and become effective. Naturally, software companies wanted to continue to mine these investments.

Why global software teams? size factors

Constantly looming in the background as a factor impelling companies to globalize their software development is *size*. Plainly, software companies have grown quite large. Almost all the Top 50 software companies now have well over 1000 employees, meaning that at least several hundred professionals are directly involved in development in some capacity. Size factors create both problems and opportunities.

Scale.   At some point, co-located software development centers become too large and unwieldy to manage. Dutch-based Baan expanded its development centers around the world seemingly overnight (Exhibit 1–1). Baan's competitor, German-based SAP, the sixth largest software organization, followed close behind—dispersing its core development activities outside of Germany—to the United States and to Japan. SAP's cofounder, Hasso Plattner, conceded in 1997 that size was a major factor in this dispersion. Another well-known case is Microsoft. The software giant held on to its geographically-centered ethos for years. Through a variety of enticements, Microsoft brought the best and brightest to Redmond, Washington. But even Microsoft is changing its ways: It has opened research and development centers in Britain, India, and Israel and has maintained (rather than liquidating) some of its acquired firms far away from headquarters.

Evolving synergies of scale.   Scale brings about opportunities for global collaborations that are unanticipated. Today, many Software 100 companies have a global infrastructure supporting a network of globally dispersed development centers working on their (often isolated) projects. Then, suddenly an opportunity arises! A synergy between two sites becomes apparent, or a talented designer in one of these remote centers envisions a new product. These kinds of unexpected opportunities for collaborating software development sites can pop up only in those firms that are already positioned globally. For example at one firm, the Israeli and Norwegian units discovered, by way of the US software conglomerate acting as a facilitator, that they had complementary products which, if meshed together, would fill a marketplace niche. At another large software organization, a distant site developed a computer network simulation that US-based executives decided should be productized, thus creating a two-site team. These collaborative projects were not the outcome of dumb luck, but the anticipated outcome of investment in a web of R&D centers working on innovative software products.

Why global software teams? "vision" factors

The software industry is both shaping and being shaped by dominant visions of our future society. Software industry decision makers are experimenting with leading organizational concepts. The first of these visions is technological, and the second one is structural.

Location transparency Eliminating the perception of distance through technology.

Virtual organization Organizing entities from different organizations around a structure resembling a network that has a weak hierarchy and a weak center.

Location transparency. Location transparency is the capability to work with another colleague or group as if you were all in the same room. Whether you are down the hallway or on the other side of the world is *transparent* as with the classic phone conversation in which your international colleague says "You sound like you're right here!" This is a technology-driven ideal enabled by massive improvements in communication technology: the Internet, video- and audio-conferencing, and other collaborative technologies.

The leap in the quality and sophistication of these communication technologies in the span of just a few short years between the early and mid-1990s is remarkable. Members of global software teams in the GDSD study were struggling to send each other a plain old, text e-mail message in the early 1990s. Within just a few years they had high-speed connections and were using e-mail with attachments, the worldwide web, and multi-site databases.

We are certainly closer today to the ideal of location transparency. The leap that we took in the 1990s, in part due to the Internet, is closely linked to a change in the way organizations are viewed by the people who work inside them.

The virtual organization and the virtual team. *Virtualness* has already permeated many facets of the business environment. US-based research company Gartner Group predicts that about 140 million global business users worldwide will be involved in remote work by the year 2003.[13] Corporations such as US-based Verifone have an organizational culture of "being virtual" that facilitates product development efforts. Grenier and Metes[14] predict in "Going Virtual" that the *virtual ethos* will become pervasive in the 21st century.

Organizations are driven to virtual forms in order to be more flexible, agile, responsive, and inexpensive. The virtual corporation is a form of a network organization (see Exhibit 1–2) created by distributing work and

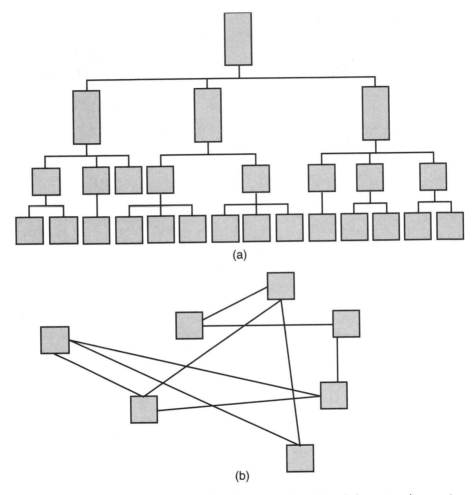

(a)

(b)

Exhibit 1–2 The traditional hierarchical organization (a) and the network organization (b).

contracting out work that was once done inside the organization to form a network of independent companies operating together as if it were a single organization.[15] As such, the organization may become geographically dispersed.

Many see virtual organizations as being *team-based* because activities will be necessarily defined by specific projects and tasks. The key difference between traditional teams and virtual teams is that members are no longer co-located (see Table 1–2). Some may be working out of their

Table 1–2 Characteristics of Teams: Yesterday and Tomorrow.[16]

Traditional teams	Virtual teams
Co-located members	Distributed members
Face-to-face interaction	Electronic communication
Members from same organization	Members from different organizations
Hierarchical	Networked
Mostly informal communication	Continuous structured communication
Position authority	Process and knowledge authority
Information distribution (push)	Information access (pull)
Information on paper	Information electronic
Sharing completed work	Continuous sharing of incomplete work
Knowledge hoarding	Knowledge sharing
Transparent process	Computer-visible process
Culture learned through osmosis	Culture learned through electronic-based communications and artifacts

home and telecommuting. Others may be working in small clusters in company offices.

Several of the global software firms in the GDSD study had some characteristics of virtual organizations. Many projects involved secondary players who were contractors, or individual consultants, some of whom telecommuted, who interacted with the principal teams from afar, sometimes even from a third or fourth country. Companies with Indian sites were often dealing with a development team that was part of a third party organization. In other cases, global collaborations were set up as joint ventures and alliances.

However, it is unlikely that we will see a leap to virtualness in the software industry. Most of the global software teams were neither virtual organizations nor virtual projects. Rather, they represented internal development units that were dispersed. Software firms may be distributing some of their core competencies, but they are reluctant to lose centralized head-quarters' control. The organizational pyramids still have many layers of hierarchy.

Why global software teams? Summary

A diverse list of factors are driving globalization of software development teams. Catalyzing factors at the executive and managerial level are: the search for specialized software talent; the shotgun collaboration brought about by global acquisitions; the drive to reduce labor costs; the company's need to project a global presence; the drive to reduce time to market for product development; and the need to be close to the customer. Sustaining factors are: the emerging development rigor required by distance; the internal freshness created by diversity; the ability to focus brought about by separation; the real experience base that the new sites have gained; and the new managerial cadre of software globalists who are influencing decisions in software companies. Size factors stem from the rapid growth of software companies, which now need to break up development centers lest they get too large. Size also leads to evolving synergies of scale—the opportunities that arise globally for companies that are already global.

The final two factors have to do with the vision of software industry decision makers experimenting with leading organizational concepts. These twin visions are transparency and virtuality. Before considering whether global software teams will continue to disperse well into the future, it is worthwhile considering where global software teams have come from.

History of Global Software Teams

The PC revolution of the 1980s brought a change to the culture of software development. No longer was software within the domain of large, dull companies—many of them selling computer hardware. Instead software development was supposed to be more fun, more creative, more entrepreneurial, smaller, co-located. The software industry, particularly the PC software sector, was not a global industry in the 1980s. Although the dominant American software companies did sell abroad, their orientation was largely domestic. "International" was handled by foreign sales offices and the budding localization market.

Co-location became a key part of the software development culture. Microsoft carried this part of the culture as far as it could in its organizational practices. Microsoft development is still largely geographically centralized on the Microsoft campus in Redmond, Washington. The Microsoft model of acquisition has typically been to buy a company, lure its best people to Redmond, and then liquidate it. As the most powerful software company of the 1990s, it was slow to globalize its core development activities.

In contrast to the software companies born with or after the PC revolution, old line companies have had global software teams for decades. Information Systems shops in large multinational corporations have been stumbling through development of linked, collaborative, and eventually global systems, since the 1960s.

IBM and a few other major computer vendors had substantial software development organizations well before the PC revolution and used global software teams well before any such term was coined. IBM, the global software company, was still the largest supplier of software in the world in 1997—just slightly ahead of Microsoft. For decades IBM has been developing its mainline systems and database software products at multiple sites. As any old-time IBMer will confirm, IBM always developed in a geographically dispersed mode. Even in the late 1970s, primitive e-mail and adequate audio-conferencing were around to facilitate work. IBM developed and still develops its premiere software products using globally dispersed teams, including AIX, OS/2, CICS, OS 8100, and DB2 (the latter developed by teams in North Carolina, California and Ireland). But IBM was not careful in maintaining control over some of these dispersed projects. In 1991, the Wall Street Journal estimated the total OS/2 development costs at $2.5 billion[17] with 1700 globally dispersed programmers working on the project. This global collaboration had four major sites: IBM's labs in Austin (Texas), Boca Raton (Florida), and Hursley (England) as well as Microsoft's Redmond campus (at the time OS/2 was a joint development program of IBM and Microsoft).

What is the difference between dispersed development at IBM today and that of the 1970s? Dave Pullin, a director of software development at IBM, posits that the difference is the collaborative technology. He points to his notebook computer:

> the entire dispersed project is sitting on my IBM Thinkpad [laptop] replicating into a Notes database—all its history, its issues, the e-mail correspondence. In that computer there is roughly four orders of magnitude more project information than we had 20 years ago.

Pullin says that because communication was so difficult in the past the task allocation—the "chunkification" of the software systems—resulted in very large pieces, which he referred to as "occasionally connected development." Now he can manage projects at much finer granules with much shorter timelines.

The Future of Global Software Teams

While much of this chapter deals with company-level reasons for dispersing software development to various points on the globe, it is important to step back and examine whether the global-collaborative software model will continue well into the future. The remainder of the chapter presents a broader perspective that includes industry, economic, government, and technology issues and trends. The question "will it continue?" is examined from different facets.

Will software continue to globalize and software teams continue to disperse?

The trajectory of the software industry is of continued rapid growth.[18] The global figures are substantial and growing at a breathtaking pace. Global spending on all facets of information technology is estimated, by various experts, at somewhere between half a trillion dollars and several trillion per year. Of this, the global packaged software industry by itself generates over $100 billion and grew between 250% and 500% in the decade of 1985 to 1995 (as compared to the US economy overall, which grew nicely during that decade, but at only about 30%). Meanwhile, software services, such as systems integration and consulting, reached roughly $200 billion by the late 1990s (see Exhibit 1–3). The two software components that are much harder to estimate, and may be the largest components, are in-house systems development (information systems) and, separately, embedded software. One heroic estimate put each of these two sectors at half a trillion dollars per year worldwide. Each year in the United States, there are approximately 175,000 software development projects.

An indicator of software development dispersion activity is the magnitude of outsourcing, which worldwide was estimated at $50 billion in 1994 and which may be growing as much as 50% annually.

As discussed earlier, there is an acute shortage in software professionals in industrialized countries. India's pool of well-trained software professionals (estimated at roughly 200,000) has so far been the critical plug to fill the gap between supply and global demand. But India's supply

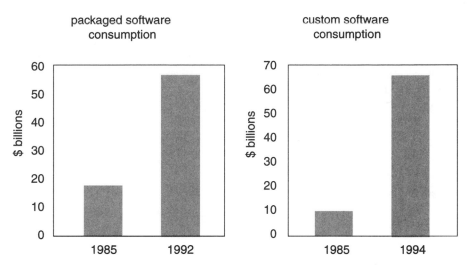

Exhibit 1–3 Growth of total consumption of software and software services in major economic blocs of US, Japan, and Western Europe.[19]

of software professionals represents only about 5% of the software labor pool in the United States,[20] so software production is likely to spread elsewhere in the years to come.

It is unlikely that the global software labor supply will be allowed to relocate to the nations with high demand (and high salaries). The United States, Europe, and other industrialized nations will not open their gates to massive immigration, but rather will continue to allow a steady trickle to come in. Therefore, most of the "excess" software labor is likely to stay put where it is currently located: in India, China, Russia, and other nations. These labor pools will continue to seek the good pay and fulfilling jobs that come from abroad via global software teams.

At the same time some real (as opposed to virtual) distances may shrink in some instances. How? One trend is *near-shore programming*. Because of visa restrictions in advanced nations, low cost programmers, primarily from India, are relocated to a nearby, typically small nation, which welcomes the extra income. Israel had a booming software industry in the late 1990s and was stymied by an acute software labor shortage. One of its largest software firms, Aurec, which develops large-scale applications for the telecommunications industry, set up a near-shore site in Cyprus, an easy one hour's flight from Aurec's headquarters in Tel Aviv. In the United States, such a near-shore development site was set up by PRT in the

Caribbean island of Barbados.[21] This is a story of a US entrepreneur who created a paradise "software island." In 1994 PRT began importing skilled programmers to Barbados, giving them housing. Like the old paternalistic corporations of yesteryear, PRT looks after many facets of employees' private lives. In the morning they play tennis. In the afternoon they create software. PRT's customers include major American financial firms, such as Merrill Lynch, Chase Manhattan Bank, and J.P. Morgan. These customers can be on the island with a five-hour nonstop flight from New York's JFK airport—shorter than most travel to California. One of the unexpected outcomes is that the customers themselves want to come and spend time with the developers in Barbados. Today these software islands may seem idyllic, perhaps tomorrow they may resemble the maquiladora towns of the Mexican-US border. In either case, software development will remain cross-border and dispersed.

Dispersion to various nations has been uneven. For most packaged software companies (as well as software service companies), country siting decisions often begin with one of the following questions: 1) Will my new site be India or someplace else? Or 2) Should I expand my India operations or try another country? The "other country" is a subject of great interest among global software managers I spoke to who often inquired about what country to site the next global development team: "What do you know about Hungary?" "We've looked at Israel and at China," and even, "I'm considering Iceland." Global R&D scholar Chiesa makes an interesting recommendation and observation about global siting of R&D units that is applicable to software.[22] The recommendation: It is legitimate to choose sites independently from other functional considerations such as marketing and production because the expertise for software development is distributed differently. The observation: At any given time a company's product development activities are dispersed as a result of decisions— centralized and decentralized—as well as accidental events.

Government officials recognize that they should support dispersed software projects. First, these projects are likely to reduce the brain-drain of highly educated professionals. The Indian government invested in satellite technology in the late 1980s after recognizing that it needed to connect the young Indian software centers with the outside world. For years the Irish government has awarded substantial tax benefits to high-technology sites on the island to slow the emigration of its young, computer-trained population to Britain and the United States. Second, the concept of globally dispersed software projects brings good projects to new, still remote sites on the world software map. Software teams far from Silicon Valley are getting a chance to work on more than just the routine tasks of porting and reengineering. The IBM JavaBeans, described in Chapter 2, brought leading edge software technologies to a collaborative project in China, India, Latvia, and Belarus.

In reflecting on the globalization of software development, it is worthwhile to examine the globalization of "general" industrial R&D. After all, global software product development and global industrial R&D have many common characteristics. Perhaps the most important commonality is the artifact itself. The artifact is a *design* artifact, rather than a tangible artifact. The artifact is shared between collaborating remote design centers. It can be decomposed into zeroes and ones and transmitted in seconds from one site to another.[23]

Many decades ahead of the software industry, R&D began globalizing, albeit slowly and unevenly. Major global players that have elaborate networks of R&D labs in multiple nations include Siemens (Germany, electronics), Ericsson (Sweden, electronics), Hewlett-Packard (United States, computers), Glaxco-Wellcome (United Kingdom, pharmaceuticals), IBM (United States, computers), Canon, with eight R&D labs in five countries, Motorola, with 14 labs in seven countries.

One such global R&D team is at Ford. In 1993 Ford introduced the Mondeo car (Contour in the United States), using global design teams collaborating using CAD. Ford continued to expand multinational design collaboration at the Turin (Italy), Dunton (England), Merkenich (Germany), and Dearborn (USA) sites for other auto designs. Ford has invested in expensive technologies and new organizational structures for several reasons: "getting people off airplanes," trimming payrolls, and reducing development time.[24]

In spite of continued globalization of industrial R&D, the majority of activity in most firms, including the firms with large global R&D networks, continues to take place in the home country. For example, in the auto industry, depending on the phase of R&D, 60% to 90% of R&D personnel still reside in the home base (headquarters nation). One study found that for American multinational companies, less than 10% of their technological activity takes place abroad—around the same level as in the 1930s. For European companies, the numbers are higher—but only at 31% on average. Of the Europeans, the British were the most likely to site key R&D abroad, with the Germans, the least. Even those multinational companies that do have a foreign presence have rather limited networks of labs with a vast majority having a presence in at most just two countries.[25]

As an initial comparison between software R&D and other industrial R&D, an aggregation of the development projects in the GDSD study shows that 39% of technical staff resided outside the headquarters' (home) nations (see Exhibit 1–4). This figure can now be compared to estimates for industrial R&D where, as noted, 60% to 90% of personnel continue to reside in the home country. It should be noted that the projects aggregated in Exhibit 1–4 represent only part of the development portfolio of most of the companies, a fact which would effectively push the number of staff in the home country up from 61%. Nevertheless, the numbers for the software industry suggest a surge of globalization that is well in excess of the trends in industrial R&D. If this trend continues, then the software industry is already charting new territory in globalization.

Finally, the software technology itself will continue to have an impact on global dispersion. Software globalization and dispersion will continue because of continued changes in underlying software technology. The industry is moving slowing, though unevenly, to a paradigm of software *components*. Small software components will be built and sold like subassemblies to be put together and made into larger, more comprehensive packages. Each of these small components will easily connect to other components. These characteristics will allow distant teams of software developers to develop software components with only minimal coordination with others. One future scenario is that low-cost nations will build the components and sell them to the software design centers in industrialized nations for assembly.

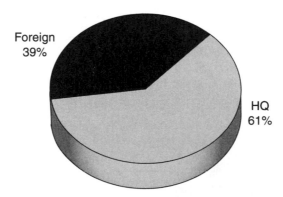

Exhibit 1–4   Distribution of technical development staff in GDSD study.[26]

Further Reading

An excellent academic book on the global software industry is Mowery, D.C. *The International Computer Software Industry: A Comparative Study of Industry Evolution and Structure.* Oxford Univ. Press, 1996.

Ed Yourdon tackles all the issues: global to multithreading. Yourdon, E. *The rise and resurrection of the American programmer.* Upper Saddle River, NJ: Yourdon Press, 1996.

Shorter articles on specific topics can be requested from the Stanford Computer Industry Project's Software Industry Research Program at: http://www-scip.stanford.edu/scip/sirp.html.

THREE TALES OF GLOBAL
SOFTWARE TEAMS

This chapter presents three short cases of global software teams: one small company—PrestigeSoft—and two large companies, Orchestral Technologies and IBM.[27] These three cases have two important characteristics in common. These companies attempted to reduce costs by turning to emerging nations—and in all three collaborations—there were attempts to do follow-the-sun development. Follow-the-sun, or round-the-clock development, takes advantage of time zone differences to hand off work between sites leading to cycle-time reductions.

PrestigeSoft's Version of Follow-the-Sun: Prototyping Around the Clock

PrestigeSoft is a $7 million US-based company with its entire programming unit in Bulgaria. The company develops low-end, low cost consumer software titles (packages). Thus far PrestigeSoft has developed about 30 such titles—all with its talented team in Sofia.

Within PrestigeSoft's niche, time-to-market is critical. The company has been able to refine a development process that minimizes time-to-market measured from concept to release. Most projects are completed in under six months. A recent cartoon character screen saver package took three months from concept to release, using only three weeks for actual programming. Time-to-market efficiencies have occurred for several reasons. First, with 30 projects under their belt, the United States and Bulgarian sites have learned to work efficiently with each other. Second, the products themselves are relatively small (e.g., the cartoon screen saver completed in 1997 was roughly 40,000 lines of code, counting reused code). Third, PrestigeSoft was able to take advantage of the ten-hour time difference between the United States and Bulgaria because the nature of the product lends itself to rapid iterations.

Specifications can be somewhat loose since some of the product is "discovered" through creativity and iterative trial-and-error. During the critical coding phase, prototypes were sent to the US-based product manager several times a week for review. The manager would review the new screens and screen effects and have responses ready for the Bulgarian site the next day. The US-based manager summed it up as follows: "Because it is a creative product, you can continue to be creative around the clock." When properly done, he said, this fast code-and-review cycle reduced total cycle time by 30%.

Orchestral Technologies' Version of Follow-the-Sun: Sharing Code Between US and Russia

In 1988, even before the iron curtain fell, Orchestral Technologies, a major US-based company specializing in graphical software, set up a joint venture in Moscow to tap Russia's enormous software talent pool. When Orchestral asked one of its seasoned managers to manage the Moscow office, he hesitated, thinking: "I'll leave my place in San Francisco for this?" Still in Moscow a decade later, this manager has made this global team one of his life's missions.

For many years Orchestral's staff in Moscow performed the traditional tasks of off-shore programming: Writing code from specs and developing small components that go into the larger product that was written in California by American programmers. With time Russian operations grew to include 35 people with sites in both Moscow and St. Petersburg. In 1994, this changed. The Russian site was tasked to develop a large (one million lines of code) brand new product (release 1.0) as equal partners to the US-based site. The global team launched into this large-scale collaborative project with five sites: Moscow, St. Petersburg (Russia), California (headquarters location), Denver (USA, consultants only), and Regina (Canada).

Design was shared by the two principal units in California and Moscow. Code was shipped back and forth (across 11 time zones) everyday during the coding phase. To accomplish this, the team set up a Software Configuration Management package at each site. A policy was instituted whereby the source code would lock up at 8 PM at either the California or Russian offices and nothing further could be added to it. An hour later the entire source would be uplinked to a satellite and ready for use by the other team. Programmers coordinated code sharing via detailed, formalized notes to each other. Generally, programmers did not work on the very same code, but rather, at a slightly higher level. For example, a pair of distant programmers would work on the same dialog box. The Russian and American programmers split up the tiles in each dialog box.

By Orchestral's account, product development was a success: It came in ahead of schedule and at lower cost than a comparable US-based project. It was the first major product in the company's recent history that did not require an immediate follow-up bug release. The global software development effort was deemed a success, and a recently acquired South African development site was added to its responsibilities.

The Case of IBM's Version of Follow-the-Sun: The Global Software Factory

In early 1997, IBM began publicizing one of the more ambitious efforts at global software teams to date: a five-site, five-country development project with round-the-clock aspirations.[28] The project involved developing small components for the IBM VisualAge application development environment.

Rather than developing one large product release 1.0, the undertaking was to develop many small components—known as beans—where each bean could be developed rapidly. Software components are the ingredients for building a new paradigm of software that no longer relies on the immense software products of today (fondly referred to as fatware).[29] Because each component is small, the development time for each one is relatively short. The project executives deliberately targeted JavaBeans because of these characteristics. IBM envisioned JavaBeans to be plugged together and used to develop functional business applications.

The organizational multi-site project had an unusual structure. IBM set up four equal size units of 31 professionals in four low-cost labor sites: at a joint venture spin-off of Tsinghua University in Beijing; at the IBM-Tata joint venture in Bangalore, India (later to become a wholly owned subsidiary now called IBM Global Services–India); at an IBM joint venture firm with the Institute of Computer Science in Minsk, Belarus; and at privately owned SWH Group in Riga, Latvia.

Why 31 on each distant unit? From past experiences with offshore sites, the key IBM managers came to the conclusion that they needed the right balance between a unit that is too small and not economically feasi-

Exhibit 2–1   The global JavaBeans sites: (*a*) Chinese site; (*b*) Belarussian site; (*c*) Latvian site; (*d*) US–based project coordinators pictured with team leads from Chinese and Latvian sites; (*e*) Indian site.

ble (e.g., in terms of setting up infrastructure) and one that is too large and unmanageable. They arrived at the number of roughly 30 per unit as optimal. IBM called this the *phalanx*. In each national site there were five core specialist areas of five people each in such areas as graphics and technical writing. Part of the original vision was to create a reusable team structure—a generic team organizational chart—to reuse when IBM expands its development to many other sites around the world.

This effort was originally envisioned as a hub and spoke structure in which a strong centralized control group would reside in the United States to initiate, review, allocate, and provide specialized services. At the outset the US site consisted of a 24-person unit in Seattle. The Seattle team played the dual role of both architects and users. Project management and other services were also centralized in the US site including Quality Assurance (QA) and user interface specialists.

Once the original (US-based) project champions left in mid-1997, a new manager came in who saw the entire project in a very different light. He reasoned that a true global development project should not be strongly centralized, but rather more closely resemble a network organization in which the various global partners coordinate more activities amongst themselves rather than through a central unit. Furthermore, he reasoned that a large control center in the United States defeats the purpose of a low-cost development project. He proceeded to change the structure to one that more resembles the classic network structure. The US command unit was moved from Seattle to IBM's large development center in Raleigh, North Carolina where it was reduced from 24 to only three people: a global manager, a budget officer, and a chief technical architect. The US site was now more of a project management unit responsible for oversight and some review functions. Whereas the US hub was initiating all projects in the early stages, with the new structure the four non-US sites began to initiate projects.

One of the project goals was to do follow-the-sun development. In fact, this was mentioned in IBM's press releases from early 1997. As it turns out, this goal was hard to achieve continuously. From the outset, development was to be iterative. The product specification and the software product itself (the bean) were to go through many separate phases, or iterations, until complete. The US command unit would set up a work specification for each JavaBean and assign it to an offshore site. The goal was to turn that spec into code by the end of the day and ship it back to the United States for successive rounds of reviews and feedback. After reviewing and testing the code, the American unit would specify new

IBM® JavaBeans Project

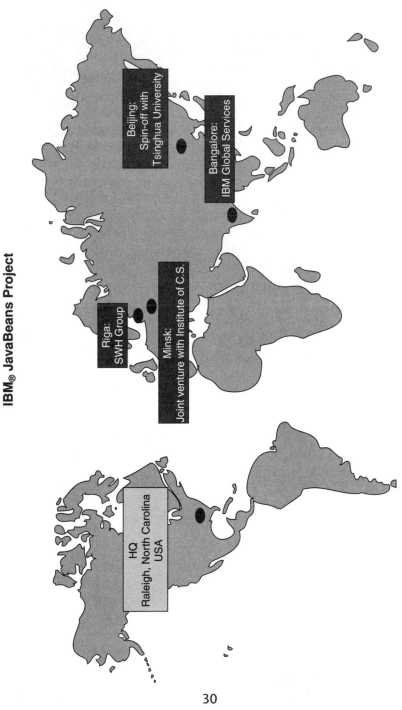

Riga:
SWH Group

Minsk:
Joint venture with Institute of C.S.

Beijing:
Spin-off with
Tsinghua University

Bangalore:
IBM Global Services

HQ
Raleigh, North Carolina
USA

Exhibit 2–2   Locations of IBM JavaBeans project sites.

changes and send those instructions back across the ocean for another iteration.

In fact, a daily turnaround (true follow-the-sun) was too ambitious for both sides—the offshore coders and the American reviewers. It was too much to digest in one day's work. The project was able to settle into a respectable two "code drops" from each remote site per week. In the meantime, the US unit had assigned about half a dozen beans to each offshore site. So, while, the Beijing site waited for review and feedback on component #1, they worked on beans #2, #3, #4, #5, and #6. At steady state, the IBM project was juggling about two dozen beans between the hub and the remote sites. The Seattle hub became the bottleneck. It was handling too many tasks and it was responsible for significant value added for each of those tasks.

With the arrival of a new US-based director, this development process changed. The US hub's overall workload was reduced significantly. The number of hand offs it received was somewhat lowered, but more importantly, instead of being responsible for each of these tasks, the US hub passed much of each task to one of the foreign sites. In most cases each bean's problem definition and coding was done by one of the four foreign sites. The final acceptance test phase was also reorganized. The symmetrical, phalanx structure was relaxed. The Minsk site became responsible for acceptance testing and integration for all beans (in addition to some of its own development).

With responsibility devolving to the distant sites and the hub delegating tasks to other sites, follow-the-sun was de-emphasized and no longer practical. Some time zone advantages still took place on an occasional basis—some quicker iterations on design and definition, as well as some quicker bug fixes in the testing phase. But these now became an incidental benefit.

With this project IBM had multiple objectives: build leading-edge technology (i.e., software components) while experimenting with a leading edge management model to build that technology. To some extent Java and the JavaBeans tied this all together—it was simultaneously the leading-edge technology end product and a new development model combined in one. JavaBeans are small components that are easier to define and for which development time is relatively short. Once finished each bean is able to communicate (or interact) with other beans. This programming model allows dispersed teams to architect (define) beans and then work fairly independently from one another on each bean. Of course, there were also many risks. IBM was simultaneously developing in five nations with inexperienced partners. And it was doing this all with Java—a very young technology with an immature set of programming support tools.

IBM executives justified this project in many ways. At the outset, one of the compelling reasons was to take advantage of low cost development centers. Indeed, the original incentive structures included incentives to keep costs down. The unloaded labor costs at the four distant sites were in the $8,000 to $15,000 per programmer per year range, far less—as little as 10%—of labor costs in North America and Western Europe. But there were additional costs, such as the high cost of travel, that are not reflected in paycheck comparisons.

Another objective that had emerged for the project was to reduce time-to-market in part through use of follow-the-sun coordination mechanisms. At the early stages of the project, IBM estimated that cycle time would be reduced by 35%. Once the project structure changed, time-to-market was no longer an overt goal. Nevertheless, bean technology allows for very rapid cycles. By early 1998, median cycle time for each bean (or close-knit bean family) was three months from original statement to acceptance.

Yet the costs and time-to-market for this individual project were not the only strategic drivers of the IBM JavaBeans project. IBM's strategic objectives for the project were largely intangible. That is, they were not to be measured strictly in cost reductions or cycle time. IBM was seeking a strong presence in all of these emerging markets in order to develop a strong base of developers who have experience working with IBM on important projects. This base would allow IBM to continue to expand in these markets. China, in particular, was an important market for IBM.

The essence of making this complicated coordination process work was a good collaborative technology infrastructure. All five sites were connected via local Internet providers to IBM's global network. The project director indicated that he could not manage such a complicated process without ubiquitous collaborative technologies. The project was structured around a groupware server, IBM/Lotus Notes, which became the project's central repository, supporting special functions for structured communications such as issues management and action management. Other coordination activities centered on the Software Configuration Management system.

THE BOTTOM LINE: ARE GLOBAL SOFTWARE TEAMS SUCCESSFUL?

In Hollywood all is forgiven—delays and production overruns—if the product is a box office hit. In software, beyond a smashing review in *PC Magazine* or *Computerworld,* true success is measured by four key process and product parameters that drive any project:

- Was the product delivered on or ahead of schedule?
- Were development costs reduced?
- Was the product innovative?
- Was the product relatively free of bugs?

Was the product delivered on or ahead of schedule?   This question is fundamental to global software teams since it is really about one of its embedded *ideals.* Given time zone differences, the ideal dispersed project can be working literally around the clock, following the sun, collapsing cycle time while mining the skills of team members in each location.

Follow-the-sun is still uncommon. Excluding the specialized functions of bug fixing and customer support, less than 20% of the projects even attempted to implement follow-the-sun, and even in those projects there was only partial implementation at best. Those project managers estimated 20% to 35% time-to-market reduction for these projects. This sounds marvelous and well worth a trip to Bangalore or Belarus. But these figures lacked any clear benchmarking and should be viewed with caution.

Not all cycle time reduction has to be done by follow-the-sun. A well run global team can achieve rapid development even without passing work back and forth every night. However, 58% of the projects reported that cycle time either was longer or there was no difference from other situations. That is, there was *no* cycle-time reduction for most projects. (In other projects there were conflicting reports about cycle-time reduction, where one management respondent contradicted another). Caution is needed with these figures because they are self-reported and (in most cases) are not based on any benchmark.

One global manager with follow-the-sun experience complained:

> Of course, follow-the-sun takes longer!!! You may be able to get it down to negligibly longer. There is no evidence that if you were able to take the same number of people and the same money you couldn't do it faster than follow-the-sun. . . . If I were to get the same programmers in one site, I would beat the three-shift team anytime.

The number of hand offs (transitions) in follow-the-sun makes it apparent why this approach is uncommon. Follow-the-sun represents a substantial communication and coordination challenge. For a product development cycle the number of hand offs may be measured in the hundreds, if not the thousands. Every hand off includes preparing the object to be understood by a colleague complete with textual explanations. At the other side, for the receiver, follow-the-sun represents a daily cognitive nightmare. Every day the receiver must immerse himself in the object and understand anew where he needs to pick up the task.

True follow-the-sun with *daily* hand offs is very difficult for *design*, particularly conceptual, innovative, or radical design. Those activities require the subtle dynamics of work in close proximity—the excitement, the mutual energy that takes place when sharp minds are solving problems. Even lower-level design activities such as conceptualizing incremental innovation or writing a low-level design document are best done in colocation. Design activities may benefit occasionally from overnight gains in perhaps 10% of the transitions. But these gains will likely be washed out by other delays resulting from dispersion.

True follow-the-sun with *daily* hand offs is very difficult for *programming,* particularly programs involving any complexity. Any programmer knows that immersing oneself in someone else's code is an enormous cognitive task. Additionally, building a program is a bit akin to an art. You cannot hand over a half finished oil painting to a friend and say: "Here, this is what I finished today, you do your best while I have myself a rest."

However, some programming work can be exchanged if planned carefully and distant programmers are paired up with each other. Each programmer works on a complementary piece of code and a daily build is done to uncover integration issues. The daily build process is really a continuous form of coordination that has now become well-known as one of the key control mechanisms at Microsoft, referred to as synch-and-stabilize.[30] The build synchronizes developers work by uncovering inconsistencies between their respective code changes.

Since follow-the-sun allocation for the core development activities of design and coding is quite difficult, it is worth noting two activities in which follow-the-sun has proven itself: bug fixing and customer support. Customer support, similar to the *global help desk*, allows 24-hour support to end users by handing off responsibility for customer support to successive sites.

Global software managers are most impressed with follow-the-sun *bug fixing*. For example, at Netherlands-based Baan, bug fixing is handed off from Barneveld (Netherlands) to Grand Rapids (United States) to Hyderabad (India). Customer problems are routed to the appropriate daytime center, and work on the bug begins. If the bug is not repaired, it may be handed over to the next center that evening (e.g., the Netherlands center hands responsibility for bug #7723 to the US center). In many ways this is the ideal application for follow-the-sun because the unit of work is so small—one bug—rather than a software component, a software program, or an entire software module. Furthermore, the problem is highly structured and unambiguous: Locate and fix the bug.

Follow-the-sun bug fixing (also called problem-resolution) benefits greatly from a multi-site bug tracking system. The system is based on a database in which each bug is given a unique identifier and tracked as it goes through the process. A good tracking system will also have workflow features attached to it, such as "Route this bug to India tonight for priority work." And, later, once the bug is fixed, it is routed to the appropriate person for approval.

Were development costs reduced?   Less than half of the projects in the GDSD study were justified on the basis of development cost reduction. In all cases in which cost was a factor, development sites were established in emerging, low-cost labor economies (China, India, and several nations from the former Soviet Union). Salaries in all these countries are far lower than comparative salaries in the industrialized nations of North America or Europe. A few cost comparisons from the study, where available, appear in Table 3–1. The cost of a global software team member if he was in an emerging nation was as low as 10% and probably as high as 30% of his team members in an industrialized country. These results are consistent with other studies. For example, the 1997 World Benchmark study found that the cost of developing one unit of software (function point) in India was 26% of the cost in the United States.[31]

Of those projects that had at least one site in an emerging economy, 57% reported reduced development costs for that site or for the project overall. The remaining projects with sites in developing countries had managers who were ambivalent about the actual cost savings because of allocated costs of travel, communication, set up, and other overhead costs. One manager said to me: "Look, we had five to ten of our [home country] software developers in a hotel in India at any given time—that adds up."

Annual and loaded costs of software developers in industrialized countries also need some clarification. The figures in Table 3–1 reflect developer costs in major metro areas in the United States (such as Silicon Valley), but loaded costs outside the largest cities are far lower, by 25% or more. Loaded developer costs in Western Europe are generally acknowledged to be roughly the same as in the United States, although one software executive reported that due to the dollar appreciation, Western European development was beginning to look cheap. Finally, loaded developer costs in Israel (categorized as an advanced industrial country by

Table 3–1   Self-Reported Cost Comparisons*

| Company | Estimated Annual Cost Per Developer (loaded cost in thousands of $US) | |
	In Emerging Economy	In Industrialized Economy
A	$15	$150
B	$30	$120
C	$24–42	not available

*(selected projects from GDSD study).

OECD) are roughly equal to those in the United States, but Israeli managers claim that costs are lower for top talent than comparative American salaries.

Was the product innovative?   Naturally, global managers and executives were proud of the creativity of their team members, but so are project managers in co-located teams. So, how does one measure the relative innovativeness of global software teams? An indirect measure is task enhancement. Task enhancement is the degree to which software companies are transferring more of their tasks to these remote global sites—particularly higher level, value-added tasks such as design. In 69% of the cases, the distant site or sites were either assuming high-level design responsibility or full product "ownership" (responsibility for the release's definition all the way through design and development). Global software teams were working on the company's flagship product or one of its primary products in 47% of the cases. In some of these cases, it was the distant site that initiated ("visioned") the product itself and then went on to design and develop the product.

Was the product relatively free of bugs?   As with the other success measures, indirect measures are needed at this early stage of the global software team evolution. First, on a relative basis, over all projects, more employees in the home country were involved in the testing phase of the life cycle. In other words, the home country's development staff was still controlling the testing phase and not dispersing it. It is likely that this occurred because of a combination of lack of resources in the remote sites and the headquarters' need to maintain standards. On the other hand, the case of the Orchestral Technologies' project may be predictive—that standards will be higher in global teams. The project manager of Orchestral's Russian-American collaborative effort stated that the joint product was the first product in a long time at the company that did not require a subsequent bug release. He attributed this success to good people, and to the more rigorous development methodology that the dispersed team used relative to their co-located colleagues back home.

Other indirect measures of success

In addition to the four key success measures, other variables hint at success or failure of the global software team concept. One such variable is growth of sites outside the home country. Software companies will not

Table 3–2   Growth of Employees at Newly Established Software Development Centers in India

Software Company	Year New Development Center Established in India	Number of Employees at New India Site
Large European	1996	300 within 2 years
Large US	1995	25 within 1 year
Large US	1995	60 within 1 year
Small US	1994	25 within 2 years

grow or expand their remote sites (and their global teams) unless they think that it is worthwhile. Most of the global software teams I came across had been growing and expanding for some time. All the Indian sites were growing very rapidly—almost at a frantic pace. Table 3–2 depicts what happened in four of the cases as core development moved to Indian sites. In at least two of these cases, product ownership was transferred to the Indian site within a relatively short period of one to two years.

Conclusions

The debate regarding the effectiveness of global software teams will most likely continue. The data here suggested that it is possible for a global software team, when well-managed, to reduce development cycle time, lower costs, improve quality, and foster innovation (although attaining all four in the same project is extremely unlikely). However, it is also possible that some projects perform at (or even below) performance levels of those projects that are co-located at the company's home country.

The Five Centrifugal Forces of Global Software Teams

Global software teams are more difficult to do right. To para-phrase one software manager: no one in their right mind would do this. A centrifugal force is a physical force that propels an ob-ject outward from the center. Software globalization is like a cen-

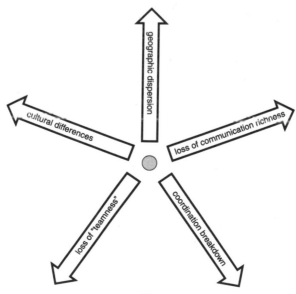

trifugal force, it disperses developers to the far corners of the world. Part II covers each of the five centrifugal forces—the problems—that pull apart the global software team: dispersion, the breakdown of traditional control and coordination mechanisms, the loss of communication "richness," the loss of "teamness," and cultural differences.

Professors de Meyer and Mizushima, who study globalized R&D, stated a truism about globalized R&D that also applies to globalized software development—that it is both an idealized objective and a managerial headache:

> . . . we have no record of companies which would indicate that it is easier to do R&D on a global scale than in a geographically centralized approach. Globalization of R&D is typically accepted more with resignation than with pleasure.[32]

Tom DeMarco, a leading thinker in the software industry, when asked in 1995 whether a team—a community—can exist where people do not see each other, said:

> No. Teams have to be together. Remoteness makes the good [community aspects] impossible. Too often we name a group of people a team. They don't acquire teamhood. They have it ascribed to them.[33]

DISPERSION, COORDINATION BREAKDOWN, LOSS OF "COMMUNICATION RICHNESS," AND LOSS OF "TEAMNESS"

The first four of the centrifugal forces are presented in this chapter beginning with dispersion. The discussion of dispersion versus co-location highlights something we know intuitively, that it is harder to manage from a distance. There is no more Management By Walking Around (MBWA) and there is no more informal adjustment by a programmer wandering down the hallway to a colleague's office saying: "Look at this piece of code; we've got a dependency problem that we need to talk about." These are all means of control and coordination, some of it formal, much of it informal. All these mechanisms fall apart when team members are far apart.

We prefer to do many of our tasks, from solving design problems to resolving a dispute, via face to face communication, because the communication is said to be "richer." When we channel communication into any electronic form, our communication degrades because we lose some richness. And losing that personal touch affects team members' relationships with other distant team members. Teams are fragile social units. On the one hand, a good team is brimming with commitment and experience to do the best job. On the other hand, once you tamper with a team by adding the burden of distance, time zone differences, and cross-cultural differences, you lose its "teamness"—that synergistic effect that makes it successful as a cohesive unit. Add to that all the "normal" factors that cause teams to fail, and global software teams become a risky managerial proposition. The discussion of teamness covers those problems that are more likely in global teams: Cross-cultural diversity leads to slower processes and, when combined with distance, inhibits the sense of cohesion. Geographic and cultural separation means that the key ingredient of trust takes longer, perhaps much longer to appear. Also, dispersed teams are often bigger than co-located teams—further hurting teamness by reducing intimacy.

Dispersion

There is no need to tell experienced managers that it is better to manage groups of people who are co-located rather than dispersed. This finding was validated in a creative way in a seminal 1977 study by technology management scholar Tom Allen.[34] Allen carefully tabulated the communication frequency of over 500 individuals in seven organizations over the course of six months. Using that data, he developed a profound relationship between distance and communication (Exhibit 4–1). Allen found that communication drops precipitously when engineers' offices are more than 25 meters from one another.

One global software manager in the GDSD study stated:

> It's hard, it's hard. No one in their right mind would split up their development effort just for the fun of it. It's much easier when someone is close to you. Technology has done a lot to ameliorate—but not to turn dispersed development into an advantage.

Co-location is, simply put, physical proximity—being within easy walking distance—whether that be down the hall, or in the adjacent building.[35] Co-location allows managers to manage by observation or the MBWA (Management By Walking Around).

"Out of sight out of mind" is one result of distance. The Holiday Inn outsourcing case of Chapter 14 describes a software development organization in which things worked nicely with an informal, comfortable, co-located style, but failed once the programming unit was moved back to

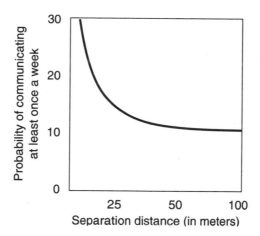

Exhibit 4–1   Relationship of distance to probability of communication.[37]

India. Problems began to bubble up, but the distant American managers were not really aware of the gravity of the situation.

Farshad Rafii[36] summarizes the advantages of co-location for product development (such as software development). Shorter project timelines result from shorter communications lines and the ability to give feedback quickly. The co-located team is less likely to squabble since co-location usually increases trust and reduces miscommunication. Co-location reduces project costs primarily because fewer organizational support services are needed to support one rather than two (or more) units. Managerial resources are also conserved. A study conducted by Stalk and Hout[38] found that a project manager of a project distributed in just a few adjacent buildings logs up to eleven miles per week in walking. Additional time is spent coordinating meetings, many of which are needed because the team members have far fewer informal lines of communications.

It is not uncommon to find American software firms, after having acquired smaller domestic companies, moving all their developers to the home location of the acquiring firm (as Microsoft has frequently done). Galbraith, the organizational designer, writes that when organizations want to foster productive relationships, they need to reduce the distance and physical barriers between people so as to increase the amount of communication.[39]

However, Rafii argues that co-location is "increasingly becoming less feasible" for many of the reasons that were introduced in Chapter 1: the need to be simultaneously close to the important customers and close to centers of knowledge (e.g., Silicon Valley). Even Tom Allen's study (Exhibit 4–1) showed that when professionals are separated by more than a few hundred feet, their informal communications drops to such an extent that they may as well be separated by hundreds of miles. One of Rafii's studies finds similar results. He observed software departments located on two floors of the same building and found very little interaction, transfer of learning, or the use of process tools.

To be fair, co-location actually has several *disadvantages*. Informal, oral communication may promote sloppiness in documentation and procedures such as passing along a half-finished task with the tacit understanding that it will be fully fixed and documented later. Furthermore, co-location leads to inbreeding, groupthink, and other group pathologies, whereas decentralization fosters independent thinking and initiative.

Co-location and dispersion are tied to the age-old continuum of centralization and decentralization of organizations. One factor affecting centralization is decision-making. Centralization is the concentration of decision-making at a single point in the organization. Older management notions assumed that decentralization of authority meant a loss of control, but with new technology this is less of an issue. Another factor affecting centralization is costs. For example, much of the historical debate in the Information Systems community on centralization versus decentralization focuses on issues that are less relevant today: the economies of scale associated with hardware and the historically high costs of telecommunications.

Then why do organizations centralize? Left to their own devices, software development managers naturally gravitate toward centralized organizations for the following reasons:

- *Control.* Control means the adherence to standards. Typically, headquarters wants to maintain a specific level of quality, that is, a certain set of standards.
- *Less duplication of effort and wasted effort.* When resources are centralized, all the specialists are easily maintained. There is no need for one specialist in each location.
- *Better ability to maintain a corporate culture.* Simply witness Microsoft's Redmond campus.

- *The need for developers to be near major customers and markets.*
- *The company focus on short product life cycles and product innovation breakthroughs.*

Decentralized software development has advantages, namely, local responsiveness to customers and the innovation of smaller, more independent groups. So the dispersion decision involves a continuum of how to find the right balance between central control and local autonomy in order to bring about the best results. Global R&D executives managing webs of laboratories deal with this issue often as they balance the need to avoid duplication and inefficiencies versus the need to allow autonomy of innovation. And it seems that cultural factors are at play here. For example, German/Swiss firms tend to centralize their R&D while firms from other nations are less inclined.

Breakdown of traditional control & coordination mechanisms

The overhead of control and coordination associated with any software project is astounding. Developers spend as much as 70% of their time working with others[40] and as much as 40% of their time waiting for resources or doing other work.[41] Some of the time working with others includes critical value-added activities such as group design meetings, but as project participants know, the coordination and control overhead is often frustrating.

Distributed/dispersed teams create further burdens on coordination and control mechanisms—primarily the informal ones. Because of distance, people cannot coordinate by peeking around the cubicle wall, nor can managers control by strolling down the hall and visiting team members' offices. With time zone differences, no longer can a quick phone call resolve an issue or clarify an algorithm on the fly. Finally it should be clear that as coordination needs for global software teams rise, so too does the load on all forms of communication—from the telephone to more subtle communications channels, such as the multi-site project management package.

Coordination is the act of integrating each task and organizational unit so that it contributes to the overall objective

Control is the process of adhering to goals or policies or standards

---

The cost of coordinating work—measured primarily in labor and management time—increases when one of two factors loom larger: when tasks are new or uncertain and, of more interest to our topic, when the work units become more interdependent. That means that as interdependence between teams increases, the need for coordination increases. This idea of increasing coordination costs is illustrated in Exhibit 4–2 and based on the work of management theorist Thompson.[42]

Today we know much more about coordination and control than did the designers of automobile mass production lines in the early 1900s. We know that control and coordination have blended to the point where they are nearly inseparable, as exemplified by Exhibit 4–3. We also know that these coordination and control concepts imply a balance between formal mechanisms (e.g., weekly meetings) and informal mechanisms (e.g., solving a problem over a cup of coffee or via a chat in the hallway). On a much larger scale the need for balance implies organization-wide structural adjustments. Global strategists Bartlett and Ghoshal[43] had an interesting insight: that global companies had reached somewhat of a coordina-

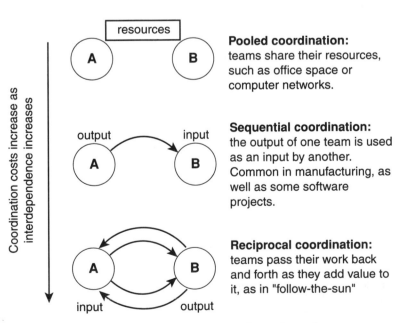

Exhibit 4–2 Coordination costs and interdependence.

Structured and formal mechanisms:

- *Departmentalization*: shaping the form of the organization, drawing organizational charts
- *Employee selection*: through hiring
- *Centralization* of decision making through the hierarchy of formal authority
- *Standardization* through written policies, rules, manuals, and charts
- *Planning* such as strategic planning, scheduling
- *Control* through measures such as technical reports, sales reports, financial performance
- *Control* via direct supervision

Informal mechanisms:

- *Lateral relations* through direct contacts, committees, and task forces
- *Informal communications* via personal contacts, conferences, and job rotation
- *Socialization* through organizational culture and team culture, shared values, training, measurement and reward systems.

Exhibit 4–3   Common mechanisms of coordination and control.[44]

tion crisis by 1980. Historical structures were no longer effective as coordination mechanisms. The companies reacted by seemingly swapping approaches: The European and Japanese firms responded by formalizing, while the American firms responded by creating informal mechanisms.

Dewane Perry and his colleagues decided that they wanted to find out what programmers really do all day long.[45] (Perhaps they were motivated by Mintzberg's seminal study, from the early 1970s, in which he followed executives around all day and found out that they do not really do what all the textbooks say they do.) They followed several developers—mostly programmers—around for several days, noting everything they did. What Perry et al. found was that these developers spend 75 minutes per day in unplanned, informal, interpersonal interactions: someone walking in, a chat by the coffee machine, a brief phone call. All of these are not part of the scheduled, more formal meetings (and the researchers did not include purely social interactions). Developers use these informal interactions for problem solving, informal code reviews, and other objectives. One of the highest number of informal interactions by a developer—14 unique contacts—took place when a developer had to modify code that had other code owners.

The loss of "communication richness"

As it turns out, we humans prefer different kinds of communication transmissions—or different media—for different kinds of tasks. A congratulations is best done in person, or perhaps with a telephone call. An inquiry to the personnel department may best be done via e-mail. A formal invitation is best sent on nice paper stationary via snail-mail. And to tackle a really wicked problem or to resolve an acrimonious dispute? That is a job that we prefer to do face to face.

We like to use "richer" communication media for tasks which require a rich message, or "high touch" as it has been called lately. Rich communication is defined as two-way interaction involving more than one sensory channel.[46] This means that common media like the telephone and e-mail are not "rich" (though we will refrain from calling them poor). In fact, the different media can be placed along a continuum of media richness, as in Exhibit 4–4. Interestingly, the continuum has been used by US-based Verifone Corporation (now part of Hewlett-Packard) to help its employees understand its own global teams' needs.[47]

Only some of the message we communicate is strictly in the explicit text that we transmit. A substantial portion—perhaps as high as 80%—is nonverbal and implicit. It consists of body language such as gestures, facial expressions, and posture. We like to use richer media to convey more information and emotion. Nonverbal communication is particularly important for (so-called "high context") cultures outside the sphere of Anglo and Northern European cultures. But the desire for rich communication crosses cultures. When intensive problem-solving, design, or conceptual collaboration needs to take place, many global software managers choose the channel of communication that allows for richest communication. First of all, they get on an airplane for a face to face meeting. As a compromised alternative, they use one of the direct conferencing techniques: audio or video.

Given the different development cycle stages, some tasks require richer communication than do others.[48] Customer contact should be face to face during requirements gathering and later during prototyping. Designers need richer media to collaborate with one another during analysis and design phases. Generally, any task requiring intense cooperation requires more communication—the richer the better. But a recent study of dispersed software teams found that team members always wanted richer medium no matter what the task.[49]

LOWEST Psychological Interaction

US Mail—Pmail (snail mail)
Courier Pmail
Electronic Mail (addressed)
Electronic Mail (bulletin board)
Fax
Voicemail
Electronic "Chat" 1:1
Electronic "Chat" 1:Many
One-way broadcast audio
One-way broadcast video
Store-and-forward compressed audio on demand
Audio annotation to files/e-mail
Store-and-forward compressed video on-demand
One-way broadcast audio w/audio back channel
Point-to-Point Telephone Call (Standard Telephone)
Point-to-Point Telephone Call (Full Duplex Audio Conferencing)
Multi-point Telephone Call (Standard Telephone)
Multi-point Telephone Call (Full Duplex Audio Conferencing)
Live Board with point-to-point audio
Live Board with multi-point audio
One-way broadcast video w/audio back channel
Point-to-point video conference (56–112 KBytes)
Point-to-point video conference (>112 KBytes)
Multi-point video conference (56–112 KBytes)
Multi-point video conference (> 112 KBytes)
Virtual Reality meeting
Face to Face meeting

HIGHEST Psychological Interaction

Exhibit 4–4   Communication richness and the continuum of psychological interaction.[50]

Communication is even more than just task-specific. A global software manager must regularly convey the team vision to all participating
groups and cultures, and to do so in a way that is certain to be understood.
Since the "vision" is one that must appeal to the emotional and motiva-
tional levels, good managers choose the delivery media very carefully.
     Some have suggested to look at media richness less as a continuum
and more as a multi-dimensional scale.[51] For example, the telephone can

be used as a complement to e-mail (as in "let's talk about the e-mail I just sent you that you can pull up on your screen"), or as a proper substitute for richer media. Furthermore, not all people see the media richness continuum in quite the same way. Some people know how to use e-mail very effectively to express themselves (using emoticons or well-crafted sentences). Naturally, masters of e-mail expressiveness may be a mixed blessing in a global team consisting of some members whose English does not allow them to appreciate graceful and subtle prose.

Loss of "teamness"

Why has there been such interest in teams in business? All kinds of new team forms have been recognized, formalized, and encouraged, such as those in the box below. A good team encompasses a set of benefits that is seductive to any organization.[52] It creates synergistic ideas and innovations; it is better at objectively evaluating ideas and finding mistakes; it provides greater access to expertise and experience; it enhances motivation and commitment to the task; it has greater access to information; and it is a very flexible unit of work. In fact, a really good team *doesn't even need to communicate much*; its members know all about each others' strengths and weaknesses, they already know the process, and they share a common vision.[53]

Teams

Multi-functional: Includes members that traditionally were in other organizational functions and roles. Now that they are part of the team they are more committed to its objectives.

Self-empowered: Members make decisions about their own work without going through the hierarchy.

Self-managed: Members take over management tasks such as scheduling and performance.

High-performing: Outperforms other teams and outperforms expectations given its composition.

What is a team, really? Does the hub and spoke modularized structure of Baan really represent a team? Does the network structure of IBM's

JavaBeans project represent a team? There is a truism: You know a real team when you see it. More formally, the list below details several characteristics of what a "real" team ought to be, though few real teams satisfy all of these characteristics. The global software teams in the GDSD study satisfied relatively few of these.

A real team:

- is perceived to be a team by its members
- is recognized as a team by non-members (i.e., it has a boundary, people know who is a member and who is not)
- has collective responsibility for its products
- shares responsibility for managing its work
- has a common goal or set of tasks
- works together on tasks that are interdependent
- demands peak performance from all members (rather than just some)
- shares its rewards
- is small in number of members

If the group of people collaborating on a project is not a team, then what is it? Some social scientists define "team" narrowly. At the extreme, an ad hoc collection of individuals is just a *group.* Most researchers see groups and teams along a continuum of "teamness" and "groupness."[54] And, of course, we frequently use the term "project"[55] (or programme in Europe) as in *project team.* After all, in many cases, the individual developers come together for a specific task—such as release 2.1. Once that release is complete, the project team is disbanded. But the term *project,* without team attached to it, suggests a more transient form of member grouping. Members may enter and leave the project at various stages of the development life cycle.

The topic of *dispersed teams* is new ground. Social scientists have been studying co-located teams (in one site) for many years and know a lot about what makes them tick. But, in spite of the promise of virtual organizations, there is still little hard research on dispersed teams and what makes them tick *together.*

Diversity's drawbacks

What is the composition of a successful team? The question usually boils down to the controversy of whether homogeneous (nondiverse) team membership is better than heterogeneous (diverse) team membership. The accepted wisdom on diverse teams is that they require more time to get consensus to implement solutions.[56] In other words, the cultural differences and miscommunication slow down the process. Of course, diverse teams bring advantages as well: They broaden thinking, they generate more problem solving options, and there is less groupthink.

Two studies illustrate findings on the topic of diversity. Belbin[57] constructed well over one hundred teams of various attributes and measured their effectiveness in managerial games. His findings were quite revolutionary in the thinking about teams: Teams we would now call diverse (or as he labeled them, "mixed") on a number of attributes, tended to be the more successful teams. Laurent[58] of INSEAD conducted an experiment measuring creativity. He created teams made up of either diverse membership or relatively homogeneous membership. He then measured their performance on creative problem solving. He found that the diverse teams formed a bi-modal distribution. That is, diverse teams were either better or worse than homogeneous teams at creative tasks.

The social science research needs to be taken with some caution because most of the teams that were studied were co-located teams. By and large, social scientists have not studied "multi-modal" teams—where the diversity is clustered in distinct and separate units. Global software teams are really multi-polar teams: each unit is culturally homogenous, but across units there is cultural heterogeneity.

Loss of cohesion

We know that successful teams are *cohesive.* Studies show that cohesiveness leads to enhanced motivation, increased morale, greater productivity, harder work, more open communication, and higher job satisfaction than non-cohesive groups. Cohesiveness means that the team has bonded, or in DeMarco and Lister's[59] words—the team has *jelled.* The team members help each other, they complement each other, they know each others' strengths and weaknesses. Successful teams develop their own culture and norms. Cohesion is one of the differences between a successful team and one that is merely plodding.

Cohesion is more difficult for cross-cultural teams due to a multitude of factors that may crop up.[60] People will mistrust each other due to excessive stereotyping, more in-group conversations, and lowered interpersonal attractiveness. Incidents of miscommunication are likely due to language. Team members cannot feel relaxed with each other. There is constant tension and alertness to linguistic and cultural messages.

Teams coalesce differently in different cultures. Most national cultures are categorized as collectivist cultures (e.g., Latin, Asian), in which individuals value the harmony and the welfare of the group above their own personal ambition. Within these cultures teams will naturally form into more cohesive units because individuals are more inclined to find meaning in team membership. Paradoxically, the notion of teams has been embraced by the American business culture. For Americans, who rate highest on individualism of *all* world cultures, team cohesiveness would seem antithetical. Individual rewards systems are strongly entrenched in the United States and are, by definition, divisive. The reflexive affinity of the computer culture toward individual freedom further aggravates this paradox.

Building trust takes time

Distance is an impediment to building relationships of trust. After all, "trust needs touch."[61] While co-located team members can build trust through formal and informal face to face meetings, trust takes time to develop.

---

trust is the peculiar belief predicated not on evidence but on the lack of contrary evidence.

—Gambetta[62]

The rather unique problem of dispersed teams is that they meet, if at all, infrequently and that they communicate primarily asynchronously. Yet it is important that you trust the message in the last e-mail and not read other ideas and hidden meanings into it. For some cultures sustaining, let alone building, trusting relationships in a detached, electronic environment is unimaginable unless solid personal relationships have been formed early.

Like a co-located team, a dispersed team needs to progress through psychosocial stages of development before it functions well as a team rather than as a collection of individuals and sub-units. The classic stage model of team development, first introduced by Tuckman,[63] is shown in Exhibit 4–5. This model assumes that the team goes through three stages until it reaches maturity and effective performance. The defining episode is the team's ability to overcome some early conflicts (the storming stage). Whether or not this model is precisely descriptive of all teams,[64] it has been broadly copied, abridged, and reused, since it is intuitively accepted that the model's notion of developmental stages to reach peak performance is essentially correct. Clearly, no team will perform instantly at its highest potential level. From what is known about team development, dispersed teams take longer to move through the early stages because of distance between members. Therefore, it can be assumed that a global software team will not even reach the "performing" stage of the model in only one product development cycle. Not until the second or even third release cycle will the team reach the higher levels of trust and psychosocial maturity.

Team size gets out of hand

Global teams in multiple sites are generally larger per task than co-located teams. Each unit at each site usually requires extra support and administrative overhead. Once the project is dispersed, it is harder for the project

Forming	The team gets together and gets to know each other. It clarifies roles, figures out the tasks and the objectives.
Storming	Conflicts break out over roles, objectives, and task allocations. Different leaders, official or otherwise, are pursuing different goals.
Norming	The team begins to form norms, roles, and protocols for working together. Some team cohesion may begin.
Performing	The team begins to perform well, working together toward a common goal. Conflicts are handled constructively.

Exhibit 4–5 The classic stage model of team psychosocial developmental maturity.

manager to ensure that each of the units remains small. Each of the dispersed units is likely to grow on its own momentum. In all, dispersing an existing project team is likely to make it larger overall. More people, in more roles, are involved.

"Smallness" is important because it ensures effective communication amongst all team members. The fewer the team members, the fewer communication links needed. The number of possible communication links grows geometrically following the formula $n*(n-1)/2$. With nine members, a team must manage up to 36 communication links (Exhibit 4–6). Of course, smallness is also associated with a sense of intimacy that, in turn, creates trust and cohesiveness.

Software managers and researchers are unanimous in advocating *small* teams. Most see a point of diminishing returns of adding extra developers (see graph in Exhibit 4–7). In a previous study of packaged software teams that I co-authored with Barbara Bird, we posited a rule: *A team of ten or above is a violation of "small is beautiful."*[65] Team leads like very

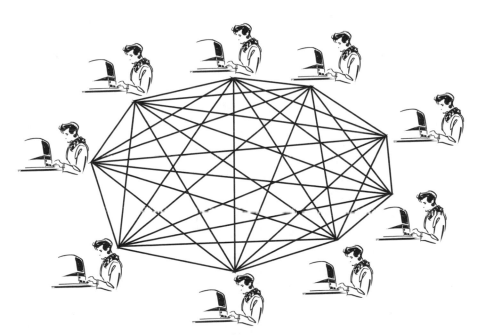

Exhibit 4–6 The maximum number of communication links required in a team of 9 members (=36).

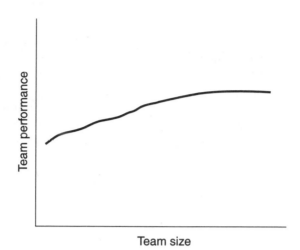

Exhibit 4–7 Performance of teams as they increase in size.

small teams: The head of Microsoft's first NT release is quoted as saying that the ideal team size is a team of *one* person.[66] In a software engineering textbook,[67] we find the statement that if a software product would take one person one year to complete, it would also most likely take three people one year to complete—and not four months—and it would most likely be of poorer quality. The Standish Group used a database of thousands of projects and found that there was an inverse correlation between project success and project size. Smaller projects (costing under $750,000) succeeded 55% of the time while large projects (over $5 million) had a success rate of only 7%.[68]

Further Reading

The best read for how to run a good team and how not to is Tracy Kidder's *Soul of a New Machine*. It's a true story of a team of engineers developing a new minicomputer. It reads like a novel. It will give you lessons for a lifetime.

A good primer on teams is *The wisdom of teams: creating the high performance organization,* by J.R. Katzenbach and Douglas K. Smith, published by Harper Business, 1993.

CULTURAL DIFFERENCES

The domain of cultural differences is likely to be a new one for most software professionals, so it merits a lengthier introductory discussion with more background information. The chapter begins by asking whether culture differences are still important these days given the "global village." Since the answer is "yes," any team member in a multi-country collaboration must begin to develop a deep awareness of cultural issues through more than just parlor talk. Unfortunately, there is no shortcut: There is no magical "grand theory of culture" that can be mastered in a quick read. Nonetheless, a useful starting point down the path of understanding culture is the principal dimensions of culture. The chapter covers ten such dimensions from the well-known works of Hofstede and Hall. The second half of the chapter is structured as a debate about whether the all-embracing computer culture dominates differences between national cultures or not.

Is culture significant?

Software professionals scatter all along the continuum of "does culture matter?" At one extreme are those that, by and large, deny cultural issues, arguing that as the world becomes a global village with dozens of

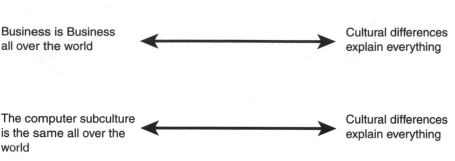

Exhibit 5–1   The continuum of "does culture matter?"

global products and services—the colors of Benetton, the burgers of Mc-Donalds—we have achieved convergence. Management and technology are by now universal and "business is business." On the other extreme are those who explain all problems as culturally induced. So what is culture?

> [Culture] provides members with images of their basic concerns, principles, ethics, and bodies of manners, rituals, ideologies, strategies, and tactics of self-survival including certain notions of good deeds and bad, various forms of folklore and legends. . . . The way we give logic to the world begins at birth with the gestures, words, tone of voice, noises, colors, smells, and body contact we experience. . . . Our culture is what is familiar, recognizable, habitual. It is 'what goes without saying'[69]

Culture may be a sensitive topic to discuss. By necessity, describing cultural differences must deal with stereotypes. A stereotype often has a negative association bordering on bigotry. However, bigotry uses stereotypes to say *all* members of a national culture are alike. At all times we must be aware that individual differences dominate cultural differences: The variance and range of personalities of individual Russians are much greater than the cultural differences between Americans and Russians. Each individual Russian and each individual American are made up of many attributes, such as the attribute "importance of material goods." When we refer to something as an "American stereotype," we are really referring to a normal distribution (a bell-shaped curve) of individuals who cluster around a hypothetical "cultural mean" of the importance of material goods. There are individual Americans who care little for material goods and there are those individuals whose sole purpose in life is to collect more of them.

To alleviate any discomfort, one could replace the word stereotype, with the word "archetype," or the term "mental file."[70] Cultural experts claim that the most effective managers are those that use these cultural mental files as starting points and continuously update them with new information. Less successful managers are those who deny having any stereotypes and those who rely strictly on the stereotypes.

Some of the software professionals I have spoken to, particularly in US firms, believe, out of a sense of idealism, that cultural differences are insignificant. They believe that that we are all equal, or should see each other as equal (and this world outlook is in itself fairly "American" as we shall see later). Others think cultural differences are insignificant because of a naïve belief (or imperialistic belief as some would see it!) that American cultural mores are somehow "neutral" and do not really carry cultural baggage. One American manager with four years of offshore experience complained to me about all those cross-cultural preparation classes. "Those cultural profiles of what Italians do and what Spaniards do are just trite," he said to me. Yet only a few minutes later, recounting the project customers he dealt with, he said: "Dealing with the Swedes and the Dutch was just like the stereotypes: The Dutch are always right and you have to do it their way; the Swedes are consensus builders, taking a long time making decisions—taking forever to make a decision! . . ."

The very notion that culture can be managed is *itself cultural:* American managers understand culture as something an organization *has*, while Europeans understand culture as something an organization *is*. Americans believe in controlling their destiny and their ability to change corporate cultures, even in relatively short time spans.[71] Americans developed the notion of "schools of management" (business schools), which until the 1980s were largely absent from the European and Asian landscapes.

Different types of culture

Although many cultures are demarcated nicely within a national boundary, other cultural attributes cross boundaries such as the Arab or Latin

American cultures. Some nations have strong internal cultural differences such as Canada (English and French), or India (there are 14 official languages in India and hundreds of dialects). Most nations have intra-regional differences such as the difference between the US Northeast and South or the states (Länder) in Germany.

Many other forms of culture exist. The first is organizational culture, commonly known as *corporate culture.* Well known exemplars of corporate culture include US-headquartered Proctor & Gamble and Microsoft, French Michelin, and Toyota in Japan. The notion of corporate culture covers many facets of organizational life, areas such as management styles, appraisals, rewards, and communication styles used by employees. It would be reasonable to assume that a strong multinational corporate culture would diminish the effects of national cultural differences. In fact, studies of multinationals versus independent companies have found just the opposite effect. Cultural differences are more pronounced among foreign employees working within a multinational corporation.[72] Perhaps the pressures to conform to the foreign corporate culture caused employees to cling tightly to what is theirs.

Corporate culture may be strong for the group but weak for individuals. An American joining, say Microsoft, will need a few months to adjust to the corporate culture. An American moving to another country may take an entire lifetime to adjust. A Frenchman may accept an egalitarian edict from corporate culture and begin using the familiar *tu* form of addressing other employees, but outside the firm, he will revert to the formal *vous* and to Monsier Directeur.[73] The corporate culture is only skin deep as compared to the intensity of national cultural norms.

A much stronger culture is the *professional culture.* Lawyers, military, academics, and programmers are all part of their professional cultures. Professional culture is ingrained in us through highly structured formal education during formative years and continued through training programs. The culture is reinforced through ongoing professional activities such as affiliation with associations. Professional culture is a strong culture since a person chooses one's profession for life and does not often move from one to another as one would move from company to company. Furthermore, professional cultures cross over national cultures. This last point is important to the topic of the software culture—does it dominate national culture?—which we'll return to later in this chapter.

Within organizations we also find *functional cultures.* A functional culture is made up of those norms and habits associated with functional roles within the organization, such as marketing, sales, finance, R&D, and manufacturing. These are the "stovepipes" or "functional silos" of corporations. Most current business thinking finds this kind of culture as a barrier to flexible organizations and business process reengineering. Furthermore, when functional cultures are ingrained they become obstacles to effective cross-functional teamwork.[74] Functional cultural differences are one of the key differences between Information Systems development and packaged software development.

Finally, good teams develop their own *team culture.* Team culture emerges from bonding through common work experiences; through disasters and successes; from a few cliquish jokes; via a team symbol or icon; and through favorite ways to let off steam together.

To summarize, each individual is a member of multiple cultures: one or more national/ethnic cultures; one or more professional cultures; perhaps a functional culture; perhaps a corporate culture; and perhaps a team culture. And all of these cultures are moving targets. None of them is totally static. Over time some cultures loosen their grip on us. I've heard the following type of refrain from a number of software professionals in the United States: "I'm more American now than I am Indian." Even for those who do not immigrate, national culture is blurring in today's global village. And is there really a future for corporate cultures with loose alliances, joint ventures, and partnerships?

The fundamentals of cultural differences: Hofstede, Hall, and others

Managing cultural differences can only be achieved by an awareness—a knowledge—of the fundamentals of cultural differences. Since there is no general theory of cultural differences, one useful approach is to detect key dimensions that distinguish cultures. We can then analyze cultures along these dimensions—with data, with observations, and with anecdotes.

Geert Hofstede and Edward T. Hall have had a profound impact on the way that we understand cultural differences. Each identified a set of fundamental cultural differences, referred to here as dimensions (Exhibit 5–2). Coincidentally, Hofstede's and Hall's work are both represented by five such dimensions. The dimensions have little overlap and nicely complement one another.[75]

Hofstede's dimensions of national culture

- Revering hierarchy
- Individualism/collectivism
- Taking care of business
- Risk avoidance
- Long term orientation

Hall's dimensions of national culture

- Space
- Material goods
- Friendship
- Time
- Agreement

Exhibit 5–2   The dimensions of national culture.

Hofstede's seminal work has been used as a basis for literally hundreds of studies and untold Ph.D. dissertations. Using data collected between 1967 and 1978, Hofstede, a Dutch scholar who was then an industrial psychologist at IBM, collected surveys from IBM personnel in 40 countries on the topic of work values. His work is important because, using a very large sample (over 100,000 surveys), he was one of the first who empirically isolated attitudes of people towards their jobs along a number of "dimensions of culture." Hofstede's work is particularly relevant to our interest in software because it was based on a single, consistent control group: employees in dozens of international offices of IBM. Some social scientists have faulted Hofstede's study for this research design, but for our own purposes, it is quite advantageous since it deals with computer professionals in a company with a computer culture. And, in spite of IBM's strong corporate culture, national cultural differences did surface.

Data for Hofsetede's five dimensions of national culture are presented in Tables 5–1A through 5–1E[76] and each of the dimensions is described below.

Revering Hierarchy (or "power distance," in Hofstede's terminology) has to do with how people think about equality and relationships with superiors and subordinates. In some cultures people see large gaps between levels of the organizational hierarchy. Individuals are careful about expressing their opinions to superiors and show proper respect to their boss. Superiors issue directives and expect subordinates to speak only when allowed to do so by a superior and are unpleasantly surprised when subordinates freely air their opinions. Other cultures do not revere hierarchy as much. Managers are less concerned with status and are more willing or even expect their subordinates to speak out. Latin Americans generally score high on revering hierarchy, with Panama, the highest. Israelis score the lowest on revering hierarchy, probably due to the socialist ethos of their founders. A related study by Hampden–Turner and Trompenaars[77] asked managers to choose the shape that most resembles their organization. The results shown in Exhibit 5–3 nicely summarize the different perspectives on hierarchy.

Some implications: In organizations that cross borders or have employees from a range of cultures, problems may arise because of different attitudes toward hierarchy. For example, in cultures that do not revere hierarchy, employees can be expected to take initiative in discussing their careers with their supervisors. Individuals from cultures that revere hierarchy are less likely to initiate this kind of dialogue.

Individualism versus Collectivism is the extent to which a person sees herself as an individual rather than part of a group. In individualist cultures people are expected to have their own opinion, are concerned with personal achievement, with individual rights, and with independence. In collectivist cultures opinions are predetermined by group membership because people see themselves first as part of the group and are concerned with the welfare of the group. In fact, they value the harmony and the welfare of the group above their own personal ambition. Anglo-Saxon cultures scored high on individualism, with Americans highest while East Asians scored highest on collectivism (or lowest on individualism).

Implications: Software teams frequently rely on group decision making techniques, most with roots in individualistic cultures. While individualists may be comfortable with a technique that inherently relies on conflict, that is not the case for someone with a "collectivist" orientation

because it would require him to be rude and to disrupt interpersonal relationships. For example, when tensions mount in an East Asian group,
members of this collectivist culture will be evasive rather than confronta-
tive. This is insulting to an individualist, who expects to be told honestly
what is the matter. So a minor meeting conflict between members of individualist and collectivist cultures could inadvertently result in mutual in-
sults through their styles of communication. This dimension also affects reward systems. Individualist cultures tend to reward individuals, while for
those in collectivist cultures, preserving harmony and equality is more important. Rewarding just the stars in the team may create embarrassment
and disrupt team harmony.

Taking care of business (or "masculinity/femininity" in Hofstede's unfortunate choice of terminology) positions the "toughness" needed in taking
care of business ("masculine") versus the softer values of taking care of
people and being concerned with quality of life ("femininity"). Japan ranks
highest on the dimension of "taking care of business." In contrast, the
Scandinavian nations rank lowest. In these cultures there is a preference
for relationships, caring and nurturing for its members, and quality of life
issues rather than bottom-line performance. These differences are apparent when comparing the Japanese norms of long work days and little uti-
lized vacation time with the Scandinavian 38-hour workweek and long
annual vacations.

  Implications: In taking-care-of-business cultures, the company counts
above all. An individual's worth is measured by related dimensions such
as competitiveness, assertiveness, promotions, and bonuses. At the other
extreme are cultures, such as the Scandinavian countries, in which employee quality of life is viewed as more important.

Risk Avoidance (or "uncertainty avoidance" in Hofstede's terminology)
has to do with people's attitudes toward risky situations, ambiguous behavior, predictability, and control. High risk avoidance cultures place
greater emphasis on stability rather than innovation and change. Their
members are more risk averse at starting companies or welcoming outsiders. Low risk avoidance cultures more readily embrace change, tend to
be more entrepreneurial, are more likely to break the rules, and are more
accepting of new ideas. The Japanese rated highest on risk avoidance
while the Danes rated lowest. As with other cultural measures, the con-

struct of risk avoidance is somewhat problematic since it is actually a composite of several attitudes toward risk which may vary quite a bit from each other.[78] For example, Americans engage in riskier behavior in changing jobs or in financial investments, but are risk-averse in seeking very detailed specific language in business contracts.

Long-Term Orientation (a.k.a Confucianism dynamism) In later years Hofstede introduced a fifth dimension of national culture to acknowledge the deep differences between Western and East Asian cultures. These have to do with the relative importance of the here-and-now versus the future—the long-term. Confucianism also includes such traits as thrift, persistence, diligence, and patience. Confucian tradition, however, also implies strong patriarchal authority, which is family centered, and is also close to the "taking care of business" dimension.

Table 5–1A Revering Hierarchy. How unequal between rank and class is normal? Low scores represent little reverence of hierarchy.

Israel	13	rank and class are less important
Germany	35	
Netherlands	38	
USA	40	
Japan	54	
France	68	
Hong Kong	68	
India	77	
West Africa	77	
Indonesia	78	
China	80	
Russia	95	rank and class are very important

Table 5–1B Individualism-Collectivism. The degree to which individuals prefer to act as individuals rather than members of groups (i.e., collectivistic). High scores indicate high individualism. Low scores imply high degree of collectivism.

USA	91	Highly individualistic
Netherlands	80	
France	71	
Germany	67	
Israel	54	
Russia	50	
India	48	
Japan	46	
Hong Kong	25	
China	20	
West Africa	20	
Indonesia	14	Highly collectivistic

Table 5–1C Taking care of business. To what degree are tough values such as assertiveness valued against paternalistic values such as relationships and quality of life.

Japan	95	Tough values
Germany	66	
USA	62	
Hong Kong	57	
India	56	
China	50	
Israel	47	
West Africa	46	
Indonesia	46	
France	43	
Russia	40	
Netherlands	14	Paternalistic values

Table 5–1D   Risk Avoidance. To what degree do people prefer structured, low risk situations versus ambiguous, higher risk.

Japan	92	Avoid risk
Russia	90	
France	86	
Israel	81	
Germany	65	
China	60	
West Africa	54	
Netherlands	53	
Indonesia	48	
USA	46	
India	40	
Hong Kong	29	

Table 5–1E   Long-term orientation. Based on values of Confucianism. To what degree do people value the future (e.g., in persistence and thrift) versus the past or present.

China	118	future orientation
Hong Kong	96	
Japan	80	
India	61	
Netherlands	44	
Germany	31	
France	30	
USA	29	
Indonesia	25	
West Africa	16	
Russia	10	past and/or present orientation
Israel	N/A	

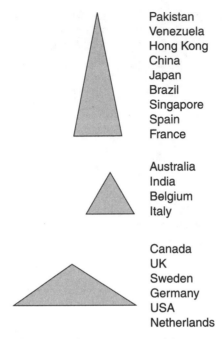

Pakistan
Venezuela
Hong Kong
China
Japan
Brazil
Singapore
Spain
France

Australia
India
Belgium
Italy

Canada
UK
Sweden
Germany
USA
Netherlands

Exhibit 5–3   What is the shape most resembling your organization?

   Hofstede's five dimensions highlight an important rule in understanding cultures: There is no easy categorization. Any one culture may appear in different places along the continuum. On some dimensions, the culture may be ranked near an endpoint, while on others it is ranked in the middle.

   Edward Hall, an American anthropologist, also introduced five dimensions of culture:[79]

   Space.   Different cultures vary in their attitudes toward space. Space manifests itself in many forms. Social distances, or "social bubbles," vary by culture. Americans need about two feet of separation to conduct a comfortable conversation with another person while Arabs are comfortable with considerably less and find an American backing away to a comfortable distance as being rude. Queuing behavior varies by culture. The British, while waiting for a bus, form nice organized queues with lots of space in between people to respect their social bubble. Israelis waiting for a bus will generally not queue or will form very vague clusters to represent queues. Seating arrangements vary by culture. While Japanese are careful about seating arrangements at a table, Americans generally sit wherever a seat is available. This is frustrating to Japanese because it gives them less information about rank and power than they are used to.

Material Goods. Material goods are used for power and status. A Danish CEO is admired by his employees for driving a battered old car. In Nordic countries pay scales are compressed relative to US pay scales. American managers battle to get the largest, most lavish office, preferably the corner office. In Japan, the boss has his desk in an open office space next to those of his subordinates, expressing the lesser importance placed on material as status.

Friendship. Friendships and relationships vary considerably across cultures. Americans are seen as being at one extreme of this dimension. Generally, they make friends and lose them quickly, regarding friendships as transitory, in part due to their high mobility. In cultures with longer-term relationships, friendships take a long time to develop but are very durable and involve a strong sense of mutual obligation. The same is true for business relationships. These cultures prefer to do business with people with whom they have developed a relationship. Only when a personal relationship is established do they engage in business.

Time. Linear time cultures ("monochronic" in Hall's terminology) take time and deadlines very seriously, in a very rationalist sense. Time is structured, sequential, and linear. Events are taken one at a time. People plan things in great details, treat deadlines very seriously, and are punctual, perhaps obsessive about keeping appointments. Expandable time cultures ("polychronic" in Hall's terminology) consider time commitments to be achieved only if possible. Time is unlimited or simultaneous. Many events can happen at once, such as multiple conversations. People change plans often and easily. Time is fluid, elastic. Delays are less important. Germans consider time to be very linear while the French consider it very expandable.

Implications: Time perceptions lead to misunderstandings. For example, a linear time person sees the expandable time person's lateness as rude—not taking the appointment seriously. However, for the person who sees time as expandable, lateness does not connote any sense of seriousness about a relationship. While a linear time person treats any deadline seriously, the expandable time person finds this attitude baffling, since time is only one of the many variables he weighs. In software development, that other variable may well be quality—and it may well be worth delaying completion since hasty software is likely to have more bugs. It is worth noting that functional cultures tend to divide along the time dimension as well: In the United States, marketing people tend to view time as expandable while IS people see time as linear.[80]

Agreement. Expressing agreement and disagreement varies by culture. In some cultures the detailed written contract is essential to agreement, while in others a handshake is sufficient. In some cultures disagreement and dissent are openly and quickly expressed, yet in others open confrontation must be avoided at all costs. Americans respect candor and frank discussion, whereas in other cultures frank discussions are to be strongly avoided.

Implications: Cultures differ in their attitudes toward contracts. Americans and Northern Europeans try to spell out all the details and contingencies in contracts, while other cultures are not used to doing so and are not necessarily being evasive.

Hall, as well as other culture social scientists, has synthesized some of these five dimensions into a single critical dimension that describes language and communication: *High-context versus Low-context* communication. This dimension defines how people communicate—how they see language, whether as neutral and explicit for low-context cultures, or as emotional and implicit for high context cultures. High-context cultures, such as the Latins, the Arabs, and the East Asians, communicate a message in which most of the information is in the person, the surroundings, and the social perspective. Much of what is communicated is not said. Ambiguity may even be valued. For these cultures the relationship of trust is of paramount importance. In low-context communication cultures, such as Anglo, Nordic, and German, people communicate in such a way that most of the information is explicitly stated in the actual message. The person, the surroundings, the social perspective are largely irrelevant. These cultures require a high degree of precision in their communication. Ambiguity is frowned upon.

High and Low communication context cultures

High Context (implicit)			Japanese Arab Latin	Chinese Mediterranean Indian
Low context (explicit)			American English	German Scandinavian

Implications: Becoming sensitized to high-/low-context culture clashes is particularly useful for understanding miscommunication. An example is a business negotiation. For the high-context partner business negotiations can really begin only after a relationship has developed. A relationship involves trust building. And trust building takes time. Americans (low-context) like to get down to business or begin coding or designing without going through steps of building a relationship. They are also obsessed with their own self-imposed deadlines. Perhaps they already have a flight scheduled and another meeting waiting. Both cultures have a duty to recognize the culture clash. The low-context partners should understand that they need to invest time and effort in relationship building. The high-context partner needs to invest in the relationship by giving the partners some indications of progress on substance.

Somewhat analogous to high-/low-context is the dimension presented by Hampden-Turner and Trompenaars[81] who distinguish between *universalist* cultures and *particularist* cultures. Universalists are those who see rules as those that everyone must follow. Particularists see situations as made up of particular individuals, unique relationships, special circumstances, and exceptional requests. The differences are best illustrated by the results of a study, presented in Exhibit 5–4, in which answers were compiled from managers from 12 nations. The results show a spectrum of universalism and particularism. Low-context cultures, such as the United States, were rated highest in universalism, while high-context cultures rated higher in particularism.

Do Cultural Differences Affect Software Professionals?

As with generic cultural differences, there is a continuum in the thinking.[82] On one hand there are those who find that, yes, there are specific norms of software development that are cultural. And then there are those who say that, no, the differences are negligible and they are washed out by the common global culture of computing. Exhibit 5–5 summarizes the varied perspectives of global software managers that were interviewed.

Managers were posed dilemmas pitting universalism against particularism

Q1. While you are talking and sharing a bottle of bear with a freind who was officially on duty as a safety controller in the company you both work for, an accident occurs, injuring a shift worker. An investigation is launched by the national safety commission and you are asked for your evidence. There are no other witnesses. What right has your friend to expect you to protect him?

① a definite right   ② some right   ③ no right

no right	USA	NL	Aus'l	Can	Ger	Swe	UK	Bel	Jap	Sin	Italy	Fr
	94	92	91	91	90	89	82	67	66	59	56	53

Q2. You run a department of a division of a large comany. One of your subordinates who you now has trouble at home, is frequently coming in significantly late. What right has this colleague to be protected by you from others in the department?

① a definite right   ② some right   ③ no right

no right	USA	Ger	Swe	UK	NL	Aus'l	Can	Sin	Bel	Jap	Italy	Fr
	95	94	91	84	82	82	81	61	57	56	47	43

Exhibit 5–4 Managers were posed dilemmas pitting universalism against particularism.

- "In our Canadian-American-British collaboration the organizational cultures were more powerful than the national cultural differences."
- "There has never been much love lost between Americans and Russians."
- "Even after 6 years of managing the relations with the Japanese I have not learned to understand them."
- "French and Americans are very very different."
- "We had ups and downs."
- "There were a few *delicate* episodes."
- "Eventually we learned to work together."
- "The hardest part of global teams is culture."
- "Language was a problem in the beginning."
- "There were small cultural problems."
- "Language was the hardest part."
- "Culture was not a problem."
- "There is a difference why people wake up in the morning and go to work in America and in Europe."
- "Distance—and the resultant turf wars—was a greater problem than language or culture."
- "There were many minor cultural issues—each of them was minor, but together they add up."
- "English is the second language of engineering, so we don't have a big language problem."
- "I really don't know if culture has been a problem."

Exhibit 5–5   Is culture a problem?*

No, there are essentially no cultural differences amongst software professionals

Software professionals worldwide belong to the *computer subculture.*[83] Using the formal terminology—this is a *professional culture*—just like lawyers and zoologists. Software guru Larry Constantine argues that the computer subculture is stronger than national culture and that the programmer in Moscow is more similar to his American programming peer

*Responses given to question, "Were there cultural problems in your global software teams?" 17 Managers from 12 different software companies from the GDSD study.

than to other Russians. If we accept that the computer subculture is a sub-set of the engineering culture, it is worth noting that the R&D scholars de Meyer and Mizushima[84] make an identical argument to Constantine—that in globalized R&D, the scientific culture dominates national culture and that the management of intercultural teams is relatively unproblematic.

Engineers, like software professionals, place high value on work and on achievement and relatively low value on social relationships. The stereotype of the antisocial programmer has a kernel of truth. Engineers self-select to the profession and are socialized from high school, through university and technical schools, and then through their respective func-tional cultures. Engineers are more likely to treat time linearly (rather than see it as expandable) and have low reverence for hierarchy, regardless of their national culture.

Very few studies have examined the intersection of software and cul-ture comparatively. Two studies, together encompassing the United States, Canada, Denmark, Austria, Israel, and Singapore confirm the strength of the computer subculture. In an interesting four-country study, Cougar and colleagues[85] used a modified Job Diagnostic Survey that measures per-sonal motivation and need for personal growth. The survey was adminis-tered to several hundred programmer-analysts in each of the three coun-tries—Austria, Israel, and Singapore and compared it to a US database with several thousand respondents. The researchers found surprisingly lit-tle difference in the motivation levels of programmer/analysts in these four nations. In all four cultures the work itself was the strongest motivator, with opportunity for advancement, pay, and opportunity for achievement also ranked high. Interpersonal relations, or social interaction, was a low scor-ing factor. This confirms the programmer stereotype of low social need and broadens it to the international arena. The software profession attracts peo-ple who do not need to express a strong cultural component in their work.

In a comparative survey of Canadian and Danish software designers conducted in the late 1980s[86], both groups of designers exhibited roughly the same set of values. In both cultures, technical values (e.g., system reli-ability) were most important to the individual designers, followed by eco-nomic values (e.g., operational costs). Sociopolitical values (e.g., provid-ing learning and growth for user jobs) ranked lowest. Of course, some cultural differences did exist, such as the Dane's greater relative value of users' job security.

Two comparative studies of tool use, techniques, and software devel-opment practices find no significant differences around the world. A 1996 study[87] comparing US, Japanese, and European choices of software development tools (i.e., development environments, languages) found no significant differences in choice of software tools. A second study[88] in the early 1990s, compared the European Community (mostly Britain in this case) and Japanese software practices. In general, for most factors of software development and process, the respondents were in remarkably close agreement. Some minor differences were found: Japanese managers did use more indicators and measures in their management. For example, use of lines of program code by unit of time was very common in Japan and far less so in Europe. Measures of Function Points/unit of time in Europe, although much more popular than in Japan, did not make up the difference. Another difference was that more European managers met deadlines. Finally, European responses showed that their software life cycles used fewer stages than did the Japanese life cycles, but they seemed to be better defined.

Yes, there certainly are cultural differences amongst software professionals

The starting point on this side of the debate is Hofstede's seminal study done with IBMers in offices around the world. In spite of the IBM corporate culture with its implicit American values, significant national cultural differences still surfaced.

The differences argument is strengthened by the amalgamation of anecdotes that one is exposed to when dealing with international software development, anecdotes such as: The French are better at object-oriented development; the Japanese are better at metrics; while Jackson methodology is well known in Britain, it is virtually unknown in North America; the Belgians are more process oriented than the "gun-slinging" cowboy Americans, who shoot first (code) and design later. Indeed, for better or for worse, the American cowboy software hacker is an interesting cultural phenomenon that I have argued elsewhere[89] is one factor explaining the sustained US hegemony in the global packaged software industry. The unique subculture of programming entrepreneurs was, and still is, a powerful innovative force.

Not all software managers experienced cultural problems in quite the same way. "Culture was never a problem" was a response from some (but by no means all) managers of global software teams. Some managers may have solved the problems quickly through experience or natural diplomacy. Conceivably, software professionals are not attentive to explaining events from a cultural perspective. In some conversations, after a few probing questions, cultural stories emerged and eventually accumulated. It is not that these managers were altogether unaware of cultural problems entirely, but they were not aggregating these incidents and then making deductions based on this dimension. Indeed, this is in line with what we know about culture: Individuals who are confident in their cultural knowledge are more inclined to explore cultural issues.

Although the studies mentioned above found virtually no differences between software professionals and their work in different countries, one found some differences. A 1996 study compared Singaporean and US firms' usage of formal software development methods (such as diagramming methods) and found that Singaporean firms make more use of formal methods.[90]

Perhaps, the real cultural differences surface in more nuanced facets of software development that are difficult to pinpoint in a study. For example, a culture that is more comfortable with ambiguity (low "risk avoidance," using one of Hofstede's dimensions) will be comfortable in early stages of design to leave some issues unspecified. Teams from linear time cultures (who tend to be more punctual) will perform better at the end of the development cycle during crunch time to meet deadlines.[91]

The most significant differences in software development culture surface vis-à-vis the Japanese. Several stories and one study point to the gulf:

- *The QA culture clash.* The differences in Japanese versus Western philosophies of quality goes back many decades. One of the principles of the Japanese Total Quality Management approach is *line stop* authority. Every worker on the manufacturing line can stop the line if he finds a problem. With this as backdrop, a European executive's comment about his Japanese counterparts and their software QA is illustrative. The executive felt that the Japanese site was very strict in recording bugs and collecting numerous metrics. He commented on their organizational structure in which QA was an independent entity and able to veto a release. The issue that he found irritating was in assessing levels of bug severity. The Japanese team did not care much about the criticality of bugs—all bugs needed to be fixed whether they were "showstoppers" or minor bugs that affected the user interface in more subjective ways.

- *The meaning of requirements.* A seasoned Japanese information systems manager described the difference between requirements in the United States and those in Japan. Particularly for contract work, Americans expect requirements to be in contract style with every deviation from contract to be subject to additional charges. In contrast, in Japan it is not the custom to charge for small changes. The customer-supplier relationship can be seen as a gentlemen's agreement that takes priority over the contract. The Japanese customer would view it as a deviation to contract if enhancements were treated as additional charges! Experienced information systems contractors cushion their contracts to take this norm into account.
- *Multicultural design sessions.* Software architects may become frustrated with design sessions with their Japanese counterparts. Western designers are more likely to approach problems using a top down approach, while the Japanese, with fundamentally different thinking styles, begin with many details, which only later emerge into a big picture—more closely resembling a bottom up approach.
- *End user computing.* Introduction of PCs and LANs in the Japanese office environment were years behind those in other industrialized nations. A study from the early 1990s found the concept of end user computing to be "virtually non-existent" in Japanese firms.[92]

Culture, User Design, and Application Knowledge

For years American programmers were accused of designing clunky user interfaces with such impossible-to-understand messages as "Abort? Retry? Fail?" The view of user interface specialists is that most programmers, if left on their own, design appalling user interfaces. Fernandes[93] provides a book chock full of examples of how clumsy and funny American cultural user designs look to those outside the United States. For example, one icon designer at Lotus created a screen icon to represent a utility that translates files. The icon shows an apple and an orange with an arrow pointing from the former to the latter. The icon represents the *English* idiom of "apples to oranges."

Now that software applications are increasingly being developed in emerging societies, the problem of poor user interfaces and baffling applications has reversed direction somewhat. Distant developers are often asked to design and program products and applications for the United States and other advanced consumer societies. Yet they do not have the consumer sophistication or the advanced business knowledge to make some design decisions. After all, even programmers writing code from specifications often have to make assumptions. It is here that global software managers in the GDSD study have run into difficulties.

The following quotes concern developers in a number of emerging nations. The tableau they create should not be surprising to an experienced software professional: One of the hardest aspects of good software is deep knowledge of the application and the customer. And this is made more difficult precisely because the developers are now so very removed from their customers' culture.

> Team manager [in emerging nation]: We have different assumptions about error messages. The guys here thought it wasn't necessary to create great, beautiful looking error messages. We thought it was enough to just warn the users [through documentation]. But that is unacceptable to the user. Some user out there got an error message and was very upset even though we had warned them that it would happen. It was a lack of [our] experience about delivering products versus custom software.

> American team leader #1: They [in emerging nation] would write programs—that if the procedure worked—it just returned a prompt—unless it blew up, you didn't know that it worked. Here [in the United States] you like to see a message saying that "it ran successfully."

> American team leader #2: They [in emerging nation] fundamentally don't understand this application since credit card usage over there is very low. So we shifted them to writing libraries. They were very good at that.

> European technical director: They [in emerging nation] are technically better than our own and well trained in I.T. In fact, that is all that is taught at their university. But they just do not understand the applications. We hire most of them straight out of school. They have no business knowledge. That is our difficulty.

> American software executive #1: We write specs. We've tried to let them do the creative stuff. But we got them to work so that they don't

question our specs on weird culture stuff. For them I'm like a builder who asks to build pink walls. […] I never give them creative control.

American software executive #2: They can't add that extra something to consumer software that people here can do.

Conclusions

What can we make of all this? Most important, there are many approaches and many shades of gray to the topic of culture and there is no one formula. For example, virtually all the cultural analyses predict that French managers, being from a culture that reveres hierarchy, give more directives, which they expect to be followed. Yet in a French-American software collaboration managed by a French manager based in Paris, the French project manager gave the American team a great deal of autonomy, claiming, "It is French to do this!" In response, also contrary to formula, the Americans demanded more and more explicit guidance.

The reader should treat texts about cultures with a grain of salt. In fact, you may have found yourself disagreeing with a few of the quantitative and qualitative findings discussed earlier. However, most of this cultural digest should feel directionally correct—and can serve as a starting point of a "mental file" into which we absorb and add new information about our colleagues from other countries. Working in a multicultural environment requires continuous learning about cultures. Cultural differences are significant. Fortunately, our common (professional) software culture is a unifying force.

Further Reading

The most enjoyable reading on this topic is Schneider, S.C. and Barsoux, J. *Managing Across Cultures*. London: Prentice Hall 1997.

An argumentative but entertaining book is: Hampden-Turner, C. and Trompenaars, A. *The seven cultures of capitalism*. New York, NY: Currency Doubleday, 1993.

Other good references are:

Adler, N.J. *International Dimensions of Organizational Behavior,* Cincinnati, Ohio: Southwestern College Publishing, 1997.

Phillips, N. *Managing International Teams*. Bur Ridge, Ill: Irwin Professional Publishing, 1994.

The Six Centripetal Forces for Successful Global SoftwareTeams

Each of the six chapters of Part III cover, respectively, one of the six centripetal forces—the solutions—that exert force inward within the global software team making it more effective. Centripetal is from the Latin "to seek the center." Global software teams need to create centripetal forces in order to counter the centrifugal forces (the unique problems) that propel the team outward from the center.

Chapter Six discusses the telecommunications infrastructure—the foundation for many of the other strategies, techniques, and solutions that come later. Chapter Seven is about the cement that holds it all together, the collaborative technologies, from groupware, through e-mail, to the family of specialized tools for software engineering. Dispersion means that the informal coordination of co-location will not work any longer. Coordination must be channeled through the many forms of collaborative technologies. Chapter Eight covers the software development methodology, which becomes the common language developers share, bridging different sites. When one programmer sends an e-mail to a distant programmer with "we'll do that during the alpha stage," there is a tremendous amount of information that is con-

The centripetal forces of global software teams

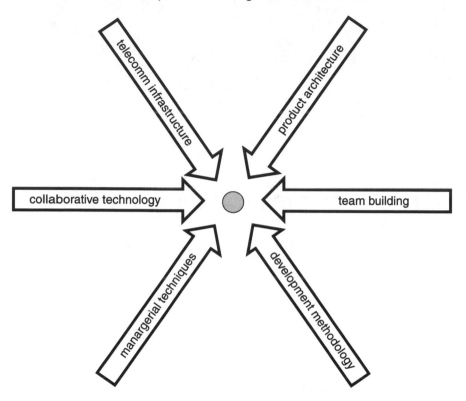

veyed if both understand alpha in the same way—when it will arrive and what exactly is supposed to be done by then.

Chapter Nine is about product architecture and task allocation. The chapter begins with the concepts of architecture and modularity, followed by an introduction to the three task allocation strategies of stage, module, and a hybrid strategy—integration. Chapter Ten addresses the question of whether the organization can create a real team from disparate work units. Creating an effective global team from multiple sites involves several key success factors: building trust, encouraging open communication, building personal relationships, and bridging cultural differences. No team can really be a team without these factors in place. Chapter Eleven covers a potpourri of management topics includ-

ing: how to architect your global team; how to measure its unique attributes; how to choose a global manager.

Elements of these six "centripetal forces" can and should be put into motion at the earliest phase possible—right after the acquisition, or when hiring begins at a new distant site. The telecommunications infrastructure needs to be established, the product architect should be designated, the team members from distant sites should meet, and so forth. However, other elements of the centripetal forces are less concentrated on the early phases: Molding distant sites into a mature, cohesive, well-oiled, high performing global software team must be viewed as continuous process.

A note on convention used throughout the book that is particularly important in Part III: a team consists of two or more (geographically dispersed) sites.

TELECOMMUNICATIONS INFRASTRUCTURE

The telecommunications infrastructure is analogous to the foundation of a house. It is the foundation on which all else rests. As with reliable telephone service, the end users of these services—the developers—will be indifferent to the physical or topological set-up of the network, so long as it serves them well. A global software team requires a reliable, reasonably high bandwidth network.

Of the "centripetal forces," this infrastructure is the least difficult managerial decision to make and implement when setting up global software teams. This short chapter recounts some of the global software teams that had difficulties with their telecommunications and introduces Virtual Private Networks, the increasingly common channel connecting global software teams.

Given the high cost of coordination overhead, *no* serious collaborative software effort should be set up unless the team is using reliable, high-speed connection for all forms of data communications. For sites in emerging nations, the same maxim holds true for Plain Old Telephone Service (fondly known as POTS). Reliable POTS is needed for voice, fax, and perhaps some data.

A minority of the firms in the GDSD study[94] did not have reliable high speed connections between sites during early years of collaboration. They suffered through enormous grief as a result. Several cases describe their difficulties.

> Ivory Systems is a very small US-based firm that decided to establish its core development in India in 1994. It hired a small group of developers in Bangalore. Lacking adequate telecommunications support, Ivory began working collaboratively. Their phone connections were so unreliable that faxes had to be routed through their Indian accountant's office in town and sent via courier to the firm's development site. With no Internet Service Providers (ISPs) yet in India until several years later, data communications was all but impossible. Code transfer was done for several years in a fashion that is far from the ideal of the virtual organization: Each Friday the Bangalore site backed up the entire code-set to magnetic tape, delivering it to the local Federal Express office. The back-up code was then flown to the United States, arriving over the weekend, ready to be used by the Americans on Monday morning.

> The Russian-American collaboration at Orchestral Technologies suffered for years from poor quality telephone service, making even a routine phone conversation difficult. Recently the Moscow office's phone system was upgraded and telephone connections from the United States to Moscow became satisfactory.

> At Sharp Applications, the US–Indian–Belgian team was unable to get the Indian site set up with sufficient and reliable telecommunications support. Sharp's executives understood that there was no point in managing collaboration without adequate communication support, so the key Indian programmers were transferred, at considerable cost, to Belgium for almost a year. By the end of the release cycle, the infrastructure was in place, and the Indian group returned home. Indirectly, this situation had a silver lining. The small Indian group became well acquainted with their peers in Belgium. Presumably, this "forced" team socialization and cohesiveness paid off later for Sharp.

Almost all firms in the GDSD study maintained connections either through *private* internal networks or through Virtual Private Networks. A private internal (global) network is created by using combinations of leased lines and/or satellite links. Private internal networks in Europe and North America will continue to use mostly terrestrial leased lines or ISDN, which are widely available at reasonable cost. Costs for private lines vary considerably: A 256K leased line costs about four times more in India than the United States. In some regions of the world poor, unreliable terrestrial infrastructure means that wireline private networks are not an option. An alternative to wireline is wireless connectivity, particularly through high bandwidth satellite links. For example, small dishes (Very Small Aperture Terminals—VSATs) can be set up to provide instant connectivity from remote locations.

A Virtual Private Network (VPN) connects dispersed offices through the Internet. Each office is connected to the Internet via its local ISP. Connection from the software development site to the local ISP is set up via dial-up or leased lines. The IP-based network then uses encryption, tunneling (a technique in which one protocol is carried inside another), and authentication to connect users securely into their own private network. Rather than setting up an entirely private network, constructing a VPN is less costly because it reduces remote access and connectivity costs as well as some equipment costs. However, relative to a private network, there is a trade-off between cost and performance (and security).

Currently, the Internet provides "best effort" service. There can be delay, deterioration in performance, and problems in transmitting large files from remote areas. The Internet community is moving to address these technical limitations. One approach is a new standard called Resource Reservation Protocol (RSVP) that will provide guaranteed quality of service to remote areas via a VPN, even allowing remote parties to engage in real-time video conferencing. However, RSVP is criticized as being a resource hog that may not scale well. Other alternatives include using connection-oriented technology such as frame-relay and ATM.

Potential cost reduction is driving more firms to the VPN/Internet option to handle their data communications for collaboration. But the technical issues alone are not the only hurdle as the story of Sharp Applications below illustrates. The path to where Sharp is today—with connections from all its worldwide development centers, through ISPs into the Internet—was not an easy transition.

At Sharp Applications, 1996 was the year that the dispersed team was molded together. At first the Belgian site resisted moving to a VPN, preferring to set up links using private leased lines that cost about $120,000 per year to India alone. Then the Belgians expressed a preference for a locally-owned ISP (rather than one owned by an American multinational corporation) for reasons that the Americans perceived as having to do with national pride. The trouble with that ISP, claimed those on the US side, was that it went through too many hops along the way and was too slow. Meanwhile, as described above, the Indian site's full operations were delayed until 1997 because of local ISP problems. But this delay had other consequences. Sharp's Indian development center was to be linked directly to the ISP via an ISDN connection, which was quite new in India at the time. One of Sharp's managers had to make sure the local Indian ISP links were set up within exact specifications. He did this through personal supervision (lots of travel) and by spelling out specifications in a detailed contract. In sum, a great deal of management attention was needed to set up the infrastructure.

Happily, many of the difficulties described in this chapter are diminishing at a fairly rapid pace (however, this should not foster complacence in planning for a new site!). Plain old telephone service is rapidly improving in countries such as China, Russia, and India. Equally as exciting for global software teams—the VPN alternative is becoming attractive in terms of cost, reliability, and availability. With the recent liberalization of the ISP market in many countries, such as India, VPNs are likely to be the first choice. There are now dozens of ISPs in India, where none existed just a few years ago.

Finally, a nontechnical qualifier on the wonders of telecommunications: Even when all sites are connected via tera-bit connections, some communication needs will not be satisfied. Electronics are only a partial substitute for human interaction. Travel is still needed between sites. In the GDSD study there was no correlation between the sophistication of the telecommunication infrastructure and the amount of travel by team members. In fact, in some of the better endowed projects, with excellent communication infrastructure, members traveled *more* than those projects with less infrastructure.

> ## Best Practices Roundup
>
> ☑ Invest in reliable, high bandwidth connections to all desktops at all sites
>
> ☑ Establish consistent hardware and software platforms
>
> ☑ Excellent telecommunications infrastructure does not negate the need for travel.

Further Reading

Prof. Jeffrey MacKie-Mason of the University of Michigan maintains an excellent reference list on telecommunications: http://china.si.umich.edu/telecom/technical-info.html.

CHAPTER 7

COLLABORATIVE TECHNOLOGY: GENERIC TECHNOLOGY AND TECHNOLOGY TO SUPPORT SOFTWARE ENGINEERING

The centrifugal forces of distance, coordination breakdown, and communication losses need to be counterbalanced by an abundance of electronic communication between the team's dispersed sites. Collaborative technology supports two key communication objectives: fostering informal inter-site communication and bringing about new forms of formal inter-site communication. Collaborative technology, commonly referred to as groupware, represents the path *to location transparency*—bringing the distant developers closer together.

The term "generic" is used in this chapter to distinguish between two categories of collaborative technologies covered here in detail. *Generic* collaborative technologies include well-known tools such as e-mail, audio-conferencing, video-conferencing, and groupware platforms. Collaborative technology to support software engineering (CT-SE) is a set of specialized tools such as software configuration management, project management, and computer aided software engineering. The chapter also covers the cultural perspective on collaborative technologies. After all, none of these tools is culturally neutral.

We have futuristic visions of new collaborative technologies that promise to collapse distance and bring us closer to a colleague far away. Better forms of two-way video usually come to mind. One vision that has become a work in progress has us walking down the hallway to the office coffee corner and coming across an entire wall that is a *team wall*.[95] The team wall is somewhat like two-way video-conferencing technology except that it is connected all day long and captures and projects an entire room or hallway to the respective distant sites. Using the team wall we casually meet with colleagues halfway around the world on an informal basis as we pour ourselves a cup of coffee.[96]

Generic Collaborative Technology

Some collaborative technologies come so naturally to us that we are hardly conscious of them. Sometimes we don't notice collaborative technology—treating it like the phone or an elevator—"it's there".[97] We notice the technology only when it breaks down. Breakdowns are intolerable for

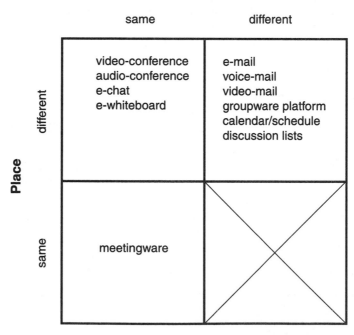

Exhibit 7–1   The time-place matrix for collaborative technology.

a global software team. A well run dispersed team will be using 10–20 types of collaborative technology (depending on how one counts them). That is, a global software team uses many types of collaborative technology all at once.[98]

"Generic" collaborative technologies include a number of well-known tools, which are listed in the time–place matrix displayed in Exhibit 7–1. The time–place matrix visually positions various collaborative technologies along the two dimensions of time and place (location). The time dimension is also referred to as synchronous and asynchronous.

The matrix helps call attention to an important interaction between a global software team and its use of collaborative technologies. Because of time zone differences, same-time (synchronous) collaborative technology tools are less useful. It is inconvenient to conduct synchronous communication, such as telephone conversations, or video-conferencing. In fact, these types of communication become an imposition on one of the participants because it is he or she that must either wake up very early in the morning, or connect late into the evening. Therefore, asynchronous collaborative technologies are more useful to a global team. The dominance of asynchronous technologies is pronounced for collaborative technology to support software engineering. With minor exceptions, there are no synchronous collaborative technologies for software engineering.

The first and obvious process that collaborative technology supports very well is *communication:* transmitting messages through a communication pipeline. Such is the case with e-mail. But what kinds of messages? Within a global software team collaborative technology tools need both to support and facilitate more formal communication and to encourage more informal communication. Why more formal communication? Because formal communication helps mitigate the inevitable communication breakdowns that occur as a result of distance and culture. Why informal? Because collaborative technology needs to emulate the co-located work environment as much as possible, with its informal mechanisms for resolving problems.

Recall the study of Perry and colleagues[99] (see Chapter 4) conducted by following several software developers (mostly programmers) for several days noting everything they did. These were developers that were *co-located.* The researchers tabulated all messages where they defined a message as being voice-mail, e-mail, phone, or face to face visit (and, yes, they took out purely "social" communications). First of all, two thirds of all messages were quite brief—less than five minutes. Each day, on average, each developer sent six messages and received sixteen. Interestingly, the median number of outgoing e-mail messages was zero(!), and incoming was nine. Now, even after we discount this finding because it took place in the early 1990s with older, less friendly e-mail, this number seems quite low. The likely explanation, as we think about collaborative technology, is that for software developers, coordination and knowledge sharing is conducted by informal lateral networks. These lateral networks are so informal that the communication between co-located team members does not even funnel through e-mail. One key implication is that once a team is dispersed, there is a need to encourage a great deal of informal (electronic) communication.

Generic collaborative technology supports more processes than just making message communication easier to use. It supports several other major team *process* categories.[100] Collaborative technology supports the team's *information access:* finding, sorting, processing, and retrieving the information that members need to solve a problem. Collaborative technology can support *deliberation:* the classic problem-solving activities of identifying the problem, evaluating alternative solutions, selecting a desired plan, and then monitoring its implementation. Moreover, collaborative technology can help organize the team's *workflow:* routing objects from one person to another in need of work, review, or authorization.

Beyond processes per se, conceptualizing collaborative technology in a dispersed environment involves three objectives:

Objectives of "Generic" Collaborative Technology (beyond merely sending messages)

1. Serves as a team memory & knowledge center. The team stores and then shares information and knowledge across a work unit.

2. Provides each team member a 360° view. All members at all sites are informed regarding task, status, people, and other dynamic team information. This is related to the concept of transparency.

3. Fosters a sense of community. The "glue" creates and maintains interpersonal relationships.

Collaborative technology *serves as a team memory and knowledge center.* The team memory, or organizational memory, is an important concept that is given many names by consultants who talk about *knowledge management* and *leveraging corporate intellectual capital*. The core of team memory is a large, well structured database for all information that can be reduced to zeroes and ones. The database (or *repository* as it is often referred to) is built from shared data and is accessible to any team member on an as-needed basis. A handful of global software teams in the GDSD study developed a team memory using a groupware platform such as Notes. For example, the IBM JavaBeans project, described in Chapter 2, maintained all of the project's documents stored on the groupware database alongside many threaded discussions and issues.

We humans have poor memories. Fortunately, the computer complements that human weakness quite well. The *team memory* is the repository of all the team's documents, communications, artifacts, code, bug reports, and more. It is also a repository for the iterations of design rationale—those documents and discussions that remind us why we decided to do what it is that we are doing. Ideally, the organizational memory can help trace the history, reasoning, and chain of thought behind every decision, large or small, that is associated with the software product being built. The team memory can also serve to draw expertise from other parts of the company. That is, the repository (team memory) can leverage the knowledge assets not just within the dispersed team sites but across the firm's entire development organization. Ideally, the repository should be shared not only by team members, but by all teams in the company.[101]

Collaborative technology *allows a 360° view for the team*.[102] In the absence of physical closeness of buildings, people, and imagery, dispersed team members need to understand where they are relative to what everyone else is doing. This is called the 360° view. Each developer can look at what people are doing above him, below him, and, laterally, on both sides. Making tasks, roles, and events explicit leads to a sense of clarity across the team sites.

Collaborative technology *fosters a sense of community*. It is the glue that maintains interpersonal relationships. The collaborative technology becomes the team's *shared context*[103]—its common kitchen in which work (its vision, work practices, and task processes) and its social life take place. The shared context creates a sense of community. Slowly at first, the repository becomes recognized and used by the team. The act of building the repository, not unlike the software artifact itself, becomes another source of pride for the team.

Selected Collaborative Technologies and Their Use

Each of seven generic collaborative technologies and its use in global software teams is introduced below beginning with asynchronous tools (e-mail, groupware platform, calendar, discussion list) followed by synchronous tools (audio-conferencing, video-conferencing, e-whiteboard).

E-mail

Of course, the most familiar form of collaborative technology is used widely in global software teams. For most projects in the GDSD study, e-mail was the most important collaborative technology. One team lead said "when we had trouble with e-mail we went insane." E-mail use was very high. For example, at one firm the manager estimated the ratio of phone to e-mail traffic at 1:20 in favor of e-mail.

E-mail is such a dominant tool in global software teams for several reasons. The first, and most compelling one is that because of time zone differences, e-mail is actually more comfortable to use because it is asynchronous. But there are several other important reasons. Clearly, software professionals are very comfortable with e-mail. It is part of the professional culture of software anywhere in the world. A humorous anecdote illustrates this point. The so-called Microsoft Lexicon[104] has the following entry for a form of communication called *Facemail*: "Technologically backward means of communication, clearly inferior to voice-mail or e-mail. Involves actually walking to someone's office and speaking to him or her face to face. Considered highly inefficient and déclassé."

E-mail is also dominant for language reasons: It is easier to use for those whose native language is not English. A real-time meeting in English is exhausting for a nonfluent English speaker. Using e-mail she can read and write at her own speed.

> At Stratigisoft several Japanese developers were assigned to the European sister development site. After a few weeks of attending face to face project meetings the (English) language burden became too much for the Japanese software engineers. They requested to minimize their participation in these meetings and to communicate with other team members via e-mail even though they remained on site!

E-mail is an excellent tool for creating more effective teams because it naturally facilitates lateral communication—communication that does not go through a formal chain of authority. It is the lateral communication between team members across sites that creates effective integration of tasks and fully and quickly addresses task problems that crop up.

Groupware platforms

Generic groupware platforms include many of the collaborative technology features packaged in one software suite: e-mail, document repositories, discussion lists, calendars, and workflow automation. The marketplace has a clear leader, Lotus Notes, arguably the premier collaborative technology of the 1990s, and several other contenders such as Novell's GroupWise, the Teamware suite, Netscape Communicator, and Microsoft Exchange.

Several global teams in the GDSD study used generic groupware platforms, mostly Lotus Notes. Those teams invested extensively in groupware as a distributed database for e-mail and sharing documents in project repositories. Significantly, these teams used the groupware platforms to create custom templates to tailor the system workflow to their needs. Some of the templates included bug tracking, change requests, approval routing, and sign-off procedures. One of the companies bought these "life-cycle templates" from a third party vendor that specializes in Notes add-ons.

One of the companies in the GDSD study is a well-known groupware platform company. Indeed, as we would expect, the global software team that developed this product used its own platform extensively. It even integrated the platform with the software configuration management (SCM) system that they purchased. Grantham and colleagues[105] also studied software teams that actually developed major groupware products. Again, the ways in which these teams used their own products are instructive. DEC's development team for its groupware product Teamlinks was dispersed in the United States, Britain, and Ireland. It used its own package for workflow management. Documents were routed with the corresponding declarations of who should review each one, who should improve it, and what the time limits for each task were. The Novell team that developed Groupwise was also dispersed. The team used its own Groupwise features to inform developers about changes to a specific document that has been previously approved.

Group calendar/ group scheduler

A multi-site group calendar is an excellent tool to inform dispersed team members of different holidays, milestones, events, and meetings. International scheduling is a coordination headache, particularly because of holiday peculiarities. For example, while Americans anticipate their own holiday norms (e.g., a long weekend at the end of November for Thanksgiving), they are unlikely to know about holiday norms of other cultures (e.g., in Israel, the week of Passover is a "semi-vacation"). The group calendar also informs team members about different work hours, time zones differences, and summertime clock changes. Schedulers are useful to overcome time zone differences to set up ad hoc audio- or video-conferences. Although some aspects of a group calendar function can be rolled into a multi-site project management package, the project management package is typically less accessible to casual browsing and is less familiar to all team members at all sites.

Discussion lists/issue lists

Text-based discussion lists were popularized in the 1980s on the Internet Usenet groups, on bulletin board systems (BBS), and then through similar constructs, on groupware platforms, and still later, on the web. Discussion lists are idiosyncratic, varying a great deal with team members' personal styles. In order to be effective, they are often facilitated by someone vested in their success, such as a team lead or project manager. One or more of these individuals needs to set up discussion topics and establish basic conventions for commenting (e.g., whether or not previous quotes should be reinserted, or how to thread comments). A team may want discussions to be closely tied to the development tasks, while another team may deliberately want to foster at least some discussions to diverge into tangential topics to foster a team social culture. Once established, discussion lists must be nurtured since some team members will inevitably delay reading them until they have some "free time"—which rarely happens.

Audio-conferencing

This technology is not considered very flashy anymore, but it still offers real value. Compared to a plane trip, or even a video-conference, audio-conferencing is quite inexpensive. Audio-conferencing was used by many global software teams for multiple purposes, especially the formal weekly telephone conference call. One of the global software managers I visited spent several minutes extolling the virtues of her sophisticated audio-conferencing equipment. On reflection this had great merit since it is very important that a lengthy audio-conference be pleasant rather than straining. New devices are now on the market to enhance communication over regular telephone lines by reducing echo and clipping effects.

Video-conferencing

An examination of the media-richness continuum of Exhibit 4–4 shows that video-conferencing is the richest media (excluding face to face communication), conveying the richest message across distance. What does video-conferencing add to lesser forms of communication?[106] Video-conferencing promises to:

- reduce need for travel.
- accelerate the process of reaching decisions.[107]
- reduce development cycles by accelerating problem resolution.
- promote creative group thinking, particularly if the sites share a common "desktop" through use of multiple channels, with one for video, another for presentation graphics display. Even Internet video-conferencing products now integrate multiple formats: file transfer, text chat, and e-whiteboard features.
- aid in assessing the value of data used in an important decision.
- foster bonding between people and building the sense of "teamness."
- convey sincerity and authority through body language or eye contact.

Given these benefits, global software teams should be rushing to use video-conferencing. In spite of the promise, video-conferencing is not used much because of a combination of five factors: technical limitations, cost issues, quality problems, synchronicity issues, and behavioral norms.

Video-conferencing is *far from being plug and play*. There is still tremendous confusion about standards in the video-conferencing world. For example, there are many variations on the two principal protocol sets: H.323 and H.324. Not all products are fully compliant with a protocol that they claim to support. Major video-conferencing vendors, such as PictureTel, have developed their own proprietary standards. Needless to say, the multiplicity of standards creates incompatibilities. Furthermore, there are a number of physical layer connectivity possibilities: POTS, ISDN, dedicated lines, and public networks.

Video-conference *costs* are still significant in spite of their multi-year decline. In the 1970s the cost of a video-conference room reached a million dollars and declined in 1997 to about $45,000. Video-conferencing mounted on a cart and rolled to the meeting room costs about $25,000. In recent years desktop video has emerged as a lower cost alternative to group video-conferencing, costing about $4000 for proprietary systems, or just a few hundred dollars for lower quality Internet solutions. But sophisticated video-conferencing requires additional costs: Pumping video-conferencing over a LAN often necessitates upgrades of network capacity and sometimes even requires platform changes. Costs also need to include specialists to maintain and set up the video-conferencing sessions. The prohibitive costs of video-conferencing lead to alienating decisions at some companies:

> At Arizona Systems' American–British–Canadian collaboration, the Canadian site was the smallest and least influential of the three. Project management decided to keep costs down: The Canadians participated in the formal meetings using audio-conferencing while the Americans and Brits used group video-conferencing. This compromise was a sore spot for the Canadians and reinforced their feelings of being a lesser player.

Video conferencing *quality* is often less than satisfactory. Pictures freeze, video or audio feeds die, pictures are jerky or jittery, audio is jumbled, the window is too small, and the picture resolution is poor. From a technical perspective, pushing a constant stream of video and audio through packet-switching (IP) networks designed for bursty traffic is still not easy. In one transatlantic collaboration in the GDSD study, the managers used group video-conferencing several times a week for regular project reviews, but often had to resort to audio-conferencing out of frustration with the video transmission quality.

Video-conferencing is a *synchronous* collaborative technology, meaning that, when parties are separated by many time zones, at least one party is using up its personal morning or evening time. In the coming years we are likely to see video-mail emerging as a sort of asynchronous hybrid between video-conferencing and e-mail. This may be more useful to global software teams, particularly when combined with other asynchronous technologies, such as file transfer for presentation graphics.

Perhaps most importantly, video-conferences are supposed to be "richer" psychologically, but they do not really feel richer in many respects. Many people simply feel awkward with video-conferencing.[108]

One reason for the discomfort is that social protocols are not commonly known. For older technology—the telephone—we all know that we pick up the receiver, say "hello," and wait for the other side to respond. In video-conferencing what are the turn-taking cues? How do people interrupt one another politely? The natural turn-taking protocols are often sabotaged by as little as a 0.2-second delay because of participants "stepping into" each other's sentences due to the pause.

Video-conferencing is not always rich because some things are missed entirely. One cannot really look people in the eye because the resolution is poor. One's vantage of the distant room is limited: It is not always possible to see everyone in the other room such as those who may be leaving or coming in. Side conversations cannot be transmitted. One cannot see the subtle cues such as the stiffening of the body in response to a question. Other cues are magnified: The speaker in the picture box gets all the attention. None of these behavioral issues are overwhelming, but together they detract from video conferences' theoretical "richness."

Managers differ in how they view video-conferencing—even within the same firm, as the following case illustrates:

> At Bordeaux Associates' French–American collaboration, the American manager found the group video-conferencing technology very useful, claiming that it reduced the need for transatlantic travel. Meanwhile, the French manager had a different view, arguing that in an established long-term relationship, as they had with their American counterparts, video-conferencing added nothing to the relationship. "It is not the silver bullet for working together," he remarked, adding that he preferred e-mail.

Electronic whiteboard

An electronic whiteboard allows dispersed users to concurrently edit, in real-time, a graphic, or a document. Electronic whiteboards are now widely available in browsers and from specialized vendors. Whiteboards can be useful during a phone conversation dealing with topics that require visualization, such as product architecture. This tool was not used by software developers in the GDSD study, who saw it as more of a toy.

The Cultural Overlay of Collaborative Technology

Much of the philosophy of collaborative technology, like much of our software today, is rooted in the low-context communication cultures of North

America and Northern Europe. One of the great fallacies about collaborative technology is that it is culturally neutral.[109] Relative to face to face communication it is indeed culturally neutral—but not absolutely. Herein lie some of the advantages and disadvantages of this technology for global software teams. In high-context cultures (e.g., Asian, Mediterranean), much of the communication is outside the body of the message—in greeting styles, gestures, posture and other cues. On one hand, collaborative technology forces its users toward a high information mode in their messages, away from the more ambiguous contextual cues of high context cultures. On the other hand, these technologies force high context culture users into communication modes in which they are less comfortable.

Relative to the other common collaborative technologies, the most culturally neutral tool is electronic mail. Additionally, e-mail has other advantages to bridge culture and language. First, e-mail allows the reader to read the English language message carefully at his *own* speed (or with assistance from a friend or dictionary if necessary). If he is an Indian software professional, who speaks English well, he has more time to dissect the idioms that may be foreign to him. If she is a nonnative speaker of English, chances are that her reading comprehension is higher than her oral comprehension. Second, e-mail allows the sender to analyze the problem carefully, the issue, or the bug, and only then to formulate a response in an English version that is understood by its intended reader. The less comfortable the party is in English, the more he or she will prefer e-mail over any other collaborative technology. For example, in a real-time meeting (face to face or video), a nonnative English speaker has to understand and contribute in real-time. This is particularly difficult in long meetings. Thus, e-mail's asynchroncity is actually a benefit.

E-mail is actually better than the other technologies for overcoming culture, but it is not neutral. Americans may be comfortable allowing electronic participants to get into a heated "fight." Such an open conflict is comfortable for Americans, but not for the Japanese. Then there is the topic of e-mail etiquette, which is highly culturally driven. Does one write "Dear Jim" at the beginning of the message even though Jim's name appears clearly on the "To" line? Americans put less fluff into their e-mail messages than into their paper-based memos and letters, but still expect some social graces. Hence, when they get very terse e-mail messages from their Indian peers, they interpret them as being rude.

We also might mistakenly view discussion *lists* as being culturally neutral. Discussion lists are useful supplements for American and Scandinavian decision making norms which debate issues openly during meetings. The discussion list becomes the public stage to continue to debate issues before and after a meeting. It effectively encourages broader participation. But the cultural process is deeply embedded in this collaborative technology.[110] Contrast this form of decision-making with the Japanese decision-making process. Decision-making in Japan is a collective process. Initiatives go through a process called *nemawashi*. Before a proposal is formally submitted, its initiator establishes consensus with all the stakeholders via informal meetings and personal contacts to gain their support. Rather than discussion lists, the Japanese make better use of electronic-nemawashi of private communications afforded by e-mail in many messages behind the scenes.[111]

Collaborative Technology to Support Software Engineering (CT-SE)

Effective collaboration cannot be achieved with "generic" collaborative technologies alone. Software development requires task-specific solutions. These are referred to here as *Collaborative Technology to support Software Engineering* (CT-SE from hereon).[112] In spite of developers' awareness of specialized software development environments and tools such as Software Configuration Management, Project Management, Computer Aided Software Engineering and others, these tools are often overlooked or rejected. Their adoption and diffusion tend to be slow within global software teams corresponding to their sluggish penetration within co-located development teams. Thus, effective electronic collaboration is far from being attained in practice.

For a global software team, CT-SE is just as important as the amalgamation of e-mail, conferencing, and other generic tools. Others have noted this as well. Failla[113] conducted a study of IBM's Rome software development center, one of many R&D labs at IBM, with the intent of studying the use of generic groupware tools. Her rather surprising discovery was that the premier groupware tool was the Software Configuration Management (SCM), discussed further below, as the tool that best allowed developers to coordinate their work.

Hawryskiewycz and Gorton[114] and their Australian colleagues who study software engineering conducted a series of fascinating experiments on small dispersed projects that became known as the Global Work in Software Engineering. The researchers patched together and augmented off-the-shelf packages of asynchronous collaborative technologies for software engineering and set about testing them on small projects. They simulated a globally distributed project in three sites with frequent, almost daily, hand-offs to simulate time zone differences. Their home-grown collaborative environment produced good results. First of all, only 20% of the team members' time was spent on asynchronous collaborative technology such as e-mail and Notes. Because technology was the developers' only coordination mechanism it compares favorably with the typical time spent on meetings estimated as high as 40% in some cases. Waiting and downtimes were 37% of total work time—far less than the 60% reported by other studies. Work was ready to be passed on to the next person 82% of the time. In other words, only 18% of the transfers caused wait periods.

Before we explore some specific CT-SE functions, five objectives are presented in the box below. Note that the first two of these objectives— that the technology serve as a team memory and knowledge center, and that it provide each team member a 360^0 view—both appeared among the three objectives of generic collaborative technology. The lists indeed overlap as one expect them to. CT-SE address many of the same needs, but at a more task-specific level.

Objectives of Collaborative Technology to support Software Engineering (CT-SE)

1. *Serves as a team memory & knowledge center.* The team stores and then shares information and knowledge across a work unit.

2. *Provides each team member a 360° view.* Inform all members at all sites regarding task, status, people, and other dynamic project information. This is related to the concept of transparency.

3. *Reduces duplication of effort.* Any software project is so complex that redundancy actively needs to be minimized. Software engineers need to share many types of project knowledge, otherwise they may end up fixing the same bug or working on software components that are out of date as a result of others' work.

4. *Supports coordination activities and workflow.* The software development culture does not operate on mandate, orders, and edicts. Hence the technology needs to support team members self-managing many of

their tasks via electronic lateral coordination and via electronic work-flow procedures.

5. *Supports Quality Assurance.* Functions, such as bug tracking, version control, and requirements tracking are essential to maintaining quality levels as the product flows through the development cycle.

Providing each team member with a 360^0 view is an important and often overlooked objective of CT-SE tools. This objective ties these specialized tools to the concepts of *visibility* and *transparency* that have been discussed in other chapters. For example, knowing project status is critical for project managers, but we overlook the fact that it is also important for dispersed team members who work in their own islands isolated from other units. Team members need project status information in order to maintain relationships with developers in other sites. When a remote site does not fully understand project status, it will end up making faulty decisions with partial and incorrect information. Additionally, the remote site may feel emotionally left out and conspiracy theories will emerge. A global team can mitigate these negative dynamics by updating the project management data and making this easily accessible. Project-wide information and milestone reports can also be circulated via e-mail (with some caution regarding information overload). In summary, maintaining a 360° view requires on-going attention.

Supporting coordination through workflow automation involves categorization of tasks and automated formalization of these categories into a language that permits certain interactions and rules out others. Grinter studied programmers' use of Software Configuration automation and found that they enjoyed and appreciated both the efficiency involved and the visibility it afforded them in seeing their own work relative to others.[115]

Elementary packaged software tools for software engineering began appearing in the 1980s. It is questionable how much good some of them really did in those early years. By the mid 1990s many of the functions listed in Exhibit 7–2 evolved to become fairly mature *stand-alone* tools, but failed global software teams on two counts: They did not adequately support multi-site usage, and they were not integrated with one another. Integration was largely left to the individual customers who ended up using various utility programs to wire them together. Today, CT-SE tools are moving down the path toward a more seamless environment. Some

- Software Configuration Management (SCM)
- Project status
- Notification services
- Project scheduling and tasking
- CASE and process management
- Programming tools
- Bug and change tracking
- Team memory & knowledge center

Exhibit 7–2   Collaborative Technology to support Software Engineering:
Eight needed functions.

tools are appearing in a cross-platform format, such as a standard web browser (as with Continuous software's SCM product) or a groupware platform. Note that Exhibit 7–2 labels well-known software engineering functions as "collaborative." Besides solitary programming tools, such as compilers, software engineering automation is about the need for groups to work together and collaborate.

The list in Exhibit 7–2[116] encompasses eight needed CT-SE *functions* for a well-run dispersed team. It represents a comprehensive list of these CT-SE functions, but the functions are not to be understood as being distinct and mutually exclusive. In fact, some of these functions blend into each other. Furthermore, the current generation of off-the-shelf software tools do not have a one-to-one correspondence to the functions on this list. For example, typical off-the-shelf project management tools have features that fall into a number of these functions.

It is worthwhile pointing out several assumptions regarding the list of functions. First, supporting a rich set of collaborative technologies requires fast and reliable connections. Second, the functions are almost all asynchronous—they assume different time and different place—even if not all users are dispersed. Third, many of these functions need to provide a variety of "views." That is, the individual developer will have some private subset of information that is integrated with the larger set (which can be seen as a personal to-do list or a personal information manager). The team as a whole needs to see detailed as well aggregated (rolled up) information.

Each of the eight functions listed in Exhibit 7–2 are discussed here:

Software Configuration Management (SCM)

For global software teams, there is no tool more important in the software engineering category than SCM. Whether you believe that a software team is managed via control mechanisms or via coordination mechanisms, SCM is the tool that does both. As a control and enforcement mechanism, it establishes a formalism: It is used to control processes, set the rules, and structure the workflow within the team. As a coordination mechanism, it is an effective way to create up-front dialogue among the dispersed sites. Each project team must determine which of the many rules built into an SCM package will be used. The rules can be decided by consensus via committees made up of members of the dispersed sites. A project manager can hardly decide, let alone know enough, about all the rules and toggles that need to be determined over the course of a project.

SCM tools also provide each developer with a 360^0 view. The tool visually arranges the work in such a way that each developer can see the various components in the evolving project and the associated information of each of the project's component: its name, its version number, its state, and the current owner. Thus, each developer sees a dynamic view of the entire project.[117]

SCM deals with managing change in a controlled fashion. Software development is a chaos of change. Each of the system objects seems to be changing constantly (whether it be a stored text document, design document, or software program). Which one is the right one? Or the most current one? SCM products' growing list of features is making collaborative development easier in this respect. For example, visual "differencing" highlights, in color, what code (or text) sections are different between two files. This is useful for correcting problems on a one by one basis. But development teams really need support at a higher level. Conceptually, the two principal components of SCM are change control and version control.

Change control revolves around the check-out/check-in metaphor. The developer who needs to modify an object selects the one he needs, fills out a few key pieces of information, and copies the object to his local computer. While the object has been checked out, no other developers can make any changes to it. It is said to be "locked." When his work is complete, the object is copied back to the repository by the check-in process. If desired by a workflow component of the system (as decided by the specific project in question), approvals and reviews may be required.

Since check-out/check-in can be too rigid, SCM vendors are moving to more flexible concepts, allowing programmers to check out code either in parallel or in small groups. Programmers can create a temporary work space (a mini-configuration) of checked-out code that is shared across a number of programmers at a time. This is a step forward because it allows programmers to work better in small problem-solving units while sharing partial results of their work.[118]

Version control assembles hundreds (if not thousands) of different objects that form part of one version (e.g., "Release 2.1"). Since there are so many objects for each release, this is quite a chore for a human being to do manually. Meanwhile, of course, "Release 2.2" is already underway and hundreds of individual objects appear in several versions simultaneously.

SCM tools are fairly well diffused. For example, Intersolv's PVCS claims half a million users worldwide. But one has to wonder how well many organizations are using these tools. The SCM vendors now realize that their increasingly dispersed customers are waking up to the real need for SCM support. Most vendors today position their products with marketing jargon, such as: ". . . parallel development and software reuse across geographically distributed development teams." Rational Software's Clearcase has an add-on product called *Multisite*. These add-on products will likely be integrated into the core products in the years to come.

The distribution/replication philosophy differs among products. Some SCM products maintain replicated copies of the repository while others centralize the repository at one site (for example, Rational Software in the former and StarTeam, the latter). If communication is less reliable, then a replicated strategy is better, but if communication is reliable and bandwidth is abundant, then centralized seems like the way to go.

Replication and synchronization of SCM was a difficult issue for several of the global teams in the GDSD study. While most of them used an SCM tool, at a number of the projects it was not synchronized across sites, meaning that the management of synchronization had to be done by fallible human beings. Sometimes synchronization was overlooked because of management decisions, but in at least one case it was due to the limitations of the SCM package. As it turned out, one SCM's check-out authorization was too coarse for the global software team—it could go down only to the module level while the team needed check-out at the object level. Because only a small percentage of the code was needed by the two sites, the team decided to segment and manage the code separately at the two sites.

Amongst the global software teams in the GDSD study, there were several cases of process failures due to lack of effective change control. Here is one of these:

Arizona Systems' large-scale global project had a three-country nexus and several additional minor sites. The project had no centralized SCM system, relying instead on different source trees at each major site. Not surprisingly, the project encountered numerous messy differences between source and binary files during the periodic builds.

Project status

Status information is needed for all project objects—from programs, to design documents, to user documentation. All information is graphically viewable on one set of screens with a catchy name: a war room, or a Space Mission Control Center, or a team dashboard. Using such a metaphor is useful to implementing the idea. The team dashboard includes, for example, a pie chart showing the total number of tasks completed, in progress, or yet to begin; and a bar chart with bugs per stage that are open/closed. An effective representation mixes project status information with other software development measures, e.g., a barometer of schedule overrun and an indicator of budget.

Project status is important to team effectiveness because it helps bring about the 360° view—knowing what all the other dispersed team members are up to and how the project as a whole is doing. Some aspects of project status are available in today's SCM packages, but most implementations are home-grown integrated front-end displays.

Notification services

This is a workflow function that is centered around notifying team members when something takes place that has an impact on their tasks. Some of these notifications feed into a private to-do list, while others are changes that may have an indirect impact on one's work. Notification is useful for two task types. First, when a change is made to an object that affects others (e.g., Erin needing to remember all of her object dependencies and informing Enriqué and Sergei informally), notification is done automatically. Second, when a task is complete, the approval process can be triggered either manually or automatically. For example, when Raj completes his program, he changes the status to "ready for review" and initiates an automatic review process that notifies the designated reviewer. An example state diagram of task/object status appears in Exhibit 7–3.

Notifications of this sort present the familiar information overload trade-off. Developers do not like too many progress reports, because they clutter up mailboxes and lead to information overload. The danger with

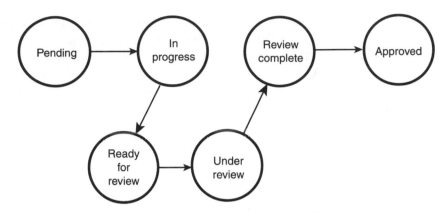

Exhibit 7–3   Task status workflow scheme to support collaborative software engineering.

automatic notification is that changes in one object (e.g., a program) ripple and impact other objects (e.g., a document), requiring all team members who are owners of those objects to be notified. However, not all changes are worthy of a notification, such as when a spelling change was made to one of the design documents.

Project scheduling and tasking

This function encompasses the core features of current project management packages, including task allocation, Gantt charts, and milestone planning. Each individual's tasks are specifically described in table and graphical format so that each individual can see the relationship of her task to all predecessor and successor tasks. This is another means to provide each team member with a 360° view of the team and its project.

Although most projects in the GDSD study made use of project management tools, most used these tools in isolated fashion, primarily by the project managers, with little cross-site integration. Project Management tools meet resistance from the hard core technical people. For example, one team lead explained that the project manager wanted him to use a project management tool but that he "didn't have time for it." Project management tools have become quite complex, loaded with features encompassing managerial concepts that are difficult without training.

Project tasking also implies role assignment and answers the question: "Who will carry out what tasks?" Roles are particularly important for reviews and approvals. A role assignment defines the specific responsibilities of each team member and ensures that the workflow features, of automatic routing, take place.

CASE & Process Management
Computer Aided Software Engineering (CASE) is an umbrella term for a broad set of features—from requirements tracking and modeling through database design. (Unfortunately, the marketplace has abandoned the term CASE, since historically it was over-hyped and has not replaced it with another popularly accepted broad term.) Many mature packages in the CASE category, such as requirements tracking, support multi-site and locking (through check-out/check-in). As with SCM, these are critical features to support a globally dispersed team.

In the 1980s US-based Texas Instruments (TI) was one of the early leaders in the CASE marketplace with a package then called IEF. TI was also an early user of global software teams with sites in the United States, India, and other locations. TI set up a globally distributed CASE environment with a central repository accessible to both the United States and India sites.[119] But CASE vendor TI was an exception. Penetration (and actual usage) of CASE in packaged software companies lagged far behind that of IS organizations until the mid 1990s. Only 21% of the global teams in the GDSD study used a CASE package, and not all used these tools on a multi-site basis, but rather as local tools.

The other dimension of this function is process management. Automated process management both instills and informs a process model (or development methodology) for the team. Typically, each organization has its own customized process model and some of its own technical terms. These organizational and team models need to be graphically depicted in a common, accessible repository. The specific stages need to be linked to supporting text documents describing the development norms. Some of the more stable documents should be translated to local spoken languages to reduce the jargon burden on the distant developer.

Programming tools
This function includes code generators and code analysis tools. Most tools in this category are solitary, single programmer tools. However, if task allocation is such that developers share code, then synchronous, collaborative tools can be used (however, beware of time zone differences). Some synchronous specialized tools have emerged in recent years: collaborative debugging, collaborative inspections, and even collaborative coding. Most

of these functions are implemented through multi-site windows. Programmers work on the same objects in a number of open windows with a variety of specialized metaphors, such as different color pens.

Bug and change tracking

Once the product is integrated at a major milestone, bugs (defects, errors) are found, and changes are requested. It is useful to concentrate all bug and change reports in one location—one database. Each bug has a myriad of related data associated with it (description of bug, date, results, severity). The data are used for addressing the individual errors and managing the process as a whole. Bug categories (severity) are very important when thousands of "open" (unresolved) changes are in progress. This database must be accessible by all team members at all sites. A desirable feature is that automatic workflow features be built into the database to route bugs and changes to the appropriate person or unit.

In the GDSD study, most global development teams that needed this kind of database had it in place early on. Unlike an SCM package, a bug database is easy to build in-house and simpler to enforce throughout the organization. Bug and change tracking is now commonly integrated in off-the-shelf SCM packages, making the coordination transition from the code stage to the test stage less difficult.

Team memory and knowledge center

This function is the complement to team memory and knowledge center for generic collaborative technology described earlier. This is the function in which the team stores and then shares information and knowledge across a work unit. One reason is that development teams often come to rely too heavily on one or two people with specialized knowledge and experience. The trouble is that these people are already overtaxed. The organization needs to off-load the more routine demands on the technical expert and reduce his distractions by building a system to augment the expert. The knowledge center is mostly document centered. For example, it stores FAQ—Frequently Asked Questions. The "center" also stores the company's technical references, as well as pointers to Internet sites with useful information.

As a final note on Collaborative Technology to support Software Engineering, it is worthwhile considering what the next generation of tools will look like. Software developers have shunned collaborative technologies, primarily those for software engineering, because they were too rigid. And they were right. Collaborative Technologies need to be adapted to each company's and each team's specific needs, while still maintaining needed formalization. The "silver bullet" to this problem may be XML—the Extensible Markup Language—a flexible metalanguage for marking up documents. It is a project of the World Wide Web Consortium (W3C), and is based on SGML, the Standard Generalized Markup Language (ISO standard 8879:1986). XML allows the user, team, or organization to design their own documents to be self-describing with their own tags and with relationships between tags. Both software engineering methodologies and collaborative technologies may well converge with XML. And it may be the way for standardizing methods of sharing data between collaborating programmers. XML is getting a further boost by an open information interchange model integrating it with the important software development framework UML, Unified Modeling Language.

The Team and Collaborative Technology

Why are global software teams not using more collaborative technologies? For example, why don't all global software teams use a groupware platform (e.g., Notes) since its represents such a good fit to the problems of dispersed development? One explanation is that developers are suspicious of collaborative technologies and the rules they seem to impose. Grantham and colleagues[120] have another explanation. After studying several US-based software companies' use of groupware platforms, they made an observation about Unix programmers that may be true about most programmers: that programmers "tend to have a bias against groupware, they see it as cute and fluffy, and not a real programming tool, and therefore how can it be of any use to them?"

Diffusing collaborative technologies within the team requires a full multi-level strategy. First, and most important, is the soft persuasion, at each site, with each team member. Second, is the example set by the project manager and her team leads. They must generate a lot of energy and enthusiasm into the discussion lists, e-mail messages, repositories, and design documents. They must make sure people are aware of and are reading the material. They must be aware of who the silent team members are and persuade them repeatedly to participate electronically.

Third, use of collaborative technologies must be rewarded. Rewards can be subtle, such as congratulations or acknowledgment of contribution, particularly if done via a quick personal and discreet message. Other creative group recognition rewards should be considered. Motivating developers to use discussion lists, electronic forums, and knowledge repositories is particularly difficult. These tools are not workflow tools, which tend to be easier to persuade and enforce, but rather involve knowledge sharing and information sharing, taking time away from one's principal task (e.g., designing or programming). Information and knowledge sharing are also key political tools that we all use tactically. We share information in order to receive other valuable information.

Another team-related issue is "buy versus build." Do you buy a collaborative technology package or do you build the functionality at home? Unfortunately, many global teams in the GDSD study patched together CT-SE tools from messaging and file systems. This was especially noticeable for SCM systems. These well-intentioned efforts relied on much ongoing team grunt work—all to create systems that were often inadequate and that could have been purchased in packaged format from software vendors.

However, there are some sound reasons for building various collaborative tools in-house. There is no software suite anywhere that covers the voluminous features described in this chapter. Integration and adaptation are inevitably needed. In addition, for software professionals, the excitement of tool use is enhanced if it is homegrown rather than off-the-shelf. Team members were proud of their homegrown tools, which they created for one of their real needs.[121]

Best Practices Roundup

☑ *Quickly standardize on collaborative technologies.* Collaborative technology tools without technical incompatibilities are hard enough to get people to use.

☑ *Introduce and use a rich set of collaborative technology.* This chapter identified seven specific types of generic collaborative technologies and eight specific functions of CT-SE, for a total of 15. How many of these are you using in your global software team? Shouldn't your team be using more? Use of collaborative technology is similar to the many features in your office telephone—people discover how valuable they are after they start using them.

☑ *Buy collaborative technologies, but leave some room for home-grown solutions.* Do a thorough market search and buy the collaborative technology that you need. Do not spend your precious team resources on work done by others. Some specialized small homegrown tools do generate a lot of team enthusiasm and pride, so don't close the door on these completely.

☑ *Use a Software Configuration Management (SCM) package.* Global teams that did not have a proper SCM system (with corresponding work practices) encountered delays. An SCM is essential if the project involves numerous hand-offs, successive "build" rounds, or use of follow-the-sun.

☑ *Train team members in use of new collaborative technology.* New technologies require training and preparation, even if they look simple on the surface. Use the tips about video-conferencing below. Buy training for most CT-SE tools such as project management and SCM.

Tips on preparing and conducting a group video-conference meeting

- Prepare and distribute printed materials (agenda, handouts) before the meeting.
- Set up many parallel channels to augment the "talking heads": electronic-mail, fax, e-whiteboard, presentation graphics.
- Prepare a list of names of all participants at all sites, depict them sitting around a table, and distribute to all sites before meeting.
- Designate one recorder (note taker) and have him update the other sites periodically over e-mail.
- Don't choose "fast topics" such as brainstorming or quick question-and-answer.
- Make sure everyone has an opportunity to speak.
- Keep meeting to one hour.

☑ *Get the team to use collaborative technology by persuasion, by example, and by reward.* Managers have no choice but to explain to their developers how these tools will make life wonderful for all. The project manager can find and bring in a developer who has worked in a dispersed development project without the benefits of CT-SE, particularly SCM, and tell (warn) your developers what a mess they got into.[122] Managers and team leads need to set an example by being very active participants of discussion lists, e-mail messages, and shared repositories. Use of technology should be recognized and rewarded.

☑ *Architect the organization memory at the outset.* When beginning a project, make a list of all the topics that should go into the organizational memory to support cross-site learning and information sharing. Do not expect it to grow by itself.

☑ *Introduce a balance of collaborative technology tools.* Think of this as you would your financial investment portfolio in which you balance different types of financial instruments. Effective use of collaborative technology requires using a multitude of channels and tools, not just a few. If your global team is already successfully using several CT-SE, balance these with a generic groupware platform or elements of such a platform, such as calendars. If the team is a heavy user of asynchronous technologies, experiment with video-conferencing and other synchronous technologies.

☑ *Integrate the collaborative technologies.* Make all the tools into a seamless suite. For example, integrate the SCM system and the bug tracking system.

☑ *Invest in specialized tech support.* A portfolio of collaborative technology, like those of other technologies, requires designated technical support. If it is a lifeline of the global software team—as it should be—then it cannot be relegated to ad hoc support by one of the team members that maintains the collaborative technology when she is not coding. The most notorious example these days is Lotus Notes. At a number of global sites, the problems of installing and implementing Notes caused them to drop Notes altogether. Support for collaborative technology is not just technical. Ideally, collaborative technology support people should also understand the "C" in collaborative technology and help facilitate its use throughout the organization.[123]

☑ *Don't overwhelm.* Collaborative technology is vital to a dispersed team, but we all live in a daily deluge of messages—mail, e-mail, phone calls, faxes, voice-mail. A 1998 US study[124] found that the average worker sends or receives 190 messages per day and is interrupted by messages three times per hour. Warn team members about the quantity of messages and information. Suggest ways to do selective filtering and scanning. It is natural for a few team members to complain about information overload and junk e-mail. Listen for signs that the deluge is really too great and that team members are reacting through stress, or by not reading e-mail.

☑ *Be sensitive to cultural differences in use of collaborative technology.* Always remind yourself that all of these collaborative technologies are not culturally neutral and are not understood in the same way by different cultures. Ask team members about how they use various collaborative technologies and listen for assumptions that are different from yours. Given all the difficulties with video-conferencing, consider the wisdom of many video-conference contrarians: "Do not expose people to video-conferencing until they have first met face to face."

☑ *Be vigilant in providing a 360° view.* Continue to inform and update all members at all sites regarding task, status, people, and other dynamic project information through various collaborative technologies.

☑ *Build workflow components into your collaborative technology.* Automated workflow increases efficiency and quality control in dispersed teams. Equally important, it formalizes some of the communication that may have been done informally before the team was dispersed. The classic workflow applications are routing objects for review and routing bugs for detection and correction

Further Reading

Madefast tells the story of an academic-engineering six-month project across a dozen US sites that produced a prototype tracker for missiles using first generation web-based tools. Cutkosky, M.R. Tennebaum, J.M, and Glicksman, J. Madefast: Collaborative engineering over the internet. *Communications of the ACM* (September, 1996) 39(9), 78–88.

Synchronous concurrent collaborative software engineering is described for distributed but private coding, collaborative debugging, use of collaborative inspection tools, and re-coding using a collaborative program editor. Dewan, P. and Riedl, J. Toward computer supported concurrent software engineering. *Computer* (January 1993).

DEVELOPMENT METHODOLOGY

The development methodology is the map that guides the team through the software development cycle. It also becomes the common language bridging developers at different sites. When one writes that "we'll do that during the alpha stage," understood between the two developers is exactly what is expected in the alpha stage as well as when it will arrive.

This chapter lays the groundwork in the area of methodology interspersed with findings from the GDSD study. Methodological rigor and maturity are introduced and contrasted with the heroics that software companies have traditionally relied on. Paradoxically, this rigor needs some flexibility in handling change. For example, when two software companies conduct a cross-border joint venture, whose development methodology should be used? This question and others are addressed below.

When we look at globalized manufacturing—of automobiles for example—studies show that companies are more likely to make the decision to globalize *if* their internal manufacturing processes are more mature and ready for the increased managerial complexity of dispersion. In software, however, it is clear that many companies with immature software development processes are taking the plunge globally. In order to manage a globally dispersed team effectively, an overall development methodology must be in place.

It is worthwhile stating explicitly why organizations—and specifically dispersed teams—use an overall development methodology (see terminology in Exhibit 8–1). An explicit development methodology gives all team members a common language of tasks and activities. Terms and milestones are understood. At any given time, all developers know where their place is in the bigger picture. It gives everyone a consistent set of expectations.

An overall development methodology (or process model) has other important benefits: It groups similar activities together; it reduces redundant activities and excessive work; it organizes activities into steps and phases; it enhances quality by assuring that the activities are comprehensive and compete; it reduces irrational activities; and it serves as effective documentation for management.

---

a methodology is a systematic approach to conducting at least one complete phase (e.g., design) of software production, consisting of a set of guidelines, activities, techniques, and tools, based on a particular philosophy of system development and the target system. An example is the Unified Modeling Language.

a process model is a representation of the sequence of stages (e.g., design, build, test) through which a software product evolves. The term "methodology" is often used synonymously with "process model."

the Capability Maturity Model (CMM) was introduced by the Software Engineering Institute at Carnegie-Mellon University (USA). It introduced and legitimized the notion of "process maturity" in software engineering. The CMM is made up of five levels of maturity to describe an organization's capabilities. An organization that is continuously improving its development practices advances through these levels. Popular in IS organizations, the CMM principles have also seeped into some packaged software companies.

a mature process means that, at a minimum, tasks are not done ad hoc. That is, they are not based on the heroics of key individuals. Many gradients of a mature process exist, such as the formal levels of the CMM. A practical determination of whether a development team uses a minimum maturity level is if the process is standardized and documented in a ring binder (or a set of web pages), has been agreed to, and is integrated across all team sites.

Exhibit 8–1 Development methodology terminology.

When I began studying packaged software companies' development practices in the early 1990s, few were using any overall development methodology or process model.[125] Most development was ad hoc. The packaged software companies and the emerging leaders in software engineering ignored each other. Once software organizations began growing and dispersing, however, they realized that they had to change their ways. It became apparent that they could not continue developing software the way they were used to when they were start-ups. They began to formalize (mature) their development practices. The project teams in the GDSD study ranged methodologically from poor to very advanced. Interestingly, the methodologically poorest were the very smallest and the very largest projects.

The software industry's development practices have improved. Informally, at least 66% of the global software projects in the GDSD study began their international collaboration using a minimal development framework (close to or roughly at Level II of the CMM). Generally, the large software organizations devoted more attention to methodology. Several of the projects were ISO 9000 certified. One of the software companies even worked closely with Watts Humphrey, formerly head of the Software Engineering Institute. The company had been training its software developers at a number of sites on derivatives of the CMM—such as the Personal Software Process.

Use of a development methodology imposes a *rigor* on the software team. It demands greater discipline than many software organizations have become accustomed to. American software firms, in particular, have a poor reputation in methodology. Their critics refer to their "cowboy mentality." In the broader context, software development—or software engineering—needs to be compared to other engineering forms, such as mechanical and chemical engineering.[126] Those engineering disciplines are much further along as industrial disciplines.

Many software companies avoid using the discipline of a process model for three reasons. First, the development team is small. With a small team, the communication and coordination overhead is reduced. An undisciplined small unit can self-correct itself with reasonable costs, if its members are sufficiently motivated. Second, the team is co-located, allowing members to improvise processes when corrections are needed. Finally, the team relies on heroics.[127] Heroics come in two forms. The first form is the end-of-cycle all-night work weeks. In the United States these sometimes reach 80 hours per week. Another heroic is actually relying on just a few heroes—exceptional people, with exceptional abilities. These heroes know the software application domain and are "super"-programmers.

Yet, once the team is dispersed—and dispersed globally—all of these informal team mechanisms for getting the job done fall apart. An overall development methodology compensates for the loss of these informal, ad hoc mechanisms. A well-understood development methodology leads to a working relationship in which many of the old coordination conversations are no longer needed. The development process is understood and agreed upon by all. There is little need to talk about it. Instead, conversations focus on solving the problem domain, such as how to squeeze more graphics onto the screen.

There are hundreds of software development process models that have been proposed. At their core, they reduce to two fundamental approaches: the waterfall/linear/sequential model, and the prototyping/iterative model. The classic model is the first of these—the waterfall/linear/sequential model—which moves through a number of stages in sequence. Generally, each stage must be fully completed before moving to the next one. The generic stages are analysis and design, then code, then test. Many managers gravitate to the classic sequential approach because it is easier to manage. For the global software manager, that also means that there are fewer hand offs where each hand off tends to be more clearly defined.

Harder to manage, but more effective, is the prototyping/iteration model, which builds successive iterations (or loops) into the process. Feedback loops are used to elicit responses from peers or customers and then revise the product. Iterations are used to enhance the product concept from within and continuously improve on specifications.

The IBM JavaBeans project (of Chapter 2) uses a process model with an iterative philosophy. Recall that instead of large, elephantine packages, this project worked on smaller applications called beans. Each bean was developed using the following process model:

1. Problem Statement Creation. A simple 1–2 line definition that can be initiated by any of the sites.
2. Problem Definition Development. This stage was considered the most difficult—working from a loose idea to high level implementation, requiring many iterations.
3. Implementation (code). Usually a small unit of three to five people are involved.

4. Acceptance. Addresses the following questions: Does it function correctly? Is it packaged correctly? Is the documentation correct and complete?

Development methodologies are somewhat like cookbooks. The cookbook analogy is useful to understand the behavior of both novice teams and experienced teams. A novice must have a cookbook and follow the instructions carefully, not always fully understanding why he is performing a certain step. A more experienced cook will use the cookbook as a foundation and, based on experience, know how to deviate from the instructions and create a dish that better suits her tastes. Another more experienced cook will combine elements from the Spanish recipe for chicken with elements from the Moroccan recipe for chicken.

The methodology-as-cookbook principle is now well accepted in software management. The methodology must never be seen as cast in stone or overly rigid. Off-the-shelf models are readily available from many sources. But they are rarely implemented in their entirety in most organizations. They are rarely used "as is." Instead, process *components* are mixed and blended along with some homegrown, successful processes to create an in-house process. Software engineering tool vendors have made their packages (e.g., modeling tools) more flexible to allow users to modify their methodologies as they see fit. Furthermore, any methodology should always be seen as an evergreen methodology. It changes as new learning is absorbed and as project conditions dictate. A flexible approach is exemplified in one of the newer iterative development methodologies DSDM[128]—Dynamic Systems Development Method. The DSDM "empowers" teams to make their own decisions. There must be prior agreement to certain levels of standards in criteria such as functionality and usability. Beyond that, each unit does not have to seek approval for minor process decisions.

When global software sites are merged together into a collaborating team, the methodological clash can be more painful than national cultural differences. Managers discover that the basic assumptions on seemingly everything seem to be different: the scope of design, how rigorous the design will be, the amount of documentation of each stage, the approach to quality assurance. Merging sites methodologically is illustrated in the following three cases from the GDSD study: The first allowed methodological differences to continue; the second imposed the headquarters standard; the third, in a joint venture, chose the methodology of one of the partners.

At US-based Arizona Systems a very large and complex three country development project with hundreds of developers pitted three major sites with three different development methodologies against each other. The sites bickered about many process issues and managed to synchronize only through the common periodic "builds" in which all the software components were brought together. Not only did the three sites maintain different methodologies, but they brought different underlying values to the methodological wars. One site took Quality Assurance much more seriously, insisting on control over its own testing because it did not trust the other sites.

At US-based Contemporary Sciences, a strong-willed global development director imposed standard methodology components on all distant sites in three countries, all of which were collaborating as a result of acquisition. All sites became ISO 9000 certified and used a gamut of common collaborative tools (e.g., a common Software Configuration Management tool, common templates). The development director showed little tolerance for deviations from standard anywhere in his organization, explaining "when we acquired [Seattle], we threw out all their Macs."

In a joint venture between a large US software company and a large European software company, the underlying methodological values were fundamentally different. The Europeans saw programming as central: Programmers were put on the pedestal. The Americans treated documentation and user design with the same level of respect as programming. These different development values and other differences led to friction during the early months of the joint venture until the two sides mutually agreed whose methodology would be used. In this case the European one was chosen.

The best approach to methodological assimilation, if politically feasible, is to impose standardization across sites. An alternative to the headquarters-imposed standard is the "blend." Methodological blending can occur because methodologies are malleable. For example, at an American–Israeli joint venture, the development methodology agreed to by both sides was blended from the two corporate parents and then documented as the official joint venture methodological approach.

What about climbing up the levels of maturity after dispersing the team globally? While dispersing without a common development methodology is a guaranteed predictor of major problems, it is natural for the methodology to mature as the pressures and experiences of global teams emerge. This became very clear from talks with global software team managers in the GDSD study. "We had to" was a refrain I would often hear about developing more mature processes under conditions of dispersion. This is common to other global software collaborations. As Texas Instruments expanded its development in India in the late 1980s and early 1990s, many procedures were phased in.[129] All process documentation began to be stored in Lotus Notes, change management control was maintained with strict sign-off procedures between customers and developers. Similarly, when Belgian-based Sidmar Steel began doing offshore development in the Philippines,[130] strict methodological and project management tracking was enforced by a company that never practiced this back home.

Recognizing that globalization required mature methodology capabilities led one organization to move faster:

At US-based VisiBusiness, a major business application software company with little global development experience, a seasoned global development executive came on board in 1997. A self-proclaimed CMM zealot, she began instituting a series of process improvements with the goal of maturing development capabilities across the organization in anticipation of an accelerated push to global development. She knew that imposing too much process rigor in a short time would lead to, as she said, an "armed rebellion." So she began by developing common terminology that, within several months, became 12 pages of methodological guidelines.

Best Practices Roundup

☑ *Impose a development framework before development begins.* Before the project standardize and document the methodological standards, store them in the team memory and knowledge center, and distribute them to all team members electronically.

☑ *Educate all team members on the chosen methodologies.* The conceptual reasoning of development methodologies and process models require repeated training, exposure, and motivation. Spend time up front with all team members, preferably in a kick-off meeting.

☑ *"Grow" the methodology.* Continue to raise the methodological capability level of your development team. Grow the documentation as new standards and terms are agreed upon.

☑ *When cross-border sites are consolidated into a team, consider one of three methodological strategies: forcing standardization, blending methodological components from the various sites into one "new" methodology, or imposing high-level guidelines only.* When cross-border sites are blended together to form a team, methodological differences are guaranteed to surface. If politically palatable, methodological standardization is the most effective route. The worldwide standard could be that of headquarters, or a blend of the best elements from the major development sites. An alternative is to allow some controlled methodological deviations within each commonly defined stage as long as the entry and exit conditions are agreed upon by all sides and documented accordingly.

☑ *Define and agree to terminology every day.* Define terms early and continue to define and clarify them as development progresses. One of a manager's artful tasks is to recognize when developers use a key term differently and then lead the way to standardizing that term. Different global sites may have different interpretations of a "code freeze," a "feature freeze," or what it means when a bug is said to be "fixed," or "verified." Term standardization is best done via the discuss-and-document[131] approach. The discussions are generally verbal (via audio-conference). Once agreement is hashed out, the terminology needs to be documented in the team memory and knowledge center.

Further Reading

The Software Engineering Institute web site is very rich in information and links: http://www.sei.cmu.edu.

Software Engineering textbooks are a useful reference source. I recommend Pressman, R. S. *Software Engineering,* fourth ed, New York, NY: McGraw-Hill, 1997.

ARCHITECTURE & TASK
ALLOCATION

Product architecture determines whether dispersed sites can work harmoniously with each other without stepping on each other's toes. Proper product architecture is based in part on the principle of modularity: designing software components that are self-contained and have few interdependencies with other modules. Module-based allocation, the first of the three task allocation strategies, assigns tasks—modules—to each site. The second strategy is phase-based allocation in which the work is passed from site to site at the end of a major phase in the development process. The third strategy is integrated allocation, which for global software teams is known as follow-the-sun. Here, tasks are tightly integrated between sites and work is passed, as often as daily, between sites. At the end of the chapter, the Stage Model of global software teams is introduced. The model illustrates how task allocation changes between headquarters and remote development sites over time.

Experienced global managers recognize that product architecture (and its corollaries, good task decomposition and then good task allocation) are a necessity for managing complex projects performed by globally dispersed teams. In fact it is the product architecture that should *determine* the team structure. "Never again," said one global software manager who took a mature product designed to be built by one co-located team and then allocated it to two global sites. He had learned his lesson the hard way and was forced to re-architect his product after a painful release cycle.

Proper product architecture is based in part on the principle of modularity. Modularity is the only way to solve and allocate big complex tasks. Modular design reduces complexity and allows for easier parallel development. And the key success factor for most dispersed global teams is the clean allocation of tasks: ensuring that each site has a significant task that relies as little as possible on other sites. By creating a minimum of *interdependence* between the sites, coordination overhead is reduced.[132] This approach is no different from other industrial product development efforts. For example, the Boeing 777 design project had 250 teams, many of which were modular, specific to body parts such as the wing, the cockpit, and the engines.

The concept of modularity—allowing a software program to be manageable intellectually—is as fundamental to computer software as it is to all engineering disciplines. So, how should software be decomposed? *Information hiding,* introduced by Parnas in 1972, is a general design concept that calls for properly structuring the software's modules such that the design logic is hidden from its user—the programmer. The less design logic the programmer has to comprehend, the fewer the communication needs with other programmers' modules. Extensions of the principle of information hiding can be found in many of the software development improvements of recent decades: structured design, and more recently, software objects.

Independence of modules can be measured by two criteria: coupling and cohesion (see Exhibit 9–1). Coupling is the degree of interaction between modules. Cohesion is the degree to which a module comprises a well-defined functional whole. Coupling and cohesion are at the core of software team task allocation.[133] Optimal modularization, and hence task allocation, minimize coupling while maximizing cohesion. Modern approaches that have to do with objects and components reduce to two principles: component independence (subdividing into loosely related subproblems) and component integrity (each component making sense as a whole). Software products are re-designed in part to increase modularity.

Large products are designed around a foundation with components (modules) all interacting with the foundation. The art is to make the foundation broad enough to support all the components while minimizing interactions between components and the foundation. The responsibility for the individual components (as well as for the foundation) is then allocated to various sites.

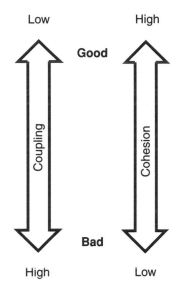

Low   High

Good

Coupling   Cohesion

Bad

High   Low

Exhibit 9–1   Coupling & cohesion.

"The software architecture of a [..] computing system is the structure or structures of the system, which comprise software components, the externally visible properties of those components, and the relationships among them."[134]

Software architecture is increasingly recognized as a distinct part of the design process. Like other design elements, architecture represents an abstraction of the system in which much of the information is hidden. Of most interest to us here, architecture defines *components* (or modules). The architecture embodies information about the ways in which components interact with each other. This means that it specifically omits (hides) information about components that does not deal with their interaction. A related design principle is to design these components in small granules (size), keeping each component's interfaces to a manageable number (e.g., less than ten).

Task allocation strategies

Allocating development tasks between sites falls into three fundamental strategies, depicted in Exhibit 9–2. The first of these strategies is based on

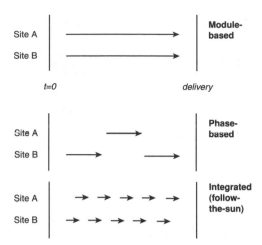

Exhibit 9–2   Types of task allocation.

modularization. In *module-based allocation,* site A and site B are each assigned one of two modules to develop from the beginning of the systems development cycle to the end. The second strategy is based on the standard stages, or phases, in the systems development cycle: design/build/test. In *phase-based allocation,* site B performs the first phase (design), while site A performs the next phase (build) and so on.[135] Lastly, *integrated allocation* takes place when (dispersed) sites work closely together, both across modules and across the development cycle. In the case of global software teams, this phase is known as follow-the-sun.

An example of a prototypical module-based allocation is the following fictional American–British collaboration. A US-based firm acquires a British software company to complement its product line. The British company's product becomes a module in an integrated suite of functions that are all marketed as one by the American-headquartered company. Once the architecture committee defines and modifies the module interfaces, and marketing has defined functional specifications, each development site, now renamed to "center of competence," is assigned design and development of its respective modules. In conclusion, module-based allocation (like that of Bordeaux Associates described in the mini-case further below) tries to decouple the sites as much as possible in order to reduce coordination costs.

The concept of "center of competence" is common to industries outside of software as well. For example, Swedish telecommunications company Ericsson's specialized R&D centers are analogous to software's centers of competence. The Swedish company evolved these based on local history of technical expertise. Thus, the silicon R&D labs reside in Australia, Italy, and Finland, while mobile systems R&D labs reside in Germany, France, Spain, and Greece.

An example of a prototypical phase-based allocation is the following fictional US–Indian collaboration. A US-based design unit works with marketing specialists and local customers. The requirements are carefully synthesized into functional specifications. The system architecture is conceived or modified. The architecture and functional specifications are shipped off to the programming site in India. The offshore Indian team leads absorb the specs and perform more detailed (low-level) design and then hand tasks over to the local programming unit. In stable situations, the Indian coding unit then requires relatively little interaction with its US-based counterparts, except for occasional clarifications. Once the software is coded and tested, it is shipped back to the United States where it is installed by a US-based unit at the customer site.

This example uses the classic "throw-over-the-wall" paradigm that is common to traditional manufacturing and software development. In throw-over-the-wall, as each phase is completed, its responsible work group hands over the deliverable product (the design document, or the system code) by throwing it over the wall and moving on to another task. In conclusion, one characteristic of phase-based allocation is that it attempts to maximize inexpensive resources (e.g., offshore programmers), while minimizing expensive resources (such as US-based architects and designers in this example).

An integrated (or follow-the-sun) allocation cannot be described at this point as prototypical. In concept, it involves passing unfinished work from site to site on a daily basis (or more pragmatically several times per week). The strategy works as follows: a US-based site finishes its work for the day and delivers it to the team repository (such as a SCM tool). A few hours later, at the start of their day, the Indian team members read through the questions, summaries, and instructions written by their American colleagues and proceed to continue their work. At the end of the day in India, the developers reverse the flow, with another day's worth of added value.

The points of weakness of each one of these task allocation schemes are in their coupling, that is, the transition, or hand-over, from site to site (depicted in Exhibit 9–3). Module-based allocation's point of weakness occurs at the end of the cycle, when the modules need to be integrated to-

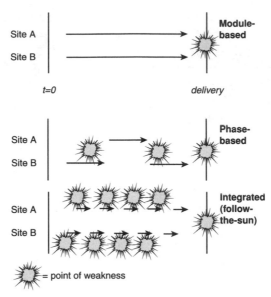

Exhibit 9–3   Types of task allocation with points of weakness in the transitions.

gether. This may happen during the first "build," or during integration testing. Numerous assumptions made by specifiers, architects, designers, and programmers prove to be faulty. For the phase approach, the point of weakness is in the hand-over from phase to phase. The third strategy, integrated allocation, theoretically has hundreds of transitions. Each one of them is a point of weakness in the time it takes each individual to package up his daily tasks and make them meaningful, asynchronously, to a distant set of colleagues who then have to make sense of their meaning.

With an understanding of the points of weakness, we move to the success factors for each of the three task allocation strategies. The requirement for successful module-based allocation is, quite simply, good architecture early on. The architectural committee must minimize the interdependencies (relationships) between the modules. A common approach uses the natural tiers inherent in software products. Site A develops the GUI (the client) while site B develops the engine (the server). Others refer to this as a layered approach. One site is tasked with the foundation, while various other sites are tasked with the various modules (e.g., applications) that fit "on top of" the foundation.

Successful phased-based allocation is based on a two-pronged approach. First, devote attention to *transitioning* (i.e., hand off). One company in the GDSD study had a semi-formal process in place in which one or more Indian managers came to the US site and worked with their American counterparts for several months, going through a long checklist of issues before receiving the functional design documents and taking them back to the Indian site for further work. Second, establish relatively stable requirements or specifications (whichever of these two terms is said to drive the changes). Closely related, the specifications have to be well defined: They must be both comprehensive and accurate.

Finally, the requirement for successful integrated allocation is to set up small granules of work and pair up individuals from distant sites to work with each other. Individual coordination of transition is simpler than passing work from group to group.

Two brief cases from the GDSD study illustrate successes and failures of task allocation. The first company set up a successful module-based allocation. The second company, also using mostly module-based allocation, could never allocate tasks properly throughout the development cycle.

> Bordeaux Associates is a France-based systems software company with two small development sites in the United States. In 1992 the company embarked on a major redesign of product architecture, which effectively decoupled the product components (along the client and server dimensions). Interdependencies among components were reduced to such an extent that the various server-side platform sites operated autonomously and only communicated with the headquarters in Paris. Bordeaux Associates' R&D manager, a reluctant global manager, said "[architecture] is a masterpiece for plugging everything together. . . . [I]f there is [too much] integration between modules it cannot work, it is a waste of money. You need to give them a significant amount of work, make them very autonomous and then limit them to a very small set of integration items."

> Arizona Systems is a large, US-based company. Its 1996 project release was more than two years in the making. It was a complex and large project with hundreds of developers in three countries. Partially because of product complexity and partially because of organizational factors, requirements kept drifting, complicating the task assignments throughout the life of the project. Ownership issues became a problem among the three sites, leading to "turf battles." One

of Arizona Systems' early objectives was to split functionality into completely separate products. This division would have simplified development by creating independent modules. However, the customer base was demanding an integrated product. So the eventual product suite became an exercise in unifying all these modules, each of which had organizational and design baggage associated with it. Naturally, the architecture committee did its best to reduce interdependencies. But once the coding began it was clear that too many interdependencies still remained. After some battles, ownership of one major module was shifted from one site to another. Another key module overlapped two sites, creating redundancy. Developers began jokingly referring to the split module as "mirror projects." Even the integration phase was not centralized at one site.

Both module and phase task allocation strategies were common among the global software development projects developing packaged software of various categories. In fact, most task allocations were hybrids of module and phase. Of the cases in the GDSD study, only 25% approached the extremes of either module-based or phase-based allocation—and significantly—none were pure phase or pure module. All the other projects used more complex task allocation: combining module with phase, module with integrative, phase with integrative; and two projects had properties of all three approaches—phase, module, and integrative.

Inter-site task allocation criteria

Project managers often voice the following complaint: I had no say in task allocation since it was all determined by historical decisions made before this specific project began. It is worthwhile dissecting these "historic" decisions into several dimensions: knowledge, cost, level of abstraction, "ownership" in the political sense, and team pride.

Two straightforward criteria have to do with knowledge and cost. The term *center of competence* is used to describe a concentration of technical or, more often, application expertise. Clearly, competency and experience play a large role in determining who gets what task/module. Many centers of competence emerge intact from an acquisition with their specialized skills and experience embodied in their members. Thus, many software companies' task allocation criteria are predetermined by acquisitions and are modular in nature. Other companies built their centers of competence from the ground up. For example, Baan built its aerospace modules in Seattle next to Boeing, and its automotive modules in Hannover near German auto manufacturing centers.

Cost issues drive certain tasks to less expensive sites, typically in emerging nations. In many cases these allocation strategies become phase-based where coding and testing tasks are allocated to the distant sites. Another factor influencing phase-based allocation is abstraction. The continuum of abstraction positions "abstract" at one extreme and "structured" at the other extreme.[136] Structured, well-defined tasks are more readily allocated by phase and more easily dispersed, while abstract tasks, if allocated at all, are better allocated by module.

Task allocation is also determined by team ownership and pride. A good global software manager rewards specific sites with increasing levels of responsibility. This is a very delicate area, because it involves not only the identity of site X, but inevitably site, organizational, and national pride issues. When ownership and pride are not accorded their due, friction arises. I heard many ways to refer to this problem; the most common is "turf war" and my favorite is "political ping-pong."

> At US-based Sharp Applications' three-country collaboration, the Belgian site wanted ownership of one of the product modules in spite of it being viewed as an "American owned" module since the original code was written by one of the American sites. After some maneuvering, the project manager was able to transfer ownership of the code to the Belgians—in exchange for freezing their headcount.

Which is better: stage- or module-based allocation? There is no correct answer because so many factors drive the task allocation decision—from costs to team history. There are good reasons for each approach. Weighing this question, Rothman[137] argues that module-based is superior because the sites are self-contained. Each site has all the development functions—from code through documentation specialists. Everyone understands what it is they have to do. In contrast, phase allocation is more prone to miscommunication at the point of transition.

Task allocation of first- and second-tier development activities

Based on data from the GDSD study, composition of staff assigned to the three generic phases of design/build/test is shown in Exhibit 9–4. "Build"

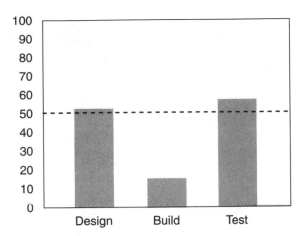

Exhibit 9–4   Percent of effort in HQ country by development phase (median percent based on 14 global projects).

(coding), at only 16% of effort in the headquarters nation, is the one major task that was assigned by most companies to the distant sites. About 50% of design effort took place in the headquarters country, while the other half took place in the various distant sites.

Somewhat surprising is that more than half the testing effort was still done in the headquarters nation. Because testing is both a less attractive and better-defined, task it seems that this ratio should have been lower. An explanation for this finding is that many of the companies were focusing their initial attention and resources on allocating the development (and some design) tasks abroad. Since the companies already had quality assurance staff at home, they relied on this existing staff to support the global efforts. Additionally, some companies combined testing with integration and this was more manageable at the headquarters nations' sites. Testing functions will likely continue migrating to distant sites. Some testing functions, such as regression testing, are relatively simple to spin off.

Software companies have a two-tier approach to task allocation. Not all development activities are seen as equally critical, glamorous, wealth-creating, or cerebral. Design/Code/Test, the core functions of development, were the primary focus of the chapter thus far. A secondary tier exists for everything else: documentation, marketing[138] (liaison role), porting (conversion from one computer platform to another), integration (integrating product modules near the end of the cycle), localization (translating software from one spoken language to another), and many quality assurance and testing activities. This two-tier model (or even three-tier in some cases) is not best practice, but rather descriptive of common practice.

Second-tier activities are in-sourced or even outsourced to other sites separately from the first tier tasks for several sound reasons. The tasks may have lower interdependence, they require specialized expertise, and they are less abstract (and therefore less ambiguous). Despite the enlightenment of software methodologists, many organizations designate documentation as a second-tier activity and allocate it to a remote site. In reality, interdependence of documentation with the Design/Code/Test axis is quite high. One project manager whose documentation unit was not in-house, but far away in Ireland, said: "It is difficult for them to be so far. The documentation unit has to learn everything from the documents we supply them. It may be more important to have them next to our software engineers than the actual software engineers sitting together!"

Porting and localization are excellent candidates for allocating to distant sites because they are well-defined tasks and the degree of interdependence with other tasks is relatively low. Other factors influence this task allocation as well. High paid programmers are reluctant to perform porting. The most abundant skills for localization are in the remote nations to begin with. Localization is an interesting special case of vertical dispersion. Some firms choose to perform centralized localization in the headquarters location while others disperse this activity to the respective local countries.

Intra-site task allocation

Task assignments to individual developers at each site are best made by local team leads based on local norms. In fact, developers who are tightly tasked may be less creative than those who are managed in a more informal style. Developers operate best when given clear objectives and guidelines and then set free with lots of latitude.

Cultural issues affect individual task allocation. In individualist cultures it is important to everyone to know who exactly is responsible, who is really being productive, and who is just free riding. However, in collectivist cultures research shows that group members work harder in order to meet the expectations of the group.[139] Moreover, the "free rider" or "social loafing" problem was most serious when individuals from collectivist cultures were assigned individual tasks since this reduced the peer pressure on them.

Change in allocation over time; Stage Model of global software teams

For any given team, allocation is not static from project to project or release to release. Allocation goes through an evolutionary process that is conceptualized in the Stage Model of global software teams (Exhibit 9–5). In Stage I all development activities are co-located at headquarters. In Stage II distant sites are added at various layers of criticality, but all are coordinated (and controlled) from headquarters. In Stage III various remote development sites assume greater responsibility for a range of tasks and coordinate some activities among themselves without funneling all decisions through headquarters. Today, some software companies are entering Stage III.

Increased and enlarged task responsibility to remote sites evolves over time. It is difficult to delegate control and decision-making to a distant site dominated by a foreign culture. It takes a certain level of acceptance that some managers develop faster than others. With the passage of time certain factors change. The newer, distant site begins to prove their professional expertise. The distant sites learn to understand the headquarters' organizational culture and its development norms and expectations.

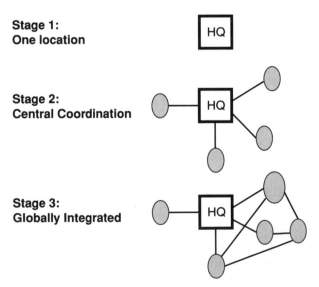

Stage 1:
One location

Stage 2:
Central Coordination

Stage 3:
Globally Integrated

Exhibit 9–5   Stage Model of global software teams.

One of the signs of a maturing relationship between headquarters and distant sites is that the distant site will "vision" a product. That is, the distant site will conceive of a product and then go through the political process of selling the concept at headquarters, getting resources, and receiving approval to move ahead. From that point the product is theirs— they "own" it politically even if not financially. I noted this dynamic at several different companies' remote sites in Europe and in Asia. Interestingly, once the remote site "owns" the product, there may be less cross-border collaboration since most all activities are done in one site.

The prototypical first step with an emerging nation site (e.g., India) is to allocate to it structured, low-level tasks such as maintenance and porting (Exhibit 9–6). Tasks are quickly enhanced to programming and redesign. Progressively, representatives from the distant site take responsibility for low-level design and some aspects of high-level design. A key milestone is involvement in producing functional specifications, typically tightly controlled by the headquarters. The final, and greatest leap is to hand over most responsibilities to the distant site. One European project manager said: "We got the Indian unit involved in some high level design within about 12 months. It was interesting to see how motivating it was for them."

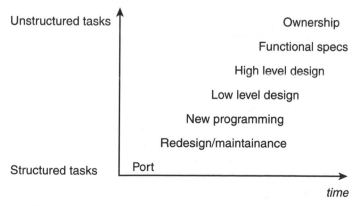

Exhibit 9–6 Enhanced responsibility of remote site over time.

Best Practices Roundup

☑ *Architect or re-architect your product before dispersing its development.* Most product architecture is too brittle to support newly dispersed development. Devote your best talent and sufficient time to architectural issues up front. Several companies in the GDSD study noted that their success, or lack thereof, hinged on the architectural design in early stages of the development process.

☑ *Architecture has to be managed.* Set up architecture support in the form of an inter-site committee or a person whose principal responsibility is architecture.

☑ *Architect the team structure after the product architecture.* Team structure should follow the product structure rather than legacy considerations. Most product architectures live longer than the teams that created them.

☑ *Modularize.* Or better yet, build small, independent software components that are easily allocated across sites.

☑ *Anticipate the points of weakness of your task allocation strategy.* The hand off is the point of weakness. For the module-base approach, the principal weakness occurs late in the cycle when modules are integrated. In the phase-based approach, it occurs during and after the hand off from phase to phase.

☑ *Do not tightly task individuals at each site.* Leave those responsibilities to the local team leads.

Further Reading

On architecture: Bass, Len, Clements P., and Kazman, R. *Software Architecture in Practice.* Reading, Mass: Addison-Wesley, 1997.

On task allocation: Meadows, C. J. Globalizing software development. *Journal of Global Information Management.* (1996) 4(1), 5–15.

BUILDING THE DISPERSED TEAM THROUGH TRUST, COMMUNICATION, AND PERSONAL BRIDGES

How can the software organization create a team—a real team—from disparate work units? Communication technology alone cannot do this. Technology merely enhances team effectiveness when team members already have established relationships and a sense of common affinity.

Building relationships means meeting face to face, shaking hands, working shoulder to shoulder, sharing a drink, building trust. Personal, face to face relationships are formed in kick-off meetings, milestones meetings, celebratory meetings, and through bridges: the traveling manager, the short foreign assignments, the cultural liaisons, the expatriate assignments.

An effective team is more than good relationships. It is about effective communication. Several sets of protocols, or ground rules are introduced in this chapter: from how to send effective e-mail messages to what is the meaning of the word "urgent."

An effective team is more than good communication. It is about giving everyone the same view—labeled the 360° view—of all people and events, their working environments, and their task progress. Team members need a clear view of their sister site across the ocean. The view needs to be transparent: The information is available; the rules are clear; the authority structures are coherent.

This chapter is the longest of those covering the centripetal forces because, more than any other chapter, it addresses the third word of the book title: *teams*. The actual design of the team structure—a managerial function—appears not here, but in Chapter 11. A final note on convention particularly important to this chapter: A *team* consists of two or more (geographically dispersed) *sites*.

The chapter includes eighteen short sections and several useful checklists:

- Building trust
- The kick-off and other milestone meetings
- Communication
- Lateral communication
- Everyone gets a 360° view
- Team communication protocols
- Communication: the many forms of English
- The principle of building personal bridges between sites
- Building personal bridges between sites: the cultural liaison
- Building personal bridges between sites: the need for constant travel
- Building personal bridges between sites: expatriates
- Creating the common team culture
- Become aware of culture's effect on the style and speed of decision-making
- Bridging and managing time zone differences
- Training
- Cultural training and preparation
- Team governance: contract?
- Maturity models for teams

Building trust

Before each member begins interacting with colleagues, implicitly he asks, "can I trust him?" Trust is essential if people are to depend upon one another to meet commitments. A team whose members do not trust each other will not function effectively—or even may fail miserably.

Trust means placing confidence in another's character, ability, strength, and reliability. Since these qualities are complex, they take time to establish. Trust takes time to build. While co-located team members can build trust through formal and informal face to face interactions, distance is an impediment to building trusting relationships. After all, "trust needs touch." Importantly, different cultures develop trust at different rates. Generally, high context cultures (e.g., Asians) are slower to develop trust than are low context cultures (e.g., Americans).

It is generally accepted that trust develops slowly as a team goes through the evolutionary stages of working together. In fact, this notion has long been legitimized in the social sciences by the Tuckman model of forming–storming–norming–performing (Exhibit 4–5) and countless similar psychosocial maturity models, such as the "team performance model."[140]

However, instead of waiting patiently while the team goes through the lengthy team maturation process, a new organizational theory of *swift trust*[141] can be applied to a dispersed team. Swift trust is used to explain how individuals who are "thrown together" quickly become productive in spite of not developing solid interpersonal relationships. The theory was developed to explain behavior in temporary teams such as film crews, theater and architectural groups, presidential commissions, and cockpit crews. Like global software teams, they form around a common task with a finite life span.

Swift trust occurs when team members assume that, like themselves, the other team members have been filtered for reliability and competence. Members set aside their suspicions and swiftly get into a trusting role. The newly formed team is keen to address the task at hand. Thus, they become productive quickly without going through the evolutionary and lengthy team maturity stages. Another example of swift trust is our trust in medical doctors. In part, we trust our health to a complete stranger because she was certified by a national board.

From the outset, global managers must engage in team members' *role legitimization* by highlighting the reputation and professional qualifications at the other sites—as units and as individuals. This highlighting is done through various cues, some overt, others subtle.

Role legitimization in a cross-national setting is difficult because the usual cues to professional status are much harder to determine, assess, and highlight: what university he attended, what company she worked for, and what products he developed. Another obstacle to swift trust is that high context cultures are less likely to reveal individual information. One would not expect a Japanese to introduce himself: "Hi, I'm Hashimoto-san, and I'm an experienced designer who worked for Hitachi for many years on major systems software development projects."

Jarvenpaa and Leidner[142] conducted an experiment with global virtual teams with interesting results. They set up 29 teams from all continents, tasked them with projects, and only allowed them to communicate via e-mail and other collaborative technologies. They found that most teams that began with low levels of trust continued operating at low levels of trust. More important was the reverse—most teams that began with high levels of trust continued in a high trust mode of operation. And what led to the initial levels of trust? The first round of electronic communication was crucial in setting the tone. The implication, as one of the authors later pointed out, is that you never get a second chance to make a good first impression.

The most useful technique to building trust is the old recipe—face to face meetings. The most effective communication at the beginning of a [dispersed] project is a handshake to create trust. The best point in time to create that handshake is at the beginning of the software development cycle—at the kick-off meeting. *"Then—and only then—can the electronics be effective."*[143]

The kick-off and other milestone meetings

The most successful trust building technique for a dispersed team is the face to face *kick-off* meeting (the metaphor comes from the "kick-off" that begins a football game), also called a *project launch* meeting. The concept is simple: Get as many members of the team together for several intensive days of working and socializing at the beginning of the development cycle. The kick-off meeting builds trust, builds team spirit, addresses some of the cultural differences, and also accelerates communication at the outset.

> A kick-off meeting was conducted at a California-based company with several foreign sites. As the project moved into high gear, after having stumbled along for some months, many of the team members from all sites were invited to the beach community where headquarters resides. Work was frequently punctuated by traditional California beach activities such as volleyball and barbecues. This was viewed as a key bonding experience for the many team leaders who participated. Unfortunately, the project was so large that the company could not afford to fly all the team members to California.

As with other social introductions, the very beginning of the kick-off meeting is critical. It is natural for team members to feel drawn to people with whom they are most comfortable. This means that, for example, the Americans will be drawn to other Americans. In a multinational team, there is little in common to begin a relationship, and thus personal relationships will take long to build or not develop at all.

Concentrate on building trust early in the kick-off meeting. Focus on the developers' respective reputation, professional qualifications, and equivalent status. This way, the members begin with professional similarity rather than differences.[144] Do some team building exercises at the outset, including some that involve forced camaraderie. Five components, introduced in Exhibit 10–1, should span much of the kick-off agenda: vision, methodological framework (see Chapter 8), communication ground rules (discussed later in this chapter), cultural training (also discussed later in this chapter), and social functions.

While some organizations begin kick-off meetings with easygoing team building exercises (e.g., the classic "knapsack to the moon" task), Leonard and colleagues write of one manager who started the kick-off meeting with a special collaborative exercise that purposefully induces stress. He assigned an aggressive deadline: Within two days write a mission statement, define the deliverables, and get executive sign-off. Knowingly or not, he was conforming to the Tuckman psychosocial model and forcing the team into early conflicts (the "storming" stage) in order to make them bond more quickly through adversity.[145]

Global managers find it difficult to make a business case for an all-inclusive kick-off meeting because such meetings are terribly expensive: Consider the costs to fly 30 developers across the ocean for ten days. In

---

- *Vision.* Elaborate on the overall project vision and how each site fits into that vision.
- *The methodological framework.* Introduce and motivate the software development framework (process model/methodology). Explain the quality standards.
- *Communication ground rules.* Explain how team members should communicate and include tips and rules about phone, e-mail, video-conferencing, and other collaborative technologies.
- *Cultural training.* Hire professional training to address specific cultural differences and how these differences can be overcome. Don't begin with this component because the topic tends to dwell on cultural dissimilarities.
- *Social functions.* Plan many of these. Most team members will not have another opportunity to meet each other in person.

Exhibit 10–1 Key components in the kick-off meeting.

such a case, consider some compromises that have been used by other global teams. First, videotape some of the kick-off meeting for those who could not attend. Second, consider back-to-back kick-off meetings:

> Sensory Systems is a large European-based software organization. The project kick-off meeting began in the home country for several days. It brought together the team leads from the remote locations as well as all associated headquarters' developers. The next week, all the key managers and team leads flew to India for the second round kick-off meeting, which included all local developers. Others participated via audio-conference.

Once the kick-off meeting is over and everyone flies back home, trust levels immediately begin falling. Trust must be reestablished through personal face-to-face communication and renewed constantly, as Exhibit 10–2[146] illustrates. The most effective formalism for renewing high levels of

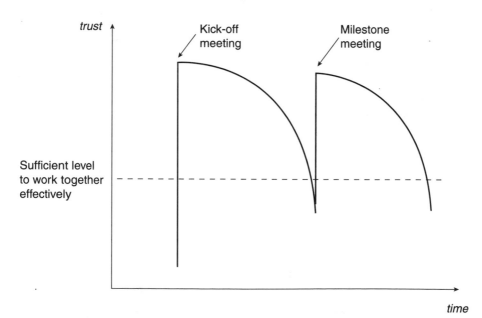

Exhibit 10–2   Change in level of trust between sites.

trust is the milestone meeting (although only some of the team members will be present—typically the team leads only). In the IBM JavaBeans project (see Chapter 2), meetings between the managers of the five sites initially took place in Seattle twice a month. Later the meeting frequency settled down to once every two months. The meeting locations rotated among all sites.

At the end of the development cycle (at the ship date, or release date) is the celebratory event. Celebrations are important for team-building. Peopleware's DeMarco and Lister urge software professionals to celebrate more in order to build the team spirit.[147] This is also an investment in the next release, since in most software organizations team members continue to work together in subsequent releases. Not everyone celebrates and those that do vary in their approach. One European software organization planned a long trip to its partner in Japan. This was a junket with families and included local sightseeing. A Russian-American collaboration exchanged vodka bottles. An Israeli-American collaboration attempted to include the American team members in the celebratory party in Israel via telephone (although this was understandably not viewed as satisfying by the Americans).

Communication

Distance causes coordination and control mechanisms to break down because what used to be done informally does not work quite as well anymore. The global team must address two communication objectives simultaneously. First, it must move from traditional reliance on informal coordination (and communication) to increased reliance on formal mechanisms. Second, it must encourage the informal communication across distance.

> An experienced global software manager confessed that he had always wanted to run a software project with more formal elements: sensible issue management, action management, and great documentation. But it never was quite compelling enough to go to the trouble of implementing these formalisms, "because you could always walk down the corridor and find Fred." But now, when his developers are all over the world, "you cannot even call Fred because he is asleep." Consequently, the team evolved a formal, deliberate issue management system "because we had to."

As this case illustrates, dispersion forces formalization. There is no choice. Discussion lists, project management software, and task lists are all elements of more formalized communications.

Distance naturally reduces informal communication between sites. Informal communication contributes to creativity, quick problem solving, and team bonding. A global software team needs to foster and encourage more *informal* communication so that communication patterns over distance emulate the co-located work environment as much as possible. One of the ways to do this is to encourage lateral communication.

Lateral communication

Some global teams cling to managerial communication styles in which the team leads handle most inter-site communication. But, lateral communication among site leaders is not enough. In a professional environment in which edicts and tight supervision are inappropriate, funneling decisions and knowledge through the formal hierarchy (known as "push") is simply not effective. The modern, integrated, network-like organization needs to foster *lateral* coordination and its corollary, lateral communication (Exhibit 10–3).

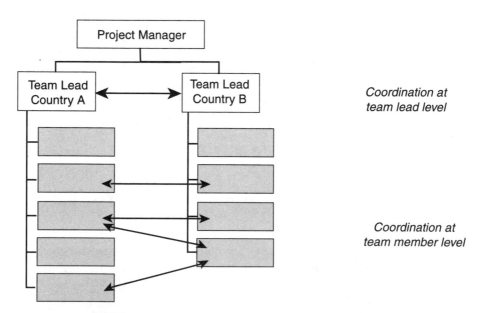

Exhibit 10–3   Lateral coordination and communication.

This means communication among team members across the organization rather than up and down the hierarchy. It is lateral communication that creates effective integration of tasks and fully and quickly addresses task problems that crop up. Lateral coordination is more flexible, makes for faster decisions, usually leads to better decisions, and does wonders for motivation and feelings of empowerment by all members of the team.

Many software companies encourage lateral communication by creating flat organizations. This structure makes it easier and less threatening for individuals to communicate across organizational lines. Even more conducive to lateralism is a network organization. As a result of effective lateral communication at US-based NetParadise's three-country project, every developer took more responsibility to solve problems by himself instead of channeling them through the chain of command.

Managers need to encourage lateral communication. Galbraith,[148] the organizational designer, offers three techniques for lateralism that are applicable to global software teams: Initiate inter-team events such as meetings or celebrations (e.g., kick-off meetings); exchange people via inter-site and inter-country rotation (discussed later in this chapter); and create a mirror organization.

A mirror organization is a symmetric organization at each site. The organizational structure and its formal roles are identical across sites. This design makes it easy for a member of one site to identify her counterpart in another site. Then it is easier (or less inhibiting) for each team member to solve problems without going through the chain of command and to build a relationship with a distant counterpart. IBM's JavaBeans project initially created symmetric 31-member *phalanxes* in each distant site. Boeing created a mirror organization to design the 777 airplane.

Everyone gets a 360° view

In the absence of physical closeness of buildings, people, and imagery, dispersed team members need to sense where they are relative to everyone else. This is called the *360° view.* Each developer can view what people are doing above him, below him, and laterally, on both sides of him. This dynamic reduces the feeling of isolation and contributes to team cohesion and effectiveness. The 360° view is closely related to the notion of organizational transparency, which requires a clear definition of individual roles, individual tasks, and group tasks. When these roles and responsibilities are not clear—not transparent—intra-team trust and communication will decrease. Additionally, communicating vision and instituting sound planning norms turn out to be effective for achieving greater transparency within the team.

Two types of information support the 360° view. Both are set up through collaborative technology such as groupware or the web, or are supported by software engineering technologies. The first view involves personal information that is fairly static. The second view is dynamic project task/status information.

The personal view provides team members with rich knowledge about each other. This knowledge is important because they cannot meet each other informally, face to face to gain that knowledge. The foundation for this personal view appears in the form of a published organization chart on-line, which includes descriptions of each person's associated roles and responsibilities (some caution may be in order here because for some cultures it is best to allow the local team leads to assign tasks and titles and set up the local organizational charts rather than having these roles determined by a distant project manager). Each team member's information includes his/her photo, background, location, and responsibility. Each member should be encouraged to add additional photographs and short voice files. Team members who go on vacation can scan a postcard and tell a short story from their vacation. Members need to *picture* the distant site's workspace. Each site can create a photo collage that shows their offices and their building. This technique is especially useful for high context cultures.[149] Finally, the team leads should be easily identifiable to all members at all sites. Each team lead's responsibilities need to be stated explicitly.

The project task/status information needs to give members rich information about their relationship to other tasks in progress. Team members must be able to access the team schedule easily, with major tasks, and major milestones—all inclusive of dates. They must be able to check project status for each task and individual. They must able to drill down several levels to see what others are doing. Both project management and SCM packages provide some of these capabilities. Team members should also be able to add some "color" to their tasks by attaching short narratives with stories about their tasks.

Finally, a 360° view is nourished by various participatory techniques, such as requiring all members to participate in video- or audio-conferences periodically. But this is not easy to do. At a General Electric

Japanese-American collaboration, the team leads met weekly via video-conference, but these meetings were shunned by the engineers because of language and culture differences.[150]

Team communication protocols

A protocol is a code prescribing adherence to correct etiquette, as is the case with a diplomatic exchange. Effective communication requires some protocols or rules. Team-wide communication protocols are presented in Exhibit 10–4. These include response norms (response protocols). Predictability, reliability, and consistency are always important for co-work and particularly important when a colleague can never be observed with one's own eyes. Because of the pervasiveness of e-mail, the protocols of broadest appeal are the e-mail protocols of Exhibit 10–5. When language differences exist, it is best to encourage e-mail over phone conversations to decrease cultural and linguistic misunderstandings.

Another application for communication protocols are conference calls that bring together different cultural meeting styles. The French begin with theory, history, and context. Americans often launch directly into the bottom line. Still other cultures begin with detail and arrive at conclusions much later. With different cultural styles, conference call protocols are quite useful. Every conference call should be facilitated with a formal checklist. Each participant should introduce his contribution as an "issue" or "action item." This is aided by the conference facilitator. Items tagged as being an issue, are later tagged as "resolved." The participant also introduces the owner of the action item, its due date, and then brings in the supporting commentary.[151]

Communication: the many forms of English

English is unequivocally the universal software language—the *lingua franca* of computing. In every global software collaboration in the GDSD study, the language of cross-border communication was English, even when no Anglos were involved. Virtually all programming languages are English-based.

However, software professionals tend to overlook language differences. Language difficulties are subtle and may emerge to become significant sources of friction. In one American-European collaboration, what began as a language misunderstanding escalated and led to the resignation

Responsiveness	• Direct the team to answer e-mail within a day and voice-mail within four hours, even if it is in the form, "I'll get to this tomorrow." Otherwise, communications breaks down because too many people are not responding to messages unless pestered. • Develop a mutual understanding of the meaning of the word *urgent*—when do you get somebody out of bed in the middle of the night?
Frequency	• Establish guidelines on mapping Task/Frequency/ Media. For example: "The weekly project management committee meets on Tuesdays (time rotated each week to accommodate time zones—0200 GMT and 1500 GMT) using video-conferencing. Meeting minutes are rotated. Length is 60 minutes. Facilitated by André and C.K. on rotating basis." And "Quality Assurance leads exchange one page summary report over e-mail every week."
Awareness	• Make everyone aware of time zone differences. Post them on the team intranet. If possible, establish regular overlap windows for synchronous communication (for voice, audio- and video-conference). • Make everyone aware of the importance of providing timely and extensive reports of what they are doing.
Handling Trouble	• Establish support mechanisms for communication problems and breakdowns. • Designate local "cultural guides" for times when interactions get into trouble or are halted. • Set up procedures for conflicts. Make everyone aware of these.

Exhibit 10–4 Communication protocols for global software teams.[152]

- Acknowledge every e-mail within one work day.
- Keep messages short: one question, one response, one announcement.
- Avoid multiple recipients unless it is absolutely necessary.
- Use descriptive subject headings.
- Avoid FYI (For Your Information). For informational purposes place the information in the appropriate Notes database or other repository.
- Spelling and grammar are *not* important (as long as nonnative English speakers are involved).
- Create and use templates for administrative messages such as meeting announcements and schedule changes.
- Become aware of idioms in your writing and try to avoid using them. For example, most football and baseball metaphors will not be understood by a non-US audience.
- Explicitly state the response you expect.

Exhibit 10–5 E-mail protocols for global software teams.[153]

of an American. Nonnative English speaking software developers operate in a world in which they rarely understand 100% of the information they are exposed to. They read manuals slowly, often missing some ideas and nuances. They cannot scan as fast—neither help screens nor program specifications. Comprehension of spoken English varies and depends a great deal on accent, speed, and use of slang.

For example, the English and Japanese languages are so far apart linguistically that there are significant day-to-day ramifications. For a Japanese software professional—even one who has a relatively good comprehension of English—every English encounter is difficult and requires enormous concentration. The computer scientist Ishii[154] wrote that he feels drained during an English language meeting in which he must both comprehend and be ready to speak in real-time. Clearly, he cannot be productive if he becomes mentally exhausted. This is why he prefers electronic mail. E-mail allows him to communicate—in English of course—but at his own pace.

Adler[155] compiled a list (in Exhibit 10–6) of useful recommendations when speaking with a colleague whose native language is not English (in fact, some items on this list are useful for better communication with native English speakers as well as for parents speaking with a two-year-old child).

One of the most commonly used techniques for overcoming cultural–linguistic misunderstandings is *active listening:* Ask lots of polite questions and listen very carefully to the responses. Rephrase what has been said. Check that they understood you and that you understood them. This approach is useful to managers during conference calls: The manager must pause the flow of discussion and check for understanding: "Sarita, did you mean that . . . ?"

> One global project manager regularly conducted multi-site audio-conference meetings with site representatives. Members of the Chinese site found it difficult to understand the Indian English because of the style and fast clip at which the Indians speak. The project manager did not immediately recognize this problem. Once he identified the problem, he found it was easy to solve. During the audio-conference, he employed a simple technique. Aware that because of cultural responses he could not directly ask the Chinese manager if he understood his Indian counterpart, he asked the Chinese participant to say what he heard: "Perhaps you can say what you expect to be doing."

Phillips[156] describes a useful technique for obtaining information in situations with language problems. He calls this a *funnel* approach. Begin by

---

- Enunciate each word.
- Don't use slang.
- Repeat important ideas.
- Avoid long compound sentences.
- Pause frequently.
- Use nonverbal communication such as pictures, gestures, acting out, and written summaries.
- Check comprehension by asking the colleague to rephrase understanding of the material back to you.

Exhibit 10–6 Recommendations for conversation with nonnative English speaker.

asking very broad open-ended questions in the form of "tell me about . . ." followed up with "what sorts of tasks did that involve?" Listen carefully, especially for emotive words. After follow-up, move to the second stage—check factual details: "What were your personal tasks on the project?" The third stage is to move to ask more about feelings: "What was it like working on a deadline?" In the fourth stage, learn about motives: "What did you like about designing that feature?"

The complement of spoken language is body language. It is important to be aware of body language such as different eye-contact norms. Europeans and Americans insist on eye contact, while East Asians find it uncomfortable or rude. Most cultural training classes will cover these communication forms.

Over the long run, all team members must communicate in a spoken language, and English seems to be the only choice. Software companies should invest in the English language skills of all employees by sponsoring English-as-a-Foreign-Language training and English refresher courses. Depending on the cultural setting, employees should be persuaded, lured, or rewarded into taking ongoing language courses.

The principle of building personal bridges between sites

There is no room for compromise on the question of team members traveling from site to site to create personal, face to face relationships—as expensive and time-consuming as it might be. Even with the best telecommunications, collaborative technologies, and methodologies in place, this is a vital ingredient to global software teams' success.

Personal face to face bridges—personal relationships—are the glue that hold distant sites together. Face to face ties foster trust by creating enduring personal relationships. They serve as a bridge between the cultures of the various sites, as well as the distant organizational cultures of those sites. Personal relationships are essential for resolving cultural miscommunications and conflicts. Furthermore, substantial time-zone differences make any synchronous (same-time) audio- or video-meeting a serious inconvenience to one of the parties, so the more "media rich" technologies are not available. It becomes a choice between e-mail or an airplane to create the bonds.

Several categories of "personal bridges" are covered in this chapter. The first is the formal, face to face meeting, such as the kick-off meeting, introduced earlier in the chapter. The other categories, covered respectively in the next three sections are: the *cultural liaison,* an individual comfortable in the two principal team cultures; managerial travel and staff rotations; and e*xpatriates,* those on foreign assignments of more than one year. The three latter categories entail just a few team representatives who act as ambassadors, fostering goodwill, mutual understanding, and trust between the sites.

Building personal bridges between sites: the cultural liaison

A successful global team relies on an individual in the role of cultural liaison—one who is comfortable in the team's two key national cultures. The liaison's *formal* role varies: Some are technical leads, some are project managers, and some are executives not involved in the projects on a day to day basis. The liaison's *informal* role is to facilitate the cultural, linguistic, and organizational flow of communication, to bridge the organizational cultures, to mediate conflicts, and to resolve cultural miscommunications. Since the liaison plays the role of ambassador, I was amused to find that at one software company the role of cultural ambassador was filled by a real ex-ambassador.

Of the companies in the GDSD study, an individual in the role of the cultural liaison was identified in about half the cases (47%). The liaisons were either expatriates (discussed separately further below) or, more commonly, *Americanized returnees.* The returnee is one who had spent a formative period in the United States. All of the returnees in this study were identified at Indian and Israeli sites. For example, US-based Rose Software picked a seasoned, Americanized Indian tech manager to be the executive in charge of its new Bombay development site. He held two degrees from US universities and worked in US high tech for more than a dozen years. Similarly, Israeli sites had managers with US high-tech work experience and advanced American degrees. In two of the Israeli cases, the individuals had worked at the parent American company and had returned to Israel to set up the Israeli development site.

While the liaison model that emerged in packaged software organizations was the key individual acting as a liaison, an alternative model appeared at the following software services firm:

> A large American software services firm with an office in Europe had an essentially entire foreign office that served as a cultural bridge. The European office's demographics were divided roughly evenly

among three groups: the local nationals, American expatriates, and a mix of other Europeans. In addition, many nonAmericans were schooled in the United States. This diverse mix meant that there were numerous liaisons back to the headquarters culture (the United States) as well as to the local and pan-European cultures.

Building personal bridges between sites: the need for constant travel

In spite of all the sophisticated communication technologies, members of the global software development team will have to travel. Air travel from site to site is a costly yet necessary part of global teams. There is no correlation between the sophistication of the communication infrastructure and the necessary amount of travel by the managers and team members. In fact, in some of the better endowed projects of the GDSD study, those with excellent communication infrastructure, team members traveled more than those projects with less infrastructure. There are two types of travel to consider: travel by managers and team leads and short-term rotations by specialists.

A global software manager needs to practice MBFA—Management By Flying Around[157] (the analogue to Management By Walking Around). One seasoned manager said that his #1 rule for globally dispersed development was: "Go meet them and make sure that they come meet you." A project manager should be traveling at least once per quarter to each of her team's sites. A number of managers in the GDSD study made regular monthly trips across 10–12 time zones to maintain close and continuous relationships with all the sites. But there is a nonfinancial cost to intense travel. Such trips are a 24-hour door-to-door ordeal, in each direction, worsened by jet lag. Individuals have different travel thresholds. Those who exceed the threshold begin to suffer morale problems, get lonely, and cross-cultural fatigue sets in. Be aware of these symptoms.

Team leads (site leads) should be traveling frequently, as well. Milestone meetings are an appropriate opportunity to gather them together in one location. One or more leads from each site should be traveling to a milestone meeting at least once per quarter. Team members who are not in managerial roles should also be traveling to establish personal relationships. Each team member should meet his counterparts: the one he woke up at night three times in the last two months and the one with whom he has been exchanging a flurry of e-mail messages on a new design approach for the database. Good managers look for excuses to send their developers to other sites to improve inter-site cohesion and communication. This is especially important if many of the team members did not participate in the kick-off meeting. Developers return from these trips with a new perspective for the people, organization, and culture they were exposed to. They now know a lot more about who is behind those hundreds of terse e-mail messages they read.

For the longer term a cohesive team is nourished by rotating some personnel to collaborating sites for more extended periods of work—usually one to four months. For example, a Japanese-Finnish collaboration involved four Finns who were rotated to Japan and ten Japanese who were rotated to Finland. Rotation was conducted in 52% of projects in the GDSD study. Most of those rotated were technical specialists and not managers. At Contemporary Sciences rotation was highly praised and called "cross-pollination," while at other companies I heard other imaginative, though less snappy, labels for this position—"assignees" and "co-locations."

Unfortunately, rotations require additional managerial attention to achieve the desired results. The rotated software professionals may not mix easily with the local professionals. A number of companies expressed dissatisfaction with foreign developers, who because of cultural or linguistic reasons, did not cross-socialize. They noticeably sat at separate tables at the cafeteria, inadvertently setting themselves apart and creating ill will.

Travel presents a risk vis-à-vis software personnel in emerging economies. Programmers in emerging economies clamor to travel and consider it prestigious and a great opportunity for shopping. Many come for longer assignments with a hidden agenda of staying in the United States. At one Russian site, travel was intentionally limited so as not to create jealousies amongst the programmers.

Building personal bridges between sites: expatriates

Only 20% of the companies in the GDSD study used expatriates. (The term *expatriate* refers to someone spending at least a year abroad on assignment.) Compared to other industries, this number is low. Why? There are several possible explanations. Software managers have more faith in communication technology's capabilities to create relationships. The American tendency is to underrate cultural issues and consider the common computer culture as a mitigating factor. Unlike in more established industries, the software manager is less primed to expect that career advancement means foreign assignment. A number of software companies used an alternative to expatriates: the returning national (or as referred to previously, the Americanized returnee common to Indian and Israeli sites).

A foreign assignment of one year or more is an important policy decision for the company and a major milestone for the individual who often has a family to bring with him. In industries outside of software, the long-term failure rate for American expatriates transferred abroad is relatively high. Twenty percent return home prematurely, before the end of the year, as compared to only about 3% for Swiss managers. Expatriates sent to Japan were found to be less successful than expatriates sent to the United States.[158] The family's lack of adjustment is the most common reason for failure. Other reasons include lack of headquarters support, the feeling of being far from the political action, and lack of training for an overseas assignment.

Studies have pointed to an over-reliance on technical skills for expatriate selection.[159] Although clearly important, technical skills should serve as just a first filter. The other decision criterion needs to be cultural. A common screening method is to go through a checklist of qualities such as prior international exposure, linguistic ability, and cultural empathy. And it is recommended that expatriates be trained.

Once the expatriate arrives abroad, she proceeds through three classic stages of adjustment. The first stage is the honeymoon period of elation and optimism in which cultural events seem charming. The second stage is known as the "morning after." The shock sets in as the familiar and reassuring are missed. Signs of irritability and frustration emerge. Emotional withdrawal may set in. Some expatriates never exit the morning-after stage. The third and last stage is "Happily ever after"—a gradual adjustment and acceptance of the new environment.

Expatriates can do more than just create bonds between team sites. One of their traditional roles is to exert control and supervision in a far away place. Another common role is to transfer corporate culture. For example, US-based 3M does not send employees overseas unless they have been with the corporation for at least ten years to absorb the corporate culture.

The prototypical multinational expatriate assignment is to oversee an office or plant in a foreign country. In fact, this scenario is unusual in software. It showed up in only one of the cases from the GDSD study. All the other expatriate cases involved, not country managers, but *technical specialists.* Some of the specialists went beyond their strictly technical role to facilitate communication. Some were tasked primarily to train.

Creating the common team culture

While a team can be productive without a common culture—without co-hesion—a team that develops a common culture tends to be more productive, more effective, and have a more enjoyable time doing its jobs.[160] A successful team creates its own culture, a kind of *micro-culture*, that may be distinct from the organizational culture, and not necessarily dominated by one of the national cultures.

Creating a common team culture is difficult. Some have written that "virtual team" is an oxymoron like "airline food" or "exact estimate." Kidding aside, there are numerous elements that draw dispersed team members together and build a common culture. This chapter has already introduced a number of these: face-to-face meetings, trust building, lateral communication, and fostering a 360° view. Several other elements are introduced below: maintaining a small, intimate team (across all sites); creating common metaphors; and creating common experiences.

A team cannot be cohesive if it is too large. As a general rule, for a given task, a dispersed global team, in multiple sites, is generally larger than a co-located team. But, having acknowledged that, it is important to strive for smallness as one of the key managerial goals at all times. Precisely because of cross-cultural differences, smaller work units are especially important for a global team. Phillips writes that the greater the cultural differences, the smaller the team needs to be to create the proper cohesion in order to overcome the cultural differences.[161]

Keeping the global team small requires a managerial vision that celebrates "smallness."[162] If that vision is absent the team will have a tendency to grow. Several years ago I wrote about one major Silicon Valley software firm that had two major product divisions: One had a core value of keeping the team small, at around ten developers, while the other division did not embrace that value—and team sizes were substantially larger, for comparable products. Microsoft is another interesting case. In spite of Microsoft's enormous growth, it has made deliberate efforts over the years to keep the small entrepreneurial culture of the firm with (relatively) small teams. These efforts include an unofficial rule of "if *n* people are needed, only *n* minus one will be used."

The team sites need to picture themselves as a common unit—a common team. It is important that the different sites are referred to as one unit, e.g., "the Atlantic 1.2 team," even though team units reside on different sides of the Atlantic. Create a common visual portrait through the wonders of digital scanning and imagery (complete with photos and name) by placing the entire team sitting around a table or some other arti-fact. Put the image on the shared team database.

A common culture is forged via common experiences. Kick-off meet-ings and all other face to face meetings are most important in this respect. Other, electronic experiences can augment these personal contacts, such as the ubiquitous electronic discussion list. This is the best tool for team mem-bers at different sites to get to know their counterparts as real people. Man-agers need to invest a lot of their own energy and excitement into these elec-tronics to get them started, to persuade some team members to participate, and to make sure people are aware of and reading the material.

Another metaphor for a common experience is the virtual "retreat." A retreat is a period of group pause for study and reflection, when team members are away from the "day to day," thinking about the big picture, or even about tangential topics like technology trends or culture. A retreat can be done periodically in chat mode (time zones permitting), or using a dispersed brainstorming tool[163], or just a plain electronic discussion tool. It is important that the retreat generate a sense of excitement and energy.

A common team culture is created via rituals, stories, symbols, and shared language.[164] Many seem corny to outsiders, but they are important to team culture. Rituals are repeated patterns of behavior. Rituals may be informal (such as a regular e-mail of the funniest bugs that one of the de-velopers began circulating), or formal (such as the celebratory party at the end of the product release). Stories need to be shared by all, such as an in-cident that all team members were part of during the kick-off meeting. Symbols (e.g., logos or mottos) are best created by the grassroots (how-ever, beware of the endless possibilities for cultural misunderstandings, e.g., the number "4" is associated with death for Chinese). Shared lan-guage is a type of team slang that evolves from team members. Software sage Larry Constantine has a story of one team that developed a special language around the data communication jargon of ACK and NAK to handle work interruptions. NAK (short for negative acknowledgment) ex-pressed "I'm busy now, don't bother me;" and ACK (acknowledgment) ex-pressed "I can see you now."[165]

In order to foster the common culture, do you impose elements of the home (usually American) culture on the distant team? With the United States playing such a dominant role in the global software industry I ob-served two phenomena. First, some American software managers were im-posing American cultural and organizational norms. This is part naiveté. At one firm the manager wanted to impose a "neutral" management style—the American management style. At other firms it was a bit more chauvinistic—the foreign sites need to learn the "American Way." The second phenomenon is that the foreign teams are not feeling resentment at this imposition—not yet, at least. They are eager to embrace Americanism because it represents the cultural pinnacle of software. I suspect that this will begin to change in the coming years. From the Moscow office of US-based Orchestral Technologies I was told "the Russians wanted to have their offices Americanized and they were afraid of it—both at the same time." The developers at the Russian site were happy to take English classes, yet Americans working for a French software firm were not pleased to be taking French classes.

Less ambiguous is the need to align the vision of the different team sites as well as the team goals and objectives. Particularly after an acquisition, it is the team manager who becomes responsible for aligning the goals and values of the remote units that are far away from headquarters and who have a difficult time internalizing the corporate or project objectives. Creating a shared vision is best done in person augmented by videoconferencing on a periodic basis. Some national cultures may be receptive to a common written team mission statement, while for others this will be a waste of time. The best form of aligning the vision of remote and acquired sites is to have members spend time at headquarters to quicken the period of organizational alignment and socialization.

Even if the team managers do not take an active role in creating a common culture, they should minimize the "out of sight, out of mind" phenomenon. The distant site is often neglected, its suggestions ignored, its influence small.[166] It is important for the project manager located in headquarters to be aware of this dynamic. Besides the various techniques listed in this chapter, regular meetings with representatives from the distant site must be maintained despite other pressures.

Become aware of culture's effect on the style and speed of decision-making

Cultural norms affect each stage of a team's decision-making and implementation process. The early stage of the decision-making process requires collecting and sharing information. In low context cultures (North American and Northern Europe), there may be a tendency to information overload—to bury everyone with lots of text (usually in English). On the other hand, high context cultures do not expect detailed textual information and feel irritated when pressed for it. What is the right balance?

Globalwork authors O'Hara-Devereaux and Johansen recommend placing a greater emphasis on visuals and graphics rather than on text.[167]

American managers, although not viewed as being slow to decide, often seek information as a way to integrate different individual perspectives and make better decisions. This takes time. Some cultures that revere hierarchy, such as the French, have more centralized decision-making and can arrive at a decision quickly. Some high context cultures view a decision made quickly as an indication that it is not important. If important, it would have been decided after careful reflection. The Japanese have a unique system called *Ringii* as a way to preserve group harmony. A position's advocate will circulate petitions and individuals are asked to support a decision. This also takes time.

While the Japanese are criticized for taking a long time to make a decision, once they make the decision they can implement it quickly. Americans and Northern Europeans, on the other hand, are criticized by the Japanese for being slow to implement because they have to sell the decision to all involved. Some highly participative cultures view decision-making as a process to promote social welfare and hence take a long time to make decisions. For example, in Germany and the Scandinavian nations, decision-making includes labor representatives in many of the decision-making steps. One of the sites in the GDSD study was in Norway. Their counterparts explained in frustration that the seven-person Norwegian development unit was *so* participative and leaderless that when it came to deciding even the smallest technical detail, it "had to be sold to *all* members individually" before it could be moved forward.

Bridging and managing time zone differences

Some global team members are wholly ignorant of time zone differences. It is as much a foreign concept to them as exotic cultures and languages. A senior Indian software manager relayed the following anecdote about a developer at his American headquarters.

> I got one e-mail saying: I'm going to lunch now—could you give me an answer by the time I get back from lunch? It was after midnight here and I am not waiting by the computer!

Global workers need to be aware of and know the tricks of working with large time differences between sites. A simple device is to publish the various times on the common team repository (and remember to update these with clock changes).

Any synchronous communication, such as a phone call, an audio-conference, or video-conference, poses inconvenience and usually imposition to one of the two parties. One manager on assignment in Europe complained: "The United States would call me and say, could you conference call at 9 PM [your time]? and I said 'yes,' but for me, it was my quality work time, my thinking time. They took that away from me." Inevitably, those not near the center of power at headquarters are the ones who are regularly inconvenienced. Over the long run, this imposition will take a toll on the distant managers and developers that are forced to alter their personal lives. The best solution is to rotate the time of audio- and video-conferences so that all sides suffer in roughly equal amounts. Another solution for handling ongoing problems is to set up an *overlap time/overlap window* in which voice or video synchronous contact can keep relationships alive. Hitachi has such a window between its Atlanta and Tokyo offices.[168]

Time zone differences can coincide with other factors to create difficulties: Various American-Israeli collaborations reported of the "Israeli black-out period." The Israeli workweek is Sunday through Thursday. When combined with the 7-hour time difference to the US east coast, this means that the Israeli site is out of touch for Americans for most of Thursday and Friday. Conversely, the American site is out of touch for Israelis for almost the entire first two days of their work week. With advanced planning, the disadvantages of these blackout periods can be minimized by scheduling substantial weekly hand offs between the two sites just before each one leaves for its respective week-end.

Strategically, time zone differences need to be one of the siting criteria when determining a new software development center. Any round-the-clock maintenance or support center typically has a center in Europe, one in the United States, and one in East Asia. Thus, the global support center, can have three shifts covering the clock, or following the sun. IBM's JavaBeans project (Chapter 2) initially chose Seattle on the US West coast so that the time zones to Asia and Europe would be roughly balanced.

In contrast, some very distant sites (measured in flying time) actually end up being in almost identical time zones, making coordination somewhat easier. In the GDSD study, there were two such instances, both of which are only one time zone apart: Moscow and Johannesburg, and separately, Israel and Norway. In both cases the team managers noted how advantageous the overlap turned out to be.

Training

Studies of teams find repeatedly that those teams involved in continuous learning perform better.[169] At Verifone, technical personnel from different cultures are trained together. Later they come across each other on distant projects and the trust-building stage is minimized. Not all training delivery should be the same: Americans like training that is practical and concrete while Europeans like training with more of a deductive approach, starting with theories and then applying them to a given situation.[170] While most learning and skills training are necessarily a site-specific experience that team members do not share, some subject areas will benefit the sense of "teamness" across sites:

English Language and English refresher courses. This will yield the best return on investment. Communication is critical to global software teams and English is the language of communication across any two sites. Depending on the cultural setting, employees should be persuaded, lured, or rewarded into taking ongoing English courses.

Process skills. Most developers have little training in team process skills, such as the art of facilitating a meeting (or even a videoconference), setting an agenda, handling disputes, or moving the team to consensus. Consider training at least one person from each site in facilitation techniques.

Software Engineering (methodologies, process models, techniques). This mix of engineering and management requires repeated refreshing. And it is likely that many developers were not educated in methods of software engineering and quality assurance. Try to incorporate general organizational topics with this training, such as a lecture on knowledge management or corporate memory.

Project management. It is likely that some team leads and project managers have never been trained in project management techniques.

Cultural training and preparation

Forward thinking companies prepare *all* global team members for cross-cultural collaboration. Since all team members are communicating with their foreign counterparts, and they are members of a global software team, they will benefit from proper training. Cultural training is particularly important for relatively isolated cultures such as Americans and Indians.

Most people may consider taking cultural preparation classes before embarking on work with radically different cultures (e.g., an American traveling to Asia). However, cultural preparation training is worthwhile even when smaller cultural differences exist (e.g., an American traveling to Denmark).

Managers traveling to a new unfamiliar country are usually adequately equipped to find differences in more overt and visible aspects of the culture, such as food and greeting etiquette. However, they have little understanding of what they will face in the deeper day-to-day aspects of their work such as decision-making, meeting dynamics, and relationship building. One of the outcomes of cultural training is that one becomes cognizant of the difference in describing a behavior ("she smiled all the time") and a culturally-interpreted message ("she likes the idea"); or misinterpreting cues: An American sees someone displaying "sulking" body language, while for some cultures that body language is perfectly normal.

Of the projects in the GDSD study, 40% conducted some sort of cultural training before their global collaboration began. Those who did were pleased with the results. One manager proudly stated "we did our homework." At one large European company that did not do cultural preparation, the project manager lamented that omission and said that he was forced to learn the material the hard way—through the trial and error of collaboration. Some software companies were naturally better prepared to launch into international projects. At one large California company, there were already many Indians in senior positions, helping to smooth the cultural adjustments and sense of bonding between the US development center and the new Indian site.

Culture preparation seminars are now offered by many boutique consultancies that tailor their offerings to the ethnicity and objectives that their paying customers request. Before embarking on their new India collaboration, key managers at US-based Contemporary Sciences received three days of cultural training on work in India. Since they were planning to work with a site in Madras they were told that people in Madras nod their head up and down (yes for Americans) when they actually mean no. Besides seminars, other cultural preparation techniques include confidential individual cultural assessment surveys, as well as books and videos.[171]

Team governance: contract?

"Teamness" is driven, in part, by the nature of the business relationship between the team sites. Teamness consists of the qualities that make the team more effective as a unit: cohesiveness, trust, rapid decision-making stemming from effective lateral communication. Today's global software teams are created via a complex network, sometimes even five or six sites. Some are wholly owned by the parent, others work on a contractual basis, still others are part of a hybrid, such as a joint venture or alliance. It is important to distinguish which of these sites are the primary development sites and which are smaller, less critical, satellite sites. A number of projects in the GDSD study had consultants dispersed at various additional locations, as individuals, or in consultant clusters. The more complex the business relationship, the less likely the many sites will feel a common sense of mission and teamness.

Within the GDSD study projects, 73% of the global collaboration was internal to the firm. That is, 73% of the principal distant site(s) were internal—wholly owned by the parent firm in the foreign country. Almost all of these came about either through acquisition or were internalized as a result of a joint venture. The remaining 27% of the projects were those in which at least one of the principal sites was part of a joint venture or other contractual relationship. All sites with a purely contractual relationship were in India. While collaboration with Indian software development operations, often set up on a contractual basis, is a common risk-reduction strategy, most managers expressed a desire to phase out of a contract and into a tighter relationship with the Indian site, by acquiring the operation. After all, for packaged software companies, any type of collaboration is unlikely to be a one-project deal, but an ongoing multi-year relationship.

The firms with sites in India encountered one pervasive problem: the high turnover rate, commonly referred to as *churn*, which is as high as 30% annually according to some sources. Unless personal relationships are developed with the Indian site as a whole—the project manager, the first-line supervisors, and the programmers themselves, the investment in knowledge and experience frequently walks out the door. The Holiday Inn outsourcing story described in Chapter 14 had such problems. Holiday Inn relied too heavily on the contract and on some *initial* relationships.

Maturity models for teams

Improving the team is not a one-shot deal, but a continuous, ongoing effort. Applying this concept into practice is the recent wave of maturity models—this time, specifically for teams as teams. A maturity model provides a guide and a benchmark to move up from inconsistent, poorly functioning teams to disciplined, continuously improving teams. These models incorporate within them many of the concepts discussed previously in this chapter. Two models are introduced here, the first is specific to software, though not to distributed teams. The second is specific to distributed teams, though not necessarily to software teams.

The Software Engineering Institute (SEI) is the author of the People Capability Maturity Model,[172] or P-CMM. The model complements SEI's own CMM in order to help software organizations integrate team development with software process improvement. The five stages in the model use the same names as the famous CMM from which they are derived (see Exhibit 10–7). Two qualities of the P-CMM's advanced levels bear explicit mention. First, teams should be empowered teams in that team members make decisions about their own work instead of having these things dele-

	Abbreviated description
Level 1: Initial	These are ad hoc, inconsistently performed practices.
Level 2: Repeatable	Instill basic disciplines into the team activities, including training, communication, and compensation.
Level 3: Defined	Identify the primary competencies and align the activities around them, including creating a participatory culture.
Level 4: Managed	Begin to manage quantitatively and engage in team-building.
Level 5: Optimizing	Continuously improve methods for personal and team competence.

Exhibit 10–7   The five stages of the People Capability Maturity Model.

	Abbreviated description
Level 1: Ad hoc	Effective work is performed only in co-located site.
Level 2: Basic	Written documents are developed for project and mission; reliable communications are put in place.
Level 3: Standardized	Organizational memory is built; detailed project specs and team member objectives are in place.
Level 4: Optimizing	Business processes are defined, aligned, and regularly reviewed; new members are easily integrated.

Exhibit 10–8   The four stages of the Maturity Model for Distributed Teams.

gated from above. Second, the compensation system should be designed, in part, to reward the team's performance.

The second model is from US-based consulting firm Management Strategies, Inc,[173] which specializes in distributed teams. It is derived from the CMM but is applied to any dispersed work team (Exhibit 10–8).

Best Practices Roundup

☑ *Actively build trust across sites.*   Facilitate opportunities for face to face encounters; encourage travel and short-term rotations.

☑ *Build swift trust.*   Swift trust comes about from team member's *role legitimization*—when colleagues respect others' professional credentials. Ensure that everyone's professional reputations and qualifications are well recognized across the team sites. Also, the first face to face and electronic communications make an important first impression.

☑ *Begin a project with a kick off meeting.*   The kick-off meeting should strive to bring all team members together from all sites. The agenda needs to include the five components of Exhibit 10–1: vision, methodological framework, communication protocols, cultural training, and social bonding.

☑ *Celebrate!* Celebrate achievements, milestones, successes, end of projects, and breakthroughs. Celebrate at the end of the development cycle to cement bonding across sites for the next cycle. Generate excitement and fun.

☑ *Communicate more and more.* Formalize some communication that used to be informal, while, at the same time, encouraging more *informal* communication between sites.

☑ *Communicate laterally.* Encourage lateral coordination and problem solving between sites without going through team management.

☑ *Communicate patiently.* Communication requires quality time.

☑ *Give everyone a 360° view.* On the team intranet, publish and update: individual, team, status, and task information. Encourage personal touches including personal pages and narratives about tasks.

☑ *Create transparency.* Every team member should be aware of and understand the goals of the project. Define the tasks and objectives clearly. Communicate the vision. Make the rules fair, visible, and stable. Set up planning norms as a means to improve information flows.

☑ *Instill communication protocols.* Instill the six communication protocols of Exhibit 10–4, which include communication responsiveness, frequency, time zone awareness, and trouble handling.

☑ *Instill protocols for e-mail communication.* Instill the nine e-mail protocols of Exhibit 10–5. These include: acknowledging each e-mail within one day, using descriptive subject headings, and more. Encourage well written e-mail over phone conversations to decrease cultural and linguistic misunderstandings.

☑ *Always remind yourself that most team members cannot comprehend or communicate in English as well as you can.* When conversing with nonnative English speakers, use the seven recommendations of Exhibit 10–6, including enunciating each word, avoiding use of slang, and others.

☑ *Always use active listening.* Rephrase answers, ask many clarification questions, check for understanding, use the funnel approach of

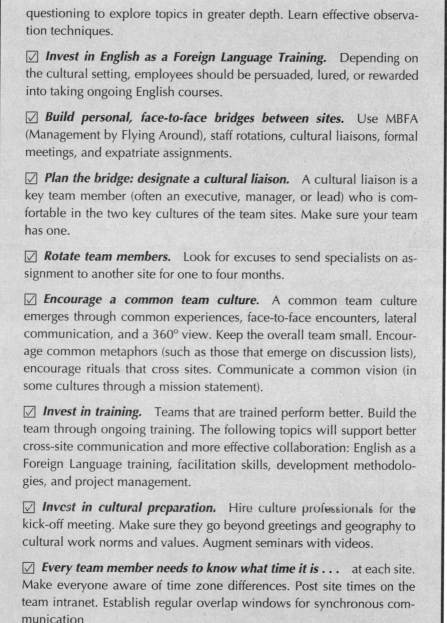

questioning to explore topics in greater depth. Learn effective observation techniques.

☑ *Invest in English as a Foreign Language Training.* Depending on the cultural setting, employees should be persuaded, lured, or rewarded into taking ongoing English courses.

☑ *Build personal, face-to-face bridges between sites.* Use MBFA (Management by Flying Around), staff rotations, cultural liaisons, formal meetings, and expatriate assignments.

☑ *Plan the bridge: designate a cultural liaison.* A cultural liaison is a key team member (often an executive, manager, or lead) who is comfortable in the two key cultures of the team sites. Make sure your team has one.

☑ *Rotate team members.* Look for excuses to send specialists on assignment to another site for one to four months.

☑ *Encourage a common team culture.* A common team culture emerges through common experiences, face-to-face encounters, lateral communication, and a 360° view. Keep the overall team small. Encourage common metaphors (such as those that emerge on discussion lists), encourage rituals that cross sites. Communicate a common vision (in some cultures through a mission statement).

☑ *Invest in training.* Teams that are trained perform better. Build the team through ongoing training. The following topics will support better cross-site communication and more effective collaboration: English as a Foreign Language training, facilitation skills, development methodologies, and project management.

☑ *Invest in cultural preparation.* Hire culture professionals for the kick-off meeting. Make sure they go beyond greetings and geography to cultural work norms and values. Augment seminars with videos.

☑ *Every team member needs to know what time it is . . .* at each site. Make everyone aware of time zone differences. Post site times on the team intranet. Establish regular overlap windows for synchronous communication

☑ *Establish "cultural guides"* for times when interactions get into trouble.

☑ *Be aware of decision making differences.* Each culture has its own style and speed of making and implementing decisions. Mitigate these differences with meeting and conferencing protocols. Each participant introduces an item as an "issue" or "action item." Items are then resolved, unresolved, or have an owner along with a due date.

☑ *Guard against giving too much power to the headquarters country site.*

Further Reading

Anyone managing a software team must, at some point, read DeMarco, T. and Lister, T. *Peopleware: productive projects and teams.* New York: Dorset House Publishing, 1987. A very thoughtful, provocative and easy read.

How to run a meeting? Look at the reprinted *How to Make Meetings Work* by Michael Doyle and David Straus, published by Berkley Pub Group, 1993.

An excellent complement to this chapter is Mary O'Hara-Devereaux and Bob Johansen's *Globalwork: Bridging Distance, Culture and Time*, San Francisco, CA: Jossey-Bass, 1994.

SPECIALIZED MANAGEMENT TECHNIQUES

This chapter presents the last of the six centripetal forces that bring the global team together. It is composed of a potpourri of techniques that are primarily in the realm of team management.

The chapter begins with the organizational design—the structure—of the global software team. The traditional team structures from the old days of co-located work will not be effective once a team is dispersed globally. Yet, not all functions should be dispersed. Some need to remain centralized. The chapter moves to another managerial concern: how to handle disputes between sites. This section includes techniques for handling conflict, but warns us that not all disputes that cross an international boundary necessarily result from national culture or language.

The global software manager also plays the traditional role of a project manager. The next section briefly introduces the fundamental project management techniques. Because it is the project manager who is principally charged with collecting and using software development measures, a list of 14 measures is presented for those qualities that are unique to dispersion and collaboration.

The last two sections cover Human Resource issues: how to reward, recognize, and compensate developers in a global team, and what qualities are needed in the global software manager. One of those tricky issues is rewards—and several examples of software managers' cultural gaffes are included here as lessons. The last section presents the unique qualities of a global software manager, represented by the acronym MERIT: Multi-culturalist, E-Facilitator, Recognition promoter, Internationalist, Traveler.

Designing the Team Structure

The traditional team structure from the days of co-located work is no longer effective when a team is dispersed globally. Software companies that are transitioning to the Stage III, *Globally Integrated,* organizational model (Exhibit 11–1) need a more flexible team structure to support dispersed modes of work and effective decision-making. Just as the software product itself needs to be re-architected internally to go global, so too does the team structure.

We begin by re-examining the Stage Model of global software teams introduced in Chapter 9 and repeated in Exhibit 11–1. To recap, Stage I, in which all development is co-located at headquarters, is, by now, an historical stage for the top 100 software organizations. In Stage II, *central coordination*, distant development sites are added, but all are largely controlled from headquarters. 85% of the projects in the GDSD study were conducted in software organizations in Stage II. However, roughly half of these exhibited some characteristics of moving to a Stage III organization: a globally integrated organization, resembling a network organization.

In Stage III the various development centers coordinate some activities among themselves. As more activities disperse globally and as the firm becomes globally integrated, less control is exerted from the headquarters central development site. Some or much of product ownership resides outside the center. Ten percent of the organizations in the GDSD study were Stage III organizations.

An interesting case is that of the IBM JavaBeans project (Chapter 2). As a result of a managerial change, it actually switched from a Stage II

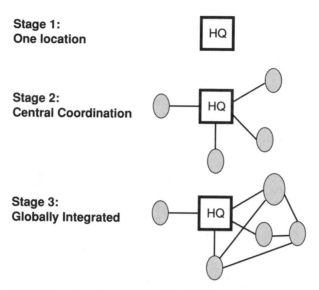

Stage 1:
One location

Stage 2:
Central Coordination

Stage 3:
Globally Integrated

Exhibit 11–1   The stage model of global software teams.

hub-and-spoke model to one closer to Stage III. And, it did this quite quickly. The speed with which the project was able to change its structure is particular to IBM and companies like IBM. First, it fit IBM's culture of a loose global network of development centers. Second, the JavaBeans project, although high profile, represented only a fraction of IBM's software business. For most software organizations, giving up headquarters control of flagship products is a wrenching process.

Industry-wide, the transition to Stage III will be a gradual one. All the centripetal forces discussed in this book need to be implemented: a solid collaborative technology foundation, good methodological practices, a solid architecture, and proper team practices. Nevertheless, the trend toward Stage III global software teams in larger organizations is inevitable. More of the distant sites will demand greater responsibility in initiating, designing, and building modules and entire products. They will no longer be content running service centers that take orders from headquarters.

A generic structure for a global software team is depicted in Exhibit 11–2.[174] The formal team structure is important as the analogue to sound product architecture: A formal structure provides the flexible foundation for efficient modular work, effective communication, and clear decision making. Also recall that one of the recurring objectives discussed in previous chapters is the notion of transparency—where everyone in the team understands what is going on. Hence, a clear team structure, depicted by an organizational chart, is one important step toward transparency. The team structure provides everyone inside and outside the team an understanding of authority relationships and information flows.

The generic team structure is based on several design principles. First, it represents a balance between a centralized and a decentralized structure. Second, some essential centralized roles are preserved, such as architecture, planning, budget, and standards setting. Third, hierarchy is not discarded entirely: Some internal decision-making hierarchy needs to remain: in the roles of the project manager, team leads, and so forth. Fourth, the structure facilitates the all important intra-team communication and lateral communication. Finally, this structure allows the various committee functions and individual functions to be collapsed if necessary. In small- and medium-size teams, the three committees may be collapsed into one, and some of the individual roles can be collapsed to one person who fills more than one role.

Note the top of Exhibit 11–2: A global software team requires an executive committee acting in oversight capacity. Specifically, the company can create a virtual product executive steering committee that reports directly to a senior executive. This committee is as an alternative to the matrix structure that otherwise complicates management of focused project activities. Matrix structures, so popular in the United States since the 1970s, have not worked well in other countries (e.g., France and Germany).[175] Nor are matrices easy to implement on a cross-border basis.[176]

At the team's center are three committee roles: project management, technical, and process. Generally, these committees are made up of one or two people from each site. The first of these committees—project management—is familiar to most software projects. The second two committees are far less common.

The project management committee is a coordinating body composed of the project manager and the leads from each site. The project

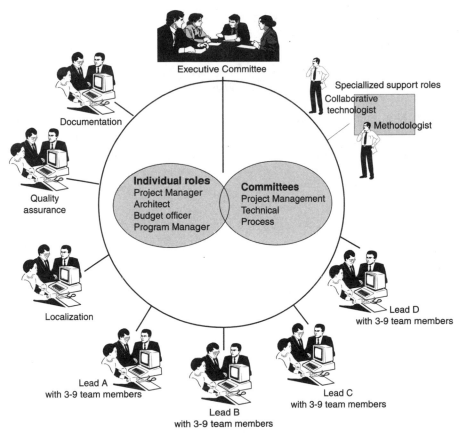

Exhibit 11–2   Generic structure of global software team.

management committee replaces the centralized role of headquarters with a looser, but still central coordinating body. The committee deals with standard managerial issues such as task commitments, goals (e.g., deadlines), resources, and problem resolution.

Most software work groups do not function on mandates. Therefore, some of the project management committee's tasks are to build and foster consensus within the dispersed sites through influence and persuasion. Depending on the cultural mix of the team, the committee can take either an Eastern or a Western approach to team consensus building. The Eastern approach is based on soliciting and getting consensus before making goals public team-wide.[177] For example, explicit deadlines should not be documented until full consensus is agreed to, not by just the team leads in the project management committee, but by all key members at all sites. Only then are the tasks and timelines made into public documents and distributed to various team members through e-mail and other electronic channels. The Western approach is based on explicit and public "buy in." Each of the team sites "buys in" to the overall goals by making a commitment to the *entire project,* not just each site's module.[178] This commitment must be a very public commitment that is communicated both in person and via electronic channels. Once the public commitment is made, then if one site-team runs into trouble or delays, it should expect assistance and problem-solving from the rest of the sites.

Also at the team's center are the four individual roles: Project Manager, Architect, Program Manager, and Budget Officer. The Project Manager role is very common, the others less so. The global team needs an Architect with overall design authority, due to the heightened importance of product architecture in a dispersed environment. In larger projects, there is need for a Program Manager,[179] who serves as a channel to other functions outside the team, particularly to marketing. Similarly, in larger organizations, with larger dispersed sites, there is need for a Budget Officer to handle administrative issues.

One of the design principles was to create a team structure that is "collapsible." The collapsibility is strongly linked to size and scale. In small projects some individual and committee roles can be collapsed. For example, in smaller projects, the individual role of Architect may be replaced by an architecture and technical committee, with representatives from different sites. Surprisingly, some teams in the GDSD study collapsed the role of the individual Project Manager (or at least weakened the authority of that individual). In such cases the Project Manager is typically replaced by a committee of team leads. In a smaller global team this committee can be effective:

> At NetParadise, the 12-person, three-country team had no person in the role of project manager. This lack led to some coordination benefits. Every developer took upon himself more responsibility for solv-

ing problems and seeing them through to resolution. When a developer discovered a problem, he informed the distant stakeholders and addressed all the issues by phone or e-mail. There was no waiting for a manager, or project milestone, to uncover the problem.

Positioned outside the center of Exhibit 11–2 are two specialized support roles critical to a global software team: a collaborative technology support specialist and a methodologist. The collaborative technology support specialist assists the software developers in implementing and using generic groupware and conferencing, as well as the specialized tools of collaborative technology for software engineering. The specialist continuously updates collaborative technology components and facilitates homegrown tools. Each globally dispersed project should have a full-time support specialist. The methodologist is responsible for updating the collective methodology and educating the developers and should be a member of the process committee.

Each of the site groups (or sub-teams) should be kept as small as possible—no larger than nine developers and preferably smaller. Each such group has a "lead" (short for leader; often referred to as a "team lead"). Some sites will have more than one such group. In most cases each site should have considerable flexibility in structuring its work units internally, as long as at the end of that process, the internal structure and members' roles are clearly defined to all developers at all sites. An alternative approach is that of a mirror organization (introduced in the previous chapter), which holds that organizational units should have identical structures and roles in order to facilitate lateral communication between team members.

Managing Conflict

Nothing is less productive than prolonged conflicts—those between team sites or those between individual members in collaborating sites. Sometimes battles are fought openly. Equally as dangerous, some parties choose avoidance mechanisms and allow disagreements to fester.

Peace and tranquillity, however, is not always a good thing. Some conflict is healthy. It can stimulate a person's energy and mental focus; it can be intellectually challenging; it can produce a better decision after issues are properly debated and challenged; it can do away with small irritants by confronting them head on; it can cause people to question unhealthy norms and procedures.

Collaboration is a constant process of negotiation and problem resolution. It is about finding a better way to resolve a problem. Resolution may not necessarily come about by one side dominating, nor necessarily by a compromise between the two parties. It is best not to think in terms of "our way" and "your way"—but by finding a third way. In the theory of negotiation, exemplified by the long-time best seller *Getting to Yes,*[180] this resolution process is called "integrative bargaining" or "creative integration."

The first step in conflict management is to set the groundwork for future inevitable conflict. Identify a trusted third party within or outside the team who can be called in to resolve inter-site disputes.[181] The project manager may be viewed as such a party in some projects. In tandem, establish the problem resolution ground rules. While low context cultures (e.g., Americans, Dutch) are comfortable with open disagreement, Asians (and some other high context cultures) tend to be much more polite and conceal disputes. The problem-resolution protocol calls for low context cultures to be unusually respectful when addressing disagreements, while Asian cultures need to be forthcoming with a full unveiling of the issues.

Once a conflict does arise, the first law of conflict resolution is: *Separate the people from the problem.* This law is particularly useful in cross-cultural settings, where cultural issues may be interwoven with substantive issues. Try to address the dispute in pieces, beginning with the technical issues first. Leave the organizational and staffing concerns to later.[182]

Humphrey, of the Software Engineering Institute, suggests a *three-step process* for handling inter-site disputes.[183] First, try to resolve the dispute between the team leads without involving the other team members. Have the team lead from each side air the various issues. Second, if the dispute remains unresolved, informally explore the respective positions separately and then bring the team leads together to discuss the dispute resolution process. The project manager needs to make media choices for these first two steps: audio- or video-conferencing? It is best, in time of dispute, not to expose one of the parties to a channel that will handicap them because of language. Consider air travel as an alternative.

The third step in handling inter-site disputes is to bring in an expert third party, a neutral, or committee to resolve the dispute. The third party is a valuable asset.

Magnetix is a large US-based systems services company with a development site in Japan. Disagreements between the American and

Japanese sites were resolved by an informal neutral board serving in the role of mediator. Initially, this board was made up of a single person—a senior American executive, on the verge of retirement, with many years experience in Japan and deep appreciation of its culture. This executive had the trust of both the Americans and the Japanese.

Conflicts that emerge from the electronic trenches have their own dynamics. In *e-mail wars,* some people will battle laterally, while others battle up the hierarchy, with copies to everyone and their boss. Some wars escalate into flaming. Flaming is a particularly angry and nasty e-mail message often out of proportion to the severity of the case at hand. Carefully monitor the electronic channels for perceived discontent and address it early. It is important to let these individuals know that part of their job is to be more careful in their communications, that not everything is a crisis, and that they need to forge relationships rather than destroy them. Focus on the concerned individuals as much as possible using e-mail or other focused communication technologies, rather than using team-wide technologies that expose the dispute.

A number of global software managers have emphasized that in a cross-cultural situation it is important to determine if the conflict has cross-cultural roots, or if the conflict is the more familiar turf battle, or is simply individual game-playing. These are three very different types of problems and need different approaches to resolving them. One of the managers pointed out that most of the conflicts he deals with were "the garden variety type" that had nothing to do with national culture. His most serious ongoing conflicts were between two groups at the same foreign site fighting a protracted ego war between programmers and testers over whether or not something was really a bug.

Project Management Techniques

When a team is dispersed, some task-related coordination can continue informally, but the team as a whole must be tasked and coordinated via formal mechanisms. These mechanisms, or techniques, are *project management techniques.* The six fundamental project management techniques are: creating a statement of work; using consistent techniques for estimating costs and task times; using consistent techniques for task decomposition and building a work breakdown structure; creating a project timeline of tasks taking into account task dependencies and critical path; creating a project budget; and conducting proper risk management.

More managers are systematically thinking about *risks*. A risk is a problem that has not yet taken place, but if it does, it will have a negative impact on the project, perhaps even threatening its continuation. For example, a technical risk is that the newly acquired Java development toolbox is too buggy. A staffing risk is that the key software engineers at each site, Avi and Giorgio, will leave the project before it is complete. Risk management involves, first, identifying risks of all kinds and evaluating each one. All risks should then be prioritized and the project manager typically focuses her attention, daily, to the "top 10 most important risks." Each risk needs to be actively mitigated, prevented, or even eliminated. This is a process that needs continuous management attention.

Too few project managers are trained in project management and fewer use the six project management techniques. Nevertheless, the techniques need to be seen for what they are: technocratic tools. They cannot replace the communication-intensive component of management. For example, it is recommended that the project manager and team leads agree verbally, during face-to-face planning meetings, to project milestones and deliverables that emerge as output from the project management software package.

A newer project management technique that addresses some of these softer issues is stakeholder mapping.[184] It can help deal with the common situation in which we hear a remark such as "they are not as committed to this task as we are." Stakeholder mapping is a political mapping exercise. The project manager needs to document and think about the following: At each site, for each team lead and other stakeholder, does he have authority to represent the group and make decisions for the group? does she have the resources to get the job done and can she can get more if necessary? does he have authority for hiring and firing? Similarly, note to whom besides the project manager the team lead and other stakeholders report. Figure out who the patrons of each site are. This mapping technique is particularly important for joint ventures and teams derived from complex organizational structures.

Once the global dispersed project is well underway, the project manager manages via milestones (also referred to as status monitoring). The manager determines the progress toward milestones. When progress is inadequate or late, then the manager takes action. But a global software project manager who does not travel frequently may rely too heavily on status monitoring and discover problems late. The project manager is also subject to reporting manipulation from distant sites. In one company in the GDSD study, one of the distant sites simply stopped reporting to the project manager for an extended period. Naturally, the site was behind schedule. But the lack of reporting caused the far-away project manager to feel helpless.

Measure!

Something that is not measured cannot be properly managed! This is the modern day derivation of Lord Kelvin's dictum: "When you can measure what you are speaking about and express it in numbers, you know something about it." This section focuses only on those measures and indices that help you understand the particular case of the *dispersed* development project rather than the entire domain of a development project, which is already taken care of by numerous other measures and metrics.

Like most other measures of software development, many of those listed below are not useful in isolation of just one project. Rather, they are useful when they can be compared to benchmarks—past projects in the firm (or outside it) that were similar (or dissimilar) to the globally dispersed project in question.

Measuring global software teams needs to focus on the construct of coordination. Coordination is at the root of effective functioning of a dispersed team. But how do you measure what it means to "coordinate well" or "coordinate poorly"? It cannot be done precisely, which is why the construct of coordination cannot be measured directly. There is no one measure of coordination. To complicate things further, the index we need to use is not necessarily indicative of good versus bad. If there is much coordination, is it good, or bad? It is good when team members are addressing and solving issues. It is bad when team members should be busy designing and programming. Therefore, coordination indices need to take snapshots from different angles (different operationalizations, in social science lingo) that, together, form a picture of coordination.

Unfortunately, coordination measures require enumeration at the level of the individual programmer, or the individual task of a programmer. This may not be palatable because it calls for filling out activity sheets, or setting up automated systems that may be viewed as too intrusive. This privacy threat can be mitigated if data can be aggregated by work unit so that no individual data is traceable. Ultimately, collecting data on individuals reduces to an issue of trust. If the individuals do not fully trust that the data collected for indices will improve their processes rather than be used to spy on them, they will sabotage their collection.

The following indices and measures deal directly with issues of dispersed development:[185]

Indices of collaborative technology use:
- *Time using collaborative technologies.* The total duration of phone calls, audio- and video-conferences. Divide by number of people on the team.
- *Quantity of sessions/messages using collaborative technologies.* The total number of sessions/messages of phone calls, audio- and video-conferences, e-mail, discussion, and issue lists. Divide by number of people on the team. Segment these figures by synchronous (e.g, phone) versus asynchronous technologies (e.g., e-mail) and by intra- versus inter-site components.

Indices of meetings, face to face time, and travel:
- *Dilbert index.* Dilbert is an American business icon—a cartoon office worker who spends too much time in meetings. Like Dilbert, software engineers do not like too many meetings. This is an index of *time per person in formal face to face meetings.* The total time in meetings is divided by total person-time on the project.
- *Team-building index.* Number of days that individuals (managers and other team members) of one site spend at other sites (net of travel days) divided by total of all person-days on the project. Anything below 1% is too low.
- *Travel days.* While raising the Team-building index, minimize this item.

Measures of hand off and transition efficiency:
- *Delay.* Count the number of times site work was delayed because of wait for dependent tasks from other sites.
- *Gain.* Count the number of times activities resulted in overnight gain. This is a follow-the-sun measure.
- *Blocking counts.* A block occurs when one site or individual compensates for time loss on one task by working on another one. Count these with duration.

Measures and indices of issue management:
- *Issues raised.* An issue is a problem of some kind. Groupware tools are useful for managing such lists and keeping track of their numbers. Once an issue is raised, it is considered open (outstanding) until it is deemed closed.
- *Number of open issues.* The number of open issues should rise over the early development cycle and at some point begin to fall toward zero by the software ship date.
- *Issue closure index.* How many days (median, moving average) it takes to close each issue.

Measures of cost that are significant to global teams:
- *Cost of telecommunications* infrastructure and ongoing usage to support the distant sites.
- *Cost of travel.* If this cost item really does become prohibitive, experiment with more aggressive video-conferencing.
- *Cost of labor.* Unloaded and loaded costs at each site.

Recognition, Rewards, and Compensation

Pay and rewards are complex in any team. The intercultural and inter-regulatory issues make this topic very touchy. Regardless of culture, it is important to link recognition and reward to performance. First, it is important to reward teamwork in global teams rather than individuals. The IBM software development center in Rome instituted a team achievement award for business achievement in which teamwork was a key factor.[186] Second, some rewards should not be monetary. Because bonuses are taxed at higher rates in Europe, an appropriate reward is a paid travel junket. An American software manager sent his European developers for a long weekend to a French château. A European software manager completed a major release in collaboration with a Japanese site. He recognized his dedicated European developers by flying them all to Japan for a combination business-pleasure trip.

Several American cultural gaffs emerged in the GDSD study that deal with recognition. Europeans see corporate icons and logos as terribly "American" and lacking in subtlety. Americans like to be congratulated and recognized for specific accomplishments. The tactile recognition comes in the form of certificates, the ubiquitous glass paperweights with the corporate logo, the marble plates, and of course, T-shirts. Several European software managers complained that they found the American corporate knickknacks insulting. Americans value public displays of congratulation. However, in most other cultures, public display is of less value, or even frowned upon; e.g., Koreans prefer not to be praised in public.

Compensation issues are no less complex. Most Human Resource consultants urge equity between team sites so that extreme variations do not create resentment. But extreme variations in labor costs is one of the driving forces that set up dispersed teams to begin with. So focus on understanding how to compensate people differently rather than equally. It is more useful to understand that different cultures have different compensation preferences: for fixed versus variable compensation, for short term versus long term, and monetary versus nonmonetary rewards. American culture is more accepting of high risk and therefore Americans are more likely to prefer variable compensation. Swedes prefer nonmonetary incentives, such as more vacation time. Japanese would not take more vacation time since they usually don't use up the time they do get (and often suffer from Karoshi—death from overwork).[187] Chinese IS professionals prefer short-term compensation, while longer term compensation is preferred in the more advanced Asian economies such as Singapore and Malaysia, and Hong Kong.[188]

Recognition should be sensitive to labor regulations. At the end of a development cycle as the deadline looms, the American work culture expects overtime from its software professionals and even rescheduling of vacations if the project slips. Europeans are less likely to work as much overtime or delay vacations. One German manager in the GDSD study expressed anger at his American counterparts for having to feel guilty that, by regulation, his developers took vacation before deadlines. Other European regulations will seem onerous to Americans: In 1998 the French government began enforcing laws that forbid *all* overtime, even for professional and managerial employees.

Selecting the Global Software Development Manager

An executive at a large US-based firm stated to me that he selects managers for large global projects based on their technical and managerial fit. When asked if any global experience or cultural factors were used to make selection decisions, the executive was startled by the question. Should he have been?

All global software managers need to become *global* managers. They must deal with more than simply managing a technical team. They must overcome the unique problems of global software teams: culture (including language), time zone, and distance.

Many checklists are used for selecting an effective global manager. For example, the Japanese firm Matsushita selects its global managers according to SMILE: Specialty, Management ability, International, Language, Endeavor.[189] International Business scholars Schneider and Barsoux[190] list nine criteria for an effective global manager: interpersonal skills, linguistic ability, cultural curiosity, tolerance for ambiguity, flexibility, patience, cultural empathy, sense of self, and sense of humor.

Global software managers in the GDSD study were asked to self-rate themselves as managers (see Table 11–1). Each manager was asked to allocate ten points among three dimensions: technical, managerial, and global orientation, according to his/her assessment of relative strengths. Separately, I classified these managers as either *effective* or *accidental* global software managers after an interview.

The effective global software managers rated themselves as (roughly) having a balance among these three dimensions. Those labeled "accidental global software managers" saw themselves as first and foremost technical managers. Generally, they did not last long. One of these "accidental managers" quit after he found the travel was too much for him. Another took an extended leave to work at a research institute.

TABLE 11–1   Self-rating by Global Software Managers.
(Each manager in the GDSD study was asked to allocate ten points to these three dimensions according to his/her relative strengths; the two columns represent averages.)

Dimension		Effective Managers	Accidental Managers
Technical	experience and knowledge in design and programming of reliable, innovative systems	2.4	6
Managerial	experience in issues of supervision, control, facilitation, and cost reduction	3.9	2.7
Global orientation	understanding national cultures, markets, and customers	3.7	1.3
		10 points	10 points

The remainder of this section focuses on those unique qualities for being a successful global software manager—rather than the entire range of qualities that make for an effective manager. These qualities allow the global software manager to handle the multicultural and dispersed components of her role. These five unique qualities are summarized in the acronym MERIT: Multiculturalist, E-Facilitator, Recognition promoter, Internationalist, Traveler.

Multiculturalist. The global software manager gracefully switches from culture to culture and from style to style. While American managers like egalitarian relationships and participatory decision-making (consensus-style supervision), Asian and other cultures that revere hierarchy expect leaders to be strong decisive leaders who do not require too much feedback (authoritarian-style supervision). Skillful global managers can switch between authoritarian-style supervision and consensus-style supervision depending on their location. One American manager of a Russian site told me that every so often he puts on a show of yelling and screaming. He explained that the Russians had lived in an authoritarian regime for so long that he needs to show who is boss.

Electronic Facilitator. The global software manager is a superb e-facilitator and e-communicator. We are all familiar with national political leaders who succeed because they have good tele-presence (television presence). The global software manager succeeds (in part) due to effective e-presence. She can communicate a vision from a distance to all sites, and then link actions to that vision.[191] She can build trust between sites and between individuals electronically, while anticipating and resolving disputes. She is a natural facilitator of all types of electronic conversations: conferences, e-mail, and issue lists. And she makes sure that everyone is participating and contributing.

Recognition Promoter. The global software manager is a master at promoting the virtues of global software teams at headquarters. He is constantly seeking recognition at headquarters. He also knows how to get resources for his various remote development sites. In the GDSD study, a manager who was a recognition promoter was present in all of the largest software organizations, including some of the largest US software organizations. At one firm this manager spent most of his time, not with the team, but at headquarters, making sure that his team continued to be in the limelight. Other senior managers spoke of making regular pilgrimages to headquarters. The recognition promoter knows that the remote sites are always vulnerable to headquarters' whims of change. After many years, one recognition promoter lost his guardian angel at headquarters and his remote site's long-term viability began to look questionable.

Internationalist. The global software manager has an intellectual appetite for all that is international. She knows about different cultures, different political systems, different telecommunications regulatory issues, and so on.[192] And, she enjoys, rather than endures, many aspects of travel. One American global software executive boasted to me that his Indian business partners were very impressed when, during a dinnertime conversation, he knew facts about twentieth century Indian political history that his hosts had difficulty recalling.

Traveler. The global software manager practices Management By Flying Around (MBFA). He makes sure to have face-to-face time with team members at all sites. He is effective at face-to-face communication in spite of not speaking all the native languages of the team members. He does much communicating in informal settings, such as sharing a lunch, or attending a social event, discussing personal, work, and career issues.[193]

Best Practices Roundup

☑ *A global team structure needs to be designed. Do not let it form organically.* Think of the structure as a network in which there is no central site. Then create the necessary central functions of project management, architecture, methodology, and budget. Fill these with individuals or committees or both.

☑ *Plan for the inevitable conflicts.* Identify a trusted third party who can mediate or arbitrate a dispute between sites. Demonstrate respect for the individual at all times. Keep alert for cultural and linguistic misunderstandings.

☑ *Once the conflict arises, manage the conflict resolution process.* Separate the people from the problem; Seek a third way— perhaps not theirs or ours. Try to resolve the conflict with the leads and project manager first. Have all sides agree to the dispute handling process. Get the dispute off of all public electronic channels. Don't hesitate to travel to resolve the dispute.

☑ *Use the six fundamental techniques of project management.* Create a statement of work; use consistent techniques for estimating costs and task times; use consistent techniques for task decomposition and building a work breakdown structure; create a project timeline of tasks, taking into account task dependencies and critical path; create a project budget; and conduct proper risk management (including the useful trick of creating a "top ten" list of most important risks). And consider a seventh technique: mapping the stakeholders at each site.

☑ *Measure the unique dimensions of a global software team and then benchmark these measures.* The unique dimensions that need to be measured are: use of collaborative technologies, meetings and face-time, site hand off efficiency, issue management, and some specific cost items: telecommunication, travel, and labor.

☑ *Rewards, recognition, and compensation norms appropriate in your culture and business climate will not be appropriate elsewhere.* Be very careful with gifts and bonuses.

☑ *Select a global software manager with a balance of global, managerial, and technical skills.* The most common mistake is to allow an individual whose main strengths are technical to fill the role of a global software manager.

☑ *Look for the five MERIT qualities in a global software manager.* Multiculturalist (ability to switch cultural styles), E-Facilitator (being an effective electronic facilitator and communicator), Recognition promoter (being a resourceful promoter of the team within the organization), Internationalist (possessing a healthy international intellectual appetite), Traveler (practices Management By Flying Around).

Further Reading

A solid book on organizational design is Galbraith's *Designing Organizations*. San Francisco, Calif: Jossey-Bass Publishers, 1995.

Phillips addresses issues of leadership and teams in Phillips, N. *Managing International Teams*. Bur Ridge, Illinois: Irwin Professional Publishing, 1994.

The best primer on conflict and negotiations is an eternal bestseller: *Getting to Yes: Negotiating Agreement Without Giving in.* Fisher, Roger and Ury, William. New York, NY: Penguin, 1991.

One of the most influential scholars of leadership in the United States is Warren G. Bennis, who with Burt Nanus wrote *Leaders: Strategies for Taking Charge*. Harperbusiness, 1997.

For more on software measures see *Measures for Excellence* by Lawrence Putnam and Ware Myers, Englewood Cliffs, NJ: Prentice Hall, 1992.

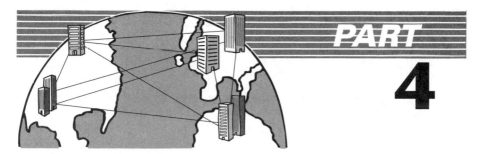

Global Information Systems Teams

The traditional portrait of information systems (IS) in global cor-porations is one in which far-flung IS units in subsidiaries develop their own applications to address primarily local needs. A more integrated approach to global IS that began in the 1980s, and continues today, requires a higher level of cross-border collabo-ration between subsidiaries and between central IS units. The 1990s brought yet more cross-border collaboration, with a differ-ent origin—outsourcing, including global (offshore) outsourc-ing. Together, these two dynamics—the global integration from within and the global contracting with the outside—have height-ened interest in global IS teams.

Chapter Twelve begins by addressing the question of why companies are globalizing their IS functions. The implication of this globalization process is that IS organizations are taking on a new structure, an Integrated Network structure, in which global systems and development efforts are shared across borders.

Chapter Thirteen presents a step-by-step guide to the PSR methodology for global applications. PSR stands for Process/Sys-tem/Responsibility. The methodology motivates corporate IS to design the global IS team only after comprehensively (and care-fully) identifying its global processes and systems worldwide. The first stage, Process, identifies the organization's core global busi-

193

ness processes. The second stage, System, identifies the systems needed to support the handful of global business processes. The third stage, Responsibility, determines what type of team will be responsible for each of the global systems.

Chapter Fourteen presents a case study of IS global out-sourcing at US-headquartered hotel chain Holiday Inn. Holiday Inn began its outsourcing by insourcing—using contract software programmers that worked inhouse. At a later phase the contracting staff were moved to India. The different management issues of insourcing versus global outsourcing provide valuable lessons.

GLOBALIZATION AND INFORMATION SYSTEMS

This first chapter devoted to Information Systems (IS) development begins by addressing the question: Why are companies globalizing their IS functions? The forces driving this globalization process include: the demands of a new global consumer and new global business customer, global sourcing, and global product R&D.

The implication of this globalization process is that the IS organization itself is taking on a new form. This new form is an *Integrated Network* in which global systems and global development efforts are increasingly shared across borders. This new organizational form will include units with worldwide systems responsibility. These units, labeled Centers of Global Applications, are assigned long-term responsibility for those systems deemed "global."

While the Integrated Network form of IS describes the globalization structures inside the organization, the global outsourcing phenomenon, described at the end of this chapter, leads to IS collaboration across the boundaries of the corporation and across international borders.

Chapter 1's introduction, devoted to the global packaged software industry, began by answering the question, "Why global software teams?" Similarly, we begin Part IV by considering what is driving global companies to globalize their IS function. Globalizing the IS function implies developing global information systems applications that support global processes rather than local or regional processes. This realignment of IS has led corporations to re-examine their IS organizational structures and thus the way that they build IS teams.

First, and most important, *globally competing companies are going through an internal globalization transformation.* It sounds like a tautology, but it is not. Globalization for Nestlé, or SKF, or Mobil means a shift away from the geographic, national focus of yesteryear. In the traditional (decentralized or "multidomestic") model of the postwar era, globally competing corporations set up national subsidiaries that operated largely independent of headquarters. Some collaboration occurred—for branding, product distribution, and manufacturing, but national subsidiaries were small empires with largely autonomous decision-making.

The traditional organizational form is changing to one that is both integrated and more similar to a network organizational structure. It is labeled the *Integrated Network* form (global strategists Bartlett and Ghoshal[194] have labeled this the "Transnational corporation"). An Integrated Network corporation can simultaneously be globally efficient (and take advantage of economies of scale) while continuing to provide local responsiveness, by tailoring products and services to the special needs of customers in any nation. It is a fine balancing act to perform. The globalization of IS and the corresponding internal transformation is driven by a number of external and internal factors:[195]

The global consumer, global business customer, and global product. The global consumer demands global airlines and global hotel chains. The global business customer demands worldwide service such as freight forwarders, package delivery firms, and telecommunications services. Meanwhile, some products are becoming essentially the same throughout the world (e.g., Coca Cola). The competitive forces of global Internet marketing will accelerate this process.

Global sourcing and integration of the supply chain. Products are being assembled from multiple sources and information systems are used to coordinate the logistics: A US computer firm may source software in the UK, monitors in Korea, and circuit boards in the United

States. An oil company has a global system for bidding on crude oil contracts. Supply chain integration is driving standardization across the corporation with the implementation of massive enterprise packages, such as SAP.

Global product R&D and shorter product cycles.   Companies, such as Ford, are integrating their worldwide automobile design centers with massive investments in CAD. Global pharmaceutical companies are integrating their far-flung R&D sites and collapsing regulatory approval time for important new discoveries.

Harmonization and standardization of reporting requirements.   Accounting and legal requirements are driving greater levels of financial consolidation.

Economies of scale for systems.   Data center consolidation combined with fast global networks reduce the need for multiple computer hosts in each country. Major global corporations, like US-based Black & Decker, reduced their European and Asian data centers to just one in each region.

Implications of Globalization for the IS Function: The Integrated Network IS Organization

Like the historical global corporation, the common IS structure was usually decentralized. Subsidiary IS units operated independently, receiving their budgets from the "country manager." Table 12–1 presents the four forms of corporate structure and the corresponding prototypical approaches for systems and IS development.[196]

The IS function has been following the lead of its global parent organization in its transition toward the more advanced of the four organizational forms, the Integrated Network organization, with its need for intensive cross-border collaboration and sharing. The journey has proven to be a difficult one. Global companies have been struggling to implement this transition strategy for many years. In the first book on multinational information systems, Ed Roche described a number of global systems implementations in the mid to late 1980s. Many of these cases were global IS failures.[197] In a study from the early 1990s, none of corporate IS entities reached this "highest" stage of IS structure and form, the Integrated Network.[198]

Table 12–1 Global Corporate Structures and Corresponding
Information Systems Approaches

Corporate Structure	Systems	IS Development
Centralized	Centralized databases and processes driven by headquarters	Headquarters centralized development and decision making
Decentralized ("Multidomestic")	Standalone, largely independent	Independent at each subsidiary
Coordinated Federation	Linked databases with some application sharing	Some joint development; formalization and standards established.
Integrated Network ("Transnational")	Integrated architecture; shared databases and shared global processes	Centers for global applications

The IS function that has completed the transition to an Integrated Network form has several important characteristics:

- Common global architecture
- Powerful telecommunication backbone
- Uniform global systems with flexible modules tailored to address local requirements
- Centers for Global Application development with responsibility for systems worldwide
- A culture of shared management
- A culture of shared application building
- A culture of shared innovation

Attaining these characteristics requires a multifaceted approach combining technological, financial, and behavioral methods. Attaining integration for global architecture, telecommunications, and applications requires some *standardization*. Why standardize? The advantages of standardization are familiar but worth re-listing: ease of communicating between corporate units, ease of communicating with trading partners, ease of transferring data, and ease of transferring (reusing) applications.

The standardization required of small teams of crack programmers in packaged software firms, described in earlier parts of this book, pales next to the scale of standardization obstacles with which global IS deals—with legacy systems and applications on a multitude of platforms. In order to integrate global applications, corporations must internally agree to standardization of architecture, hardware, software, telecommunications, systems development processes, and quality standards.[199]

Attaining uniform global systems requires the creation of global development units, labeled *Centers for Global Applications* (CGA). The CGA is a development center that unifies all development work for one or more global application systems. The center is said to "own" this global system. Ownership is assigned for an indefinite time, across multiple releases, rather than on a one-project basis. Ownership also means end-to-end responsibility for systems development—from requirements and enhancement requests through pilot testing and global roll-out.

Attaining a culture of shared systems and management runs into a difficulty: Many subsidiaries are reluctant to play along. The IS units in subsidiaries prefer independence and control of their own destinies. They want to be responsive to their own "country manager's" requirements. Yet the Integrated Network model of global information systems requires a high degree of coordination and sharing between headquarters and its dispersed worldwide development units.

The approach for bringing about effective coordination among central IS, the IS subsidiaries, and the CGA is called *constructive engagement*, which is a soft, informal method of coordination. Constructive engagement is the conversion of people's attitudes in a persuasive, yet positive, nonconfrontational way. Constructive engagement also entails a dialogue of consensus building—consensus among the various stakeholders involved in building or rolling out a global application. The consensus building process takes place without surrendering the central unit's overall direction. Some have called this approach co-optation, although this term may be too suggestive of coercion.[200] Four mechanisms are used for bringing about constructive engagement: budget, business case, liaisons, and information dissemination.

The first step toward constructive engagement is a realignment of the budget and financial incentives. Traditionally, IS budgets come from the "country manager" or some other unit that necessarily has a parochial view. Globalized applications require actions for the benefit of the larger enterprise, while the incentives of local developers are to develop locally.

An IS subsidiary in Zurich has practically no incentive to collaborate with an IS subsidiary in São Paulo if their respective budgets come from their local units to support local applications.

A pragmatic type of constructive engagement involves making the "business case," augmented with abundant personal contact and persuasion. Most employees want the company to succeed, but reflexively will present arguments to any initiative, especially from headquarters or other outside units. Local units need to see that an initiative benefits them as well as the corporation at large.

> At Caterair International (formerly Marriott's In-Flite Services Division), the four people who were assigned to worldwide IS headquarters near Washington D.C. had very little authority over the local IS units and no influence over the local IS shops' budget. The headquarters unit, however, did have a travel budget of one quarter million dollars for them to fly around the world to the dozens of sites. At each local unit they made a "business case" for their system proposal. The headquarters' representatives made the case that the new system would reduce costs and improve operating performance of the units as a whole. This pleased not only the local IS manager, but the country manager as well. When money was needed, the headquarters' representatives agreed to fund part of the development work using headquarters' funds. The face to face contact, combined with persuasion, allowed headquarters to influence the development process and the resulting applications.

Once formal CGAs are formed, constructive engagement can be institutionalized by creating a liaison role within each IS subsidiary, called the *CGA Associate(s)*. One or more individuals at the subsidiary are formally selected to work with the CGA on a permanent basis. The CGA Associates are involved throughout the development cycle of each global system release, from the requirements phase, through local tailoring, to local roll-out. The CGA needs to form a close relationship with the Associates. In turn, the CGA Associates develop a vested interest in the success of the global system. Informally, the Associates play the critical role of consensus builders at the local subsidiary by engaging local opposition from within. Also informally, the Associates channel innovation from the local unit back to the global unit.

Finally, constructive engagement requires keeping all subsidiary IS units well informed. In Chapter 10 this was called the *360° view*: allowing each unit to see what others are doing above it, below it, and laterally, on both sides. The information formats include news and information via corporate intranets. Content includes updates on global systems' development progress. Information can be diffused via tailored workshops on technology and strategic issues. Furthermore, keeping distant IS units engaged must include communicating the overall global IS vision.

IS Global Outsourcing

IS organizations are turning to outsourcing for a myriad of reasons, listed in Exhibit 12–1.[201] Of the six reasons in the exhibit, the first, cost, makes *offshore* outsourcing particularly attractive.

- *Cost savings.* Reported savings have been in the 10%–50% range (although there have been contrarian cases). Outsourcers offer economies of scale in data centers and other services.
- *Not part of core business.* The corporation decides to focus on the core business activity. There is little desire to manage something that is viewed as a commodity. IS is not viewed as a strategic activity, and its systems do not differentiate the business.
- *Functionally discrete.* Some IS functions are relatively simple to outsource because they are operationally discrete functions rather than tightly integrated into the business. Sometimes, the IS function has already begun the process of being a procurer of services rather than a provider of services.
- *Lack of internal skills.* The IS function lacks certain skills or may be tired and under-motivated. It is having problems hiring and cannot deliver systems that internal customers are requesting.
- *Improve financial reporting.* Improve short-term cash flow by liquidating the IS organization. Reduction in assets improves returns.
- *Solve internal political battles.* The IS function has turned into divisional fiefdoms, which are beyond redemption.

Exhibit 12–1   Reasons for outsourcing.

Global outsourcing has been with us for a surprisingly long time. Data entry was the first job category to go offshore. Pacific Data Services has been contracting for data entry since 1961! Later data entry jobs have gone to Korea, Jamaica, Barbados, Haiti and many other countries.[202]

Globalization of outsourcing presents problems of distance—both physical and cultural. Distance affects two types of communication and interaction: between the corporate customer (end user) and the distant outsourcer; and between corporate IS management and the distant outsourcer.

Distance from the corporate customer is often overlooked. Whereas IS developers located in CGAs may be geographically far from their corporate customers, they are still within the organizational boundaries and know how things work. This is not the case with a distant outsourcer—who is far removed from the organizational culture as well as the national culture, and is the principal reason that offshore outsourcing is most suitable for highly structured activities, such as porting, which require relatively little communication.[203]

The Holiday Inn case study of Chapter 14 illustrates the unique problems created by distance between corporate IS management and the distant outsourcer. One of the case's lessons is "out of sight, out of mind." The tale begins with a standard body shop arrangement in which IS tasks were insourced to co-located developers who worked in proximity and under direct supervision of US-based Holiday Inn IS managers. During this phase, all went well: Personal relationships were forged, and the insourced staff developed experience with and understanding of the Holiday Inn organization. In the subsequent phase, development was moved to India—half a world away. While coordination worked nicely in a co-located situation, it failed with distance. Once in India, staff turnover increased markedly. The people with whom personal relationships were formed were gone. They took with them the experience of working with Holiday Inn's applications. The authors of this case see the problem as one in which Holiday Inn relied too heavily on relationships rather than contracts.

Best Practices Roundup

☑ *Design shared global systems with flexibility for local tailoring.*[204] Design core global applications to consider that each country needs to modify core applications to support local requirements. Consider migrating these changes into the core systems to reduce the maintenance burden on the local IS shops. The many issues to consider include: different accounting needs, different tax laws, local legal and regulatory differences, different fonts (for different language scripts), different (spoken) languages, local and multiple currency issues (e.g., the euro), time representations (support multiple time zones by expressing time in terms of UTC, Coordinated Universal Time, plus the offset, including fractional offsets). Finally, develop a methodology to describe business rules in each country.

☑ *Allocate time in the development cycle for translations.* Translation can become a bottleneck unless properly managed, particularly for multilingual requirements gatherings. Business analysts may be biding their time while waiting for key documents to be translated.

☑ *Provide training at remote IS shops.* Vendor support is less accessible in many countries, so investment in on-site training will help distant teams keep up to date.

☑ *Actively develop a program of "constructive engagement" to improve cooperation among headquarters IS, the global development units, and the (sometimes reluctant) local IS subsidiaries.* Change budget allocation to support global applications. Present the business case for global initiatives (local units need to see that an initiative benefits them as well as the corporation at large). Keep the subsidiary IS units well informed of the global business and systems strategy. Institute liaisons at subsidiary IS units to the CGAs.

☑ *Address churn when outsourcing to India.* Churn, or high staff turnover, is the most frustrating component of a relationship with an Indian outsourcer. This can be partially addressed by hiring more mature programmers, by paying higher wages, by developing closer relations with the Indian staff, by instilling a sense of loyalty to the parent company, and through innovative contractual clauses with the third party outsourcer. Be aware that investment in training is a double-edged sword: It enhances work, but makes the developers more marketable and more likely to jump ship.

Further Reading

Still the most comprehensive book on global information system is Ed Roche's *Managing Information Technology in Multinational Corporations.* New York, NY: MacMillan, 1992.

The definitive book on India's software industry, with its focus on contracting and outsourcing, is Richard Heeks, *India's Software Industry: State Policy, Liberalisation, and Industrial Development.* Thousand Oaks, CA: Sage Publications, 1996. Also see Heeks' web site on the topic at http://www.man.ac.uk/idpm/isi.htm.

A METHODOLOGY FOR DEFINING GLOBAL INFORMATION SYSTEMS & DESIGNING GLOBAL IS TEAMS

The PSR methodology presented in this chapter drives corporate IS decision makers to design the global IS teams only after carefully identifying the corporation's global processes and systems worldwide. The chapter presents a step-by-step walkthrough of the PSR (Process/System/Responsibility) methodology for global applications. Process identifies the organization's core global business processes. The second stage, System, identifies the systems needed to support the handful of global business processes. The third, Responsibility, determines what type of team will be responsible for each of the global application systems. Building and maintaining any one of the global systems usually call for a central, permanent unit that is referred to as the *Center for Global Applications* (CGAs; see Chapter 12). Depending on the organizational requirements and constraints, this Center may be co-located, transnational, or virtual.

PSR—Process/System/Responsibility

A comprehensive approach—a methodology—is needed to support the global corporation's rationalization of its hodgepodge of decentralized systems. The objective of the IS function's transition is to bring about an

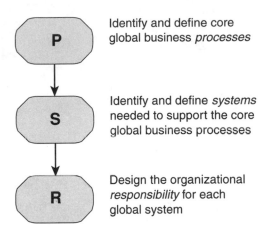

Exhibit 13–1   Process/System/Responsibility: A methodology for identifying and supporting global applications.

Integrated Network (Chapter 12) IS structure that is better aligned with the corporation's global competitiveness. The Integrated Network IS organizational form is based on a common global architecture and telecommunication backbone, uniform global systems with flexible modules tailored to address local requirements, CGA development with responsibility for worldwide systems, and a culture of shared management, shared application building, and shared innovation.

PSR is a methodology for rethinking (and often redesigning) those processes deemed global and redesigning the teams that will develop, roll-out, and support the systems for those global processes. The outcome of PSR's final stage is a redesign of IS teams' responsibility at multiple corporate sites. Clearly, this is organizationally radical. Implementing PSR requires strong support at executive levels inside and outside the IS function. Each of the three stages of the PSR methodology is described here in sequence.[205]

Stage 1: "P" (for Process). Identify and define core global business processes
The essence of this stage is to identify business processes and then ask: Is it a global process? If yes, then it is a candidate for a global information systems application.

A more precise explanation of a *core global business process* is best grasped by parsing the three key terms: core, global, and process. Core processes are those that are absolutely critical to the organization. Global processes are those that are used in multiple markets—they are not solely regional or local. Finally, a process is a set of logically related tasks performed to achieve a defined business outcome (for example, shipping orders to customers).

There are several useful rules of thumb for identifying core global processes. First, as with re-engineering approaches, it is important to think cross-functionally and to stay away from deliberating about processes along traditional, vertical functional areas (e.g., marketing, manufacturing) because these will often be too narrow and parochial. Second, some systems are *a priori* unlikely to be global, such as payroll. Others are likely be global candidates, such as sourcing, customer interaction, inventory, or financial reporting. Third, a global firm is likely to have somewhere between two and six global business processes. For example, US-based Caterair (the systems unit of Caterair International, formerly Marriott's In-Flite Services Division, which delivers food to many airlines around the world) identified two core global processes: production planning and control and, separately, the dispatch function. Finland-based Nokia Telecommunications (Nokia's division responsible for designing and installing multimillion dollar telecommunications systems) also identified two core global processes: the product process, from identification of needs to launch; and the customer commitment process, from tendering to order-delivery.

Formal approaches can be useful for identifying global processes. After all, this stage deals with defining and mapping processes and lends itself to modeling techniques quite well. One such comprehensive approach is to conduct a workflow analysis looking for all tasks that achieve a defined business outcome, such as shipping out orders to customers, or delivering innovative products to the market. Another formal approach is to rely on standard business models such as the "value chain" model, which defines the inputs, processes, and outputs of a business.

The output of the Process Stage is a short list of a handful of core global business processes along with their respective descriptions.

Stage 2: "S" for System. Identify and define systems needed to support the core global business processes

The essence of this stage is to define the system(s) to support each core global business process.

Stage 2 begins by defining a set of functional requirements for each of the core global business processes uncovered in Stage 1. It is best to perform this task first in the abstract, without regard to the current systems in place since these existing systems were often built as narrow, functional systems. The output of this task is a detailed description of each of the global processes.

In parallel, the IS unit needs to compile a comprehensive inventory of current applications, systems, and systems owners. This task does not have to be done in sequence and may begin in parallel to Stage 1. The outcome of this task is a system inventory.

By combining the two task outputs—the global business process list and the system inventory—each system is then mapped (allocated) to one of the global business processes. The mapping process uncovers four categories of current information systems: 1) those that fall completely within one of the global business processes; 2) those that span processes and may require re-allocation; 3) those that are not global and require local or regional support; 4) the gap areas—global business processes and subprocesses that are not currently supported by any existing information system.

The mapping process will uncover redundant worldwide systems, as well as global systems deemed "Best-in-breed" or "Best-in-firm." Perhaps the customer fulfillment system is superior in the US subsidiary, while the process control system is best in the Dutch subsidiary. Are they good enough to be rolled out worldwide? Do they have the flexibility and appropriate architecture to handle this? The European systems are more likely to be candidates for global roll-out because they are already sensitive to multi-currency and language issues.

From this mapping process emerges a new list of global business systems that includes the old and the new: current and future systems. The global IS teams, discussed in the next section, will then be fitted around this new mapping. Each team will have responsibility for a global system or global subsystem. The premise in the PSR methodology is that one—and only one—team be responsible for each piece of global functionality. Redundant applications in various subsidiaries are to be phased out. Ownership of the global components shifts from the local IS shop to elsewhere in the organization.

The final list of global systems will go through an iterative pruning process to make it more politically palatable. Two rules of thumb for pruning may be useful. First, keep the list of global applications short and doable. After all, global systems are costly. The costs are measured in the immense human resources needed to build and operate these systems. The costs are also measured in the length of time to deliver and implement. Also, the costs are measured in the organizational energy that these systems require. Second, avoid efforts that are too small or too large. Those that are too small lack the needed visibility, while those that are too grand are likely to fail. Some large projects may be broken down into more manageable chunks.

The output of the System Stage is a list of the corporation's global systems (with accompanying documentation of current supporting systems, future functional requirements, etc.).

Stage 3. "R" for Responsibility. Design the organizational responsibility for each global system

The essence of this stage is to define and design the global IS application team. This global IS team will be responsible for building and maintaining the global systems. The Responsibility stage includes decisions on locations of the teams, the scope of their responsibility, whom they report to, and their composition. This stage is the most ambitious and most difficult organizationally. The next section presents this stage and the menu of team choices available.

Types of Global IS Application Teams

Once global applications have been defined and mapped in the Process and System stages of the PSR methodology, it is time to define the organizational unit of responsibility for developing, implementing, and maintaining these global systems. These units are the *global IS application teams*. Teams are particularly important to global applications because lateral communication and cross-unit collaboration must be encouraged in global corporations where functional, divisional, and geographic preferences dominate. Teams tend to be more effective at cutting across the bureaucratic lines.

As with the previous stage, the first task in this stage is to conduct an inventory. However, this inventory is not of hardware, but an inventory of pockets of internal IS people capabilities worldwide. Perhaps the customer fulfillment application team is superior in the United States, while the process control specialists are best in Holland. Perhaps the customer call center application is already being de facto supported by scattered individuals: two programmers in Italy, one in Israel, a testing unit in Osaka, and a project manager in Berlin.

This assessment, labeled the *People Assessment,* needs to be made at two levels: an assessment of individuals and an assessment of current teams as a team unit (i.e., in some cases, IS people will be represented twice, as individuals and as team members). This bi-level assessment is needed because, as discussed shortly, one of the key team design choices is whether to build virtual teams or co-located teams.

The People Assessment must be multidimensional to include both hard skills and soft skills. Hard skills is the more obvious category and includes technical and application knowledge as well as experience, training, and education. The assessment must also include softer data such as managerial experience and flexibility, ability of individuals to work in cross-cultural and multicultural teams, as well as whether individuals will be open to travel, or foreign assignment.

Lastly, the People Assessment needs to come from multiple sources:[206] its data sources (e.g., via survey) need to be diverse geographically and hierarchically. The reason is straightforward: Headquarters IS decision makers will inevitably have biased views of some teams and some individuals. The bias is likely to err in both directions. For example, headquarters may not be aware of certain strengths in the European center, which the Asians and Latin Americans have known about for years. Also, headquarters may overrate the Florida team's performance. Determining the best team to be the foundation of a global applications units is an important decision. If headquarters makes uninformed decisions, it will end up building, not a center of global IS excellence, but a center of global IS mediocrity.

Once the People Assessment is complete, it is time to allocate individuals and teams to one or more of the various global IS team types that are displayed in the matrix of Exhibit 13–2.[207] The two axes have to do with time (horizontal axis) and location (the vertical axis). With respect to the time dimension, teams can be temporary or permanent. A temporary team brings together individuals for a limited time span—until the project is completed and the team is disbanded. A permanent team, or CGA, has ongoing responsibility for a global business system. The second axis has to do with location. A team can be co-located (all individuals are assigned from and work in the same site), a team can be dispersed (where two or more international sites are collaborating), or a team can be virtual (composed of dispersed individuals from different sites).

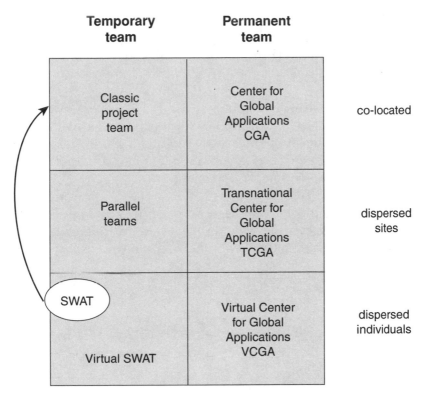

Temporary team | Permanent team

Exhibit 13–2 Global IS teams matrix.

The matrix' seven team types are introduced here and then discussed further below:

- *Classic project team.* Individuals are assigned from and work in the same site. The team is disbanded upon project completion.
- *Parallel teams.* Each team is chosen from *one* of the company sites to develop a subsystem. One subsystem is developed in each country and then integrated together with other subsystems. The team is disbanded upon project completion.
- *SWAT team.* A commando team of specialists, who are recruited from development sites worldwide for their expertise and parachuted into one location to complete a critical project. (SWAT is a term orig-

inally used in the US military for Special Weapons And Tactics and it has been adopted by the field of management to label any elite task team.) The IS SWAT team often uses variations on rapid application development (RAD). The team is disbanded upon project completion.

- *Virtual SWAT team.* A dispersed team of specialists, who are recruited from development sites worldwide for their expertise. The individuals remain in their respective locations and collaborate electronically, but may travel at various milestones or phases. The team is disbanded upon project completion.
- *Center for Global Applications (CGA).* The CGA team is chosen from *one* of the company sites to develop and be responsible for a global business system. The CGA has ownership of the global application and has responsibility for that application at worldwide locations.
- *Transnational Center for Global Applications (TCGA).* The TCGA team is chosen from *two or more* of the company sites to develop and be responsible for a global business system. The center is composed of subteams at each of the sites. The TCGA has ownership of the global application and has responsibility for that application at worldwide locations.
- *Virtual Center for Global Applications (VCGA).* The VCGA team is a dispersed team of specialists, recruited from development sites worldwide for their expertise. The individuals remain in their respective locations and collaborate electronically, but they may travel at various milestones or phases. The VCGA has ownership of the global application and has responsibility for that application at worldwide locations.

Selecting global IS team types requires analyzing various trade-offs and consideration of special issues peculiar to the organization. These issues are listed here and discussed below:

- Acceptance of long-term system ownership
- Selecting individuals versus teams
- Potential to create a cohesive team
- Preserving an organizational balance
- Managerial experience and interest in new team forms

- Time-to-completion
- Legacy architecture

The organizational stakeholders need to accept that one unit is assigned long-term system ownership. Generally, each system that was categorized as a "global system" (in the System stage of PSR) needs to be supported by a global IS team in CGA structure. In fact, many global corporations have begun experimenting with variations on this organizational form under various labels, such as *center of excellence* and *center of competence*. However, these corporate centers tend to be centers of *expertise*—of methodologies, best practices, or technologies, rather than centers of application development and support.

The CGA may take on any one of three location-related forms: co-located, transnational, or virtual. The CGA concept implies *long-term ownership* of the global system across multiple releases, rather than one of the more transient team types listed in the team matrix. The center has responsibility for continuous improvements to the system at worldwide locations. In contrast, the various temporary team types imply that some system ownership resides outside the teams themselves, with central IS or with local units. This separation leads to dilution: When there are multiple owners, there are effectively no owners. The CGA concept also means that budget is allocated for global rather than for one-site projects. Finally, the CGA concept means end-to-end responsibility for systems development—from requirements and enhancement requests through pilot testing, and global roll-out. A mission statement or charter legitimizes the CGA's responsibility and scope of authority.

As with any organizational change, there will be opposition to the CGA concept in general, or specific CGAs in particular. Four success factors will determine the CGA's long-term viability. First, it must be viewed as a more prestigious unit within the larger IS function, commanding the respect of an elite unit. Second, the CGA needs to report to a senior nonIS executive sponsor, preferably a line manager and global process owner. Third, the CGA's composition needs to be organizationally diverse. The CGA requires diversity that is multinational, multi-operational, and at multiple types of experience.[208] It is not so much for the diversity of ideas, but for the ability to establish consensus throughout the organization. The CGA and its members must craft their message slightly differently depending on the situation. Fourth, one and only one team develops each piece of global functionality. Redundant applications in various subsidiaries must be phased out. Ownership of these global components shifts from the local IS shop to the CGA.

The choice between a team of dispersed individuals (i.e., SWAT, virtual) and other team types boils down to whether the teams should be chosen based on the expertise of a team as a whole or on the expertise of individuals scattered at different sites. Both SWAT and virtual teams' main advantage is the ability to gather the company's best individual talent from around the world to work on a project. But selecting individuals may break apart existing work units, which, particularly in collectivist cultures (those outside the North American/North European axis) may be counter-productive. Co-located or dispersed sites contribute as coherent units or sub-units with established working relationships, while dispersed individuals have to form an entirely new work structure and relationship structure from scratch.

The newly created global IS team needs to function as a cohesive team. Team morale, or esprit de corps, is vital for an effective team. Cohesion is enhanced by the prestige of being in an elite, commando-like unit of the SWAT, or the selected experts of the Center for Global Applications. One assumption that needs to be carefully examined at the onset is that a team that already works well together will continue doing so once it becomes the core of a CGA. Harder to predict is how a team that is not physically co-located will perform. Those teams need to be artificially fused together, often cross-culturally. Instead of creating cohesion, the sites of a Transnational CGA may feel as if they are competing against one another (which can be both good and bad). Creating a sense of team cohesion is even more difficult for virtual teams, who need to develop working norms and relationships from scratch. Particularly acute is the SWAT team, which must be composed of individuals who perform well in a multiculturally diverse team.

The CGA concept is susceptible to the need for a natural organizational balance. Choosing just *one* site for a co-located CGA may be unpalatable for political reasons. If current expertise is skewed within the organization toward one or two sites in one or two countries, there will be IS units left without representation in a CGA—fueling resentment. Therefore, the Transnational CGA represents somewhat of a political compromise. Instead of one co-located site, two or more sites are chosen and fused together.

Most of the team types in the matrix are somewhat new organizational forms. Few IS managers are experienced with CGAs and SWATs. Virtual development teams are largely untested, particularly the Virtual CGA, in which individuals will be working remotely with others over many years rather than over a finite period. The most challenging position is the SWAT team leader—parachuted into a remote site for a project. The person in charge of that team has to be a true leader and not just a manager. There are very few of those in any organization.

Some teams perform development tasks faster than others. As a general rule, co-located teams will have shorter time-to-completion than will dispersed teams. SWAT teams are designed in a commando mode, to arrive and work quickly and professionally. The SWAT team concept is often combined with fast methodologies such as RAD.

Legacy system architectures were designed piecemeal and can be maintained effectively only by co-located teams who can problem-solve quickly and informally. A system with a brittle architecture should not be dispersed to two sites (as with Parallel teams or Transnational CGA). Of course, systems can be designed from the ground up to be modular and globally integrated, although few firms can afford this luxury in time and costs.

Global versus local application development decision processes can be routinized once the organizational mechanisms are in place for global coordination as this case illustrates:

> US-headquartered Seagate Technology has IS development centers in Thailand, Singapore, Malaysia, and the United States. At Seagate applications development decisions are cleared via a networked global database of applications, in order to avoid duplication. When a similar application is found on the database, its expert gives a remote tutorial of some kind to the interested team. If the interested team rejects the existing application and decides to propose a new system, an interesting process kicks in. At that point Seagate relies not on a committee, but on an outside consultant to endorse or reject the proposed system. Once the project is approved, the next step is to decide who develops it. In the case of the Thai local currency accounting system, it was clear that most resources and requirements were local, but some application package expertise was in the United States. One US expert took several long trips to Thailand to

work on the project. Meanwhile, coding was done with contractors in Bangalore, India, who worked over leased lines to Seagate's VAX computer in Singapore.[209]

Other specialized global IS teams

Global application development is not the sole activity for which corporations need global IS teams. Two other types of cross-border teams are required: global roll-out teams and global infrastructure teams.

Global roll-out teams.   Once the global application is in its final release phases, the global application team (e.g., the CGA) morphs and expands into another structure—into a roll-out structure. Members of the global unit begin to coordinate activities with local IS units via the selected local IS liaisons, the CGA Associates (described in Chapter 12), as well as additional personnel from the local IS units. Together, members of the global and local units form a temporary project team—a roll-out team—to tailor, test, install, and launch the application. Members of the global unit are parachuted to the various global sites to work together with the local units. This roll-out sequence of coordination/parachute/launch/return-to-base is staggered throughout worldwide units.

Global Infrastructure teams.   Global infrastructure teams roll-out global standards and platforms—from e-mail to Lotus Notes to PictureTel, from NT to IP WANs. Global applications teams (those responsible for core global processes described above) are somewhat different from global infrastructure teams. Whereas global application processes are relatively stable, infrastructure building projects tend to be shorter in duration (up to two years). While global process applications require work upfront on design and coding, infrastructure projects are focused on roll-out. Global Infrastructure teams resemble the roll-out teams described previously in the common modus operandi of coordination/parachute/launch/return-to-base. Some corporations designate Global Infrastructure teams as Centers of Excellence.

Best Practices Roundup

☑ *Build Centers for Global Applications around core global business systems (and not the project du jour).* The CGA has ongoing responsibility for a global business system that does not go away when a project is complete. The CGA structure and mandate give the team stability, responsibility, resources, coherence, and pride in its work.

☑ *Approach the design of Centers for Global Applications methodically.* Following a comprehensive methodology, such as the PSR methodology described in this chapter, leads to better organizational designs. Perform a corporate IS People Assessment at the final stage of the PSR methodology to identify the individuals and the teams at the level of global "excellence." Do not create inflation in the number of global centers. If there are too many, they become centers of global mediocrity rather than global excellence.

☑ *Invest in the human side of the Center for Global Applications.* Think of the CGA as a multimillion dollar system that needs constant care and feeding. Invest in training, in travel for face to face work, in team celebrations, and in team symbols. Invest in a network of CGA Associates at subsidiary IS units.

HOLIDAY INN'S 'A PASSAGE TO INDIA'

by
Kuldeep Kumar [210]
Professor in Information Management, Erasmus University, Netherlands

Leslie Willcocks
University Lecturer and Fellow, Oxford Institute of Information Management, Templeton College, University of Oxford, United Kingdom

Acquisition and the Move to Atlanta

In 1992, United Kingdom-based Bass plc, as a part of its ongoing strategy of diversification and expansion, acquired the Memphis, Tennessee-based Holiday Inn hotel chain. Immediately after the acquisition, Bass plc decided to move Holiday Inn head offices from Memphis to Atlanta, Georgia, for a number of reasons. First, Atlanta's location as an airline hub with direct connections to most international and US cities provided Bass and Holiday Inn executives convenient and direct access to their worldwide locations. Second, the highly developed telecommunications infrastructure in Atlanta provided Holiday Inn with a suitable technological base for developing their own worldwide communication network. Third, with a vigorous business climate, a large number of corporate head offices, a large business applications software industry, and four world class universities, Atlanta provided a ready pool of trained business and technical talent. Fourth, the availability of high quality office space in Atlanta at reasonable prices meant that appropriate office space could be acquired. Finally, Atlanta's growing reputation as a cosmopolitan, international city meant a high quality of life for Holiday Inn's local and international executives and employees.

To house its corporate headquarters in a building befitting its image as an international corporation, Holiday Inn acquired a major property on the North Side of the city. The property, called the Ravinia, consisted of a complex of modern office buildings among a forest of tall green trees. This complex included the former Hyatt Regency Ravinia hotel, which was converted into the flagship Holiday Inn Crowne Plaza Hotel. The new Holiday Inn executive offices were in the next building. Despite the attractiveness of the new locale, about 80% of the IS/IT staff from Memphis decided not to relocate to Atlanta. No specific reasons for the unwillingness of this large number of people to move are available. However, it is our conjecture that despite Memphis being larger than Atlanta, the latter had a reputation as a big city (rated world's fourth best city for international business by Fortune magazine in November 14th, 1994), and Memphis employees were reluctant to leave a relatively cosy smaller-city atmosphere and also face higher cost of living and real estate prices. Most of the operational staff (operators, programmers, analysts) and the senior staff (CIO and assistant vice-presidents) did not relocate to Atlanta.

Consequently, Holiday Inn hired a number of new senior and lower-level IS/IT staff. At the senior executive level, they recruited Dick Smith from Memphis-based Federal Express and appointed him as the Sr. VP/CIO of Information Systems. Smith brought Greg Tollander with him from Federal Express and appointed him as the Holiday Inn vice president of technology and operations. Michael Kennedy, an executive from the Holiday Inn user community, was recruited as the vice president in charge of applications and strategic systems. Through an appointment to the Bass plc executive committee, and in keeping with his role as the CIO, Smith was connected closely to the Bass decision-making structure. Consequently, a large percentage of his time was spent in working with Bass headquarters. At the same time he had considerable autonomy in running the Holiday Inn IS/IT operation. Most of the day-to-day operational and tactical IS/IT decisions were made by Kennedy and Tollander.

Unlike the senior and operational staff, most personnel at the middle management level did relocate from Memphis to Atlanta. Holiday Inn hired one new middle-level manager, Daniel Newton, from outside Holiday Inn. Originally hired as the Senior Manager of Databases, in 1994 Newton was promoted to Director of Strategic Systems. The case concerns his group's experiences of outsourcing. A brief discussion of his background is provided as a context for understanding his decisions. He was recruited in 1993 from Lithonia Lighting, another Atlanta company. At Lithonia he had been a key player in the development and implementation of the innovative LightLink System. Thus he was experienced in building and implementing high profile strategic systems using advanced technologies. Prior to working at Lithonia Lighting, he had worked and studied in the United Kingdom. Newton was originally from Sri Lanka, a fact which could have been a factor in his willingness to experiment with offshore outsourcing.

Dealing with legacy issues: 1993–summer 1994

As indicated, the move from Memphis to Atlanta was a consequence of Holiday Inn being acquired by a UK firm—Bass plc. Moreover, 80% of the IS/IT staff and most of the top IS/IT management were recruited from outside immediately after the move. However, the middle management, along with the legacy systems and legacy data did move from Memphis to Atlanta. This made for a complex dynamic. While the people brought in from outside brought in new ideas and practices, they had to function within an established framework of day-to-day management practices and technology brought over from Memphis.

An analysis of the Holiday Inn data very quickly established that the usual problems of legacy data, data fragmentation, data redundancy, lack of data integration, and lack of consistency in data quality, access, and security standards also existed in the Holiday Inn data files. As a result of this analysis, Newton initiated a new Database Re-engineering project. The objective of this project was to develop an enterprise data model for Holiday Inn worldwide. Based upon this data model, the existing corporate data would be converted to a relational (DB2) database. This step would be followed by modification and rewriting of all legacy software interfacing with the relational database. Given the strategic and operational importance of data to Holiday Inn, Newton also set a very high ambition level for the project by establishing a goal of completing the re-engineering in a one-year time frame. It is our conjecture that this ambitious time frame was partly motivated by Newton's desire to prove himself in a new job.

However, it should be recognized that the project did not involve any re-engineering of the underlying business practices. It was conceived primarily as a technical conversion project, in which existing files and databases were to be redesigned and implemented as an integrated relational database. Newton developed a database re-engineering strategy in which data models were to be reverse-engineered from existing file and database definitions, fragmented data views integrated, and the relational databases forward-engineered from these integrated data models. In addition, all legacy programs accessing these files were to be identified, and their data interfaces modified to accommodate the move to relational databases.

Very soon it became clear that except for Newton and a few others in his group, the IS/IT department at Holiday Inn had neither expertise nor headcount to undertake a project of this magnitude. The high labor turnover due to the move had left Holiday Inn critically short-handed. Furthermore, the remaining in-house staff lacked the data modeling and database redesign skills crucial to the project. It was apparent that creative strategies were needed to cope with this lack of expertise and human resources and the ambitious self-imposed deadline. A two-part strategy was developed to meet these challenges.

First, a set of computer-aided software engineering (CASE) tools were acquired to support the database re-engineering methodology. Originally Holiday Inn had acquired the Bachmann reverse-engineering tool. However, the limited scope of the Bachmann tool (it did not address the software re-engineering component of the project), coupled with the perceived high learning curve, resulted in its being supplanted by the LBMS CASE tool. The LBMS CASE tool was based upon the SSADM development methodology developed by LBMS. At that time, the SSADM was considered to be the de facto development standard in the UK data processing industry. It is likely that Newton's UK-based training and experience and the parent company Bass plc's UK roots had some influence on this decision.

The second part of the strategy was to rely on outside consulting firms to supply the necessary expertise and labor. Accordingly, after a short search, two firms, California-based Codd and Date Associates, and Bangalore, India-based CompTech were engaged to support the project.

Codd and Date Associates, a consulting firm founded by the two relational database pioneers E.F. Codd and Chris Date, was hired based upon the reputation of its principals. CompTech, an Indian DP consulting firm founded in 1982 by seven Indian IS professionals, was hired based upon its cost estimates and an excellent reputation with offshore clients. CompTech had clients and offices in Tokyo, Sydney (Australia), Maastricht (The Netherlands), Boston, and San Francisco. They also had a local Atlanta presence through half ownership of a joint venture firm with another Atlanta management consulting company, Kurt Salmon Associates. Krishna Patil, one of the seven founding partners of CompTech, represented CompTech in this joint venture firm and also provided high-level liaison between Holiday Inn and CompTech.

While Codd and Date Associates were to supply database programming as well as logical database analysis and design expertise, CompTech's original role was to supply programmers for modifying and/or rewriting the legacy programs. Classic "body-shop" or "insourcing" arrangements characterized both consulting contracts. Codd and Date and CompTech were to supply the necessary labor that would then be deployed under the Holiday Inn (Newton's) management and control. CompTech, however, did supply an onsite project manager/coordinator to coordinate with Holiday Inn's requirements and to help manage their CompTech's staff.

The contracts themselves were not very specific as to the services to be provided by the vendor. Newton reasoned that given the complex and reciprocal nature of the re-engineering task, and the relative uniqueness of the re-engineering process, specific and detailed requirements could not be developed in advance. He expected that by developing a working relationship with the vendors, Holiday Inn and the vendors should mutually be able to adjust to the evolving requirements. At this point it should be recognized that while each of the parties brought complementary expertise to the project, none of them had any actual experience in integrating all these components of the strategy into a database re-engineering project of this magnitude and ambition. While Newton had devised the overall strategy, methodology, and CASE tools to support the project, the details of the methodology and project tasks could only be filled in as the project evolved. Thus, rather than using prespecified outcome standards or process standards as coordination mechanisms, he decided to rely upon mutual adjustment and personal supervision as the primary coordination strategies.

Evolving and deteriorating relationships: 1994

The working relationship with Codd and Date Associates went quickly downhill. The firm was not accustomed to working in an evolving recipro-cal environment and insisted upon detailed prespecification of all work. Furthermore, Newton felt that Codd and Date were not supplying ade-quately trained people for the project, that the quality of effort and work delivered by Codd and Date was below par. Although work was con-tracted with and paid for in advance, Newton felt that Codd and Date was unable to deliver on promises, and the relationship was dissolved.

On the other hand, as the working relationship with CompTech matured, Holiday Inn (Newton) realized that CompTech had design and project management expertise beyond straight programming skills. The CompTech project manager was brought into the DB design process. The actual database re-design and software re-engineering process was inter-leaved. While the components of the relational database were being re-designed, specifications were produced on an ongoing basis for program re-design, and programs were modified or rewritten as needed. The close working relationship between Newton's group and onsite CompTech per-sonnel, coupled with the CompTech project manager's involvement with the logical design team, meant that CompTech could anticipate Holiday Inn's needs and adjust its services and staff assignments on an ongoing basis. CompTech pulled out all stops to service the Holiday Inn account. They brought in a number of experienced and qualified programmers and analysts from India to support the re-engineering effort. Newton's satisfac-tion with and trust in CompTech had grown to the point that he started mentioning the CompTech's project manager as his own man.

New problems

However, by this time some new problems were becoming evident. First, CompTech realized that although the cost of Indian programmers in India was low, when they were brought to the United States, the cost of trans-portation, housing, and per diem expenses quickly increased these costs to be at par with the costs of local consulting firms. Thus, competing on costs alone was not feasible. Next, about this time there was a tightening of US regulations on issuing visas to foreign professionals. US professional asso-ciations were lobbying against the entry of foreign programmers. As a re-sult the US embassy in India made it very difficult for Indian IS/IT firms to obtain work permits for Indian professionals to work in the United States.

Finally, some signs of tensions were beginning to appear between the regular Holiday Inn staff and the Indian expatriates. These tensions seemed to be the result of cultural differences between the two groups.

While the Indians' knowledge of English has been a key advantage for the Indian software industry, the cultural differences between the US and Indian IT professionals became apparent when they met face to face. First, the work style of Indian programmers and analysts was very different from that of their American counterparts. Compared to most US professionals who had acquired their expertise on the job, most of the Indian professionals had formal, graduate level training in development methodologies. Thus, while the work style of the Americans relied upon informally learnt practices and improvisation, the Indian work style reflected a greater degree of methodology formalism. Second, being away from home, the Indians did not have as many day-to-day living concerns as their US counterparts. Thus they tended to devote longer hours to work and in general worked harder. One of the senior Holiday Inn executives remarked that a new plantation culture seemed to be developing at Holiday Inn. Finally, with their foreign accents, habits, and color, the Indians were a very visible reminder of the foreigner taking away US jobs.

From Insourcing to Offshore Outsourcing: Passage to India

The increasing costs of maintaining a staff in the United States and the problems associated with obtaining visas for its staff prompted CompTech to seek alternatives to bringing Indian professionals into the States. With Holiday Inn's concurrence, they decided to move their programming staff back to CompTech headquarters in Bangalore, India and work on the programming tasks from India.

Four issues were associated with the move. First, as the process of developing program re-engineering specifications, developing the programs, and testing them was an interactive process involving both Holiday Inn and CompTech staff, mechanisms were needed for the "to and fro" transfer of specifications, software, test data, and test results. Second, as the personnel involved in the process could no longer interact face to face, direct clarification of the usual specification ambiguities and incomplete specifications was no longer possible. Third, as the Indian staff was now halfway around the world, direct supervision of the staff was no longer feasible. Finally, the 10½-hour difference in time zones between

Atlanta and Bangalore meant that the normal working hours at the two lo-cations did not overlap. The coordination procedures needed to take these geographical and time differences into account.

A combination of technical, procedural, and administrative mecha-nisms were established to resolve some of these issues. First, a high-speed data link (a T1 line) was set up between Atlanta and Bangalore to transfer specifications, programs, and test results. To utilize the expensive line ca-pacity, CompTech shared this line with another offshore outsourcing proj-ect it was conducting for another major corporation in the United States. Second, both Holiday Inn and CompTech decided to use the LBMS CASE tool as a basis for communicating specifications. The use of the CASE tool formalized and standardized the specification process, thereby reducing some of the ambiguities and imprecision of informal specifications. Fi-nally, a common time window was established such that the Holiday Inn staff in Atlanta could communicate in real-time with CompTech staff in Bangalore, India. They communicated usually by telephone, but also via faxes and the high-speed data link when necessary.

By summer of 1994 these mechanisms were in place and seemed to be working well. CompTech's human resources costs were under control and the visa problems considerably reduced. There was another un-expected bonus. The 10½-hour time difference was exploited by the re-engineering team to reduce the delivery time. As the working hours of the American and Indian teams no longer overlapped, each team could pass work to the other to be worked on by the other team overnight, and shipped back next morning via the transmission lines. This in effect meant that project work could now be performed around the clock, thereby re-ducing the delivery times considerably.

Departures and developments: autumn 1994–summer 1995

During this period a number of new developments took place at Holiday Inn and CompTech, which affected the course of the project. On the Holi-day Inn side, a number of senior IS/IT executives left Holiday Inn. Mike Kennedy, vice president in charge of applications and strategic systems, left Holiday Inn to accept a senior position at another hotel chain. Greg Tollander, the vice president of operations, also left Holiday Inn. Dick Smith, now the executive vice-president of IS/IT, was involved primarily in strategic issues and setting up a Holiday Inn IS/IT subsidiary. This left the middle managers, previously from Memphis, very much in charge of day-to-day operations of the IS/IT group.

Daniel Newton decided to form his own consulting firm with Phil Fasone, senior manager of IS quality and methodology at Holiday Inn. He tendered his resignation to Dick Smith who asked him to stay on until the database re-engineering project was completed. For some time Newton worked in a dual capacity, running his consulting firm and managing the strategic systems group at Holiday Inn. Finally, in the spring of 1995 he resigned from Holiday Inn to manage his company "PowerSolv" on a full-time basis. His clients from that date included some user groups in Holiday Inn.

During this timeframe CompTech was also undergoing major changes. First, CompTech decided to dissolve its Atlanta-based joint venture by selling its shares in the joint venture to its former partnering company, Kurt Salmon Associates. Second, CompTech decided to focus on developing and marketing logistics and distribution software packages. It recalled Patil, CompTech's founding partner in Atlanta, to head up the research and product development group in Bangalore. Thus the high-level liaison between CompTech and Holiday Inn no longer existed. Third, in the summer of 1994 CompTech went public on the Bombay stock exchange and within a week its stock was trading at ten times the initial opening price. This surge in stock prices reflected the strong growth in new business for CompTech. This growth was putting additional demands on CompTech's human resources. As a result CompTech reassigned people from the Holiday Inn project to other projects and replaced them with new personnel. Given this rapid growth, the change of focus to package software development, and the closing of its Atlanta office, Holiday Inn was no longer a significant account for CompTech.

By early 1995 the situation had started to deteriorate. As Newton was no longer in face to face contact with the Indian team, he was not aware of the personnel changes in Bangalore. Only after a few software conversions blew up did Newton become aware that the original CompTech staff, experienced with Holiday Inn systems, were no longer working on the project. They had been replaced by relatively inexperienced newcomers. While in the past Newton could rely on the Indian project manager's and team's intimate understanding of the project requirements, the new staff needed detailed specifications. An example mentioned by Newton illustrates this point. CompTech was assigned to create a certain set of relational tables by combining data from a variety of sources. Newton maintains that persons familiar with the requirements of the re-engineering project would have developed a customized merge utility that would check for duplicate records, inconsistent data, missing data, and unacceptable data before this data was loaded onto the relational database. The inexperienced CompTech staff instead used a standard merge utility without these checks to create the relational tables, thereby corrupting the database. The problem was found only after reports based upon this data were distributed to Holiday Inn sites worldwide.

This incident also illustrates another problem. While these staffing changes were being made by CompTech in its Bangalore Holiday Inn team, Newton and his staff were no longer closely monitoring the work produced by CompTech. Newton admits that he became a bit too comfortable with CompTech and therefore started relying upon them for interpreting the specifications and monitoring the quality of the results. It is also likely that during this time Newton was preoccupied with other priorities and thus was not as careful as he would have otherwise been.

By spring 1995 Newton had left Holiday Inn to form his own consulting company. One of his major clients was the marketing group at Holiday Inn who retained him to develop and implement a Data Warehouse for strategic marketing information. In this case he worked directly with the marketing group and not through the IS/IT department. He still maintained a good relationship with Dick Smith who became increasingly involved with Holiday Inn's plan for spinning off an information technology based subsidiary. As mentioned above, except for Smith, most of the senior staff hired from outside after the move had left Holiday Inn by mid-1995. Newton's relationships with the remaining IS/IT group at the Holiday Inn were not so cordial. The Database re-engineering project was complete by mid-1995. Glory Cung, Newton's right-hand man and the key analyst on the database re-engineering project, who was also brought in from outside, had also left Holiday Inn to form his own consulting company. CompTech has been retained by Holiday Inn to maintain the software it helped modify and develop.

Despite his problems with CompTech, Newton believed that offshore outsourcing had great potential. He suggested that where coordination and monitoring problems were recognized and solved, the combination of lower costs, higher quality, and reduced cycle times would make it profitable for firms to use offshore personnel.

A

RESEARCH & DATA COLLECTION METHODOLOGY

This book is based on a long-term research study called the *Globally Dispersed Software Development* study and referred to as the *GDSD* study throughout the book. The study's research and data collection are presented in this appendix.

Composition

Number of sites. The research consisted of 20 projects at 17 different firms. The sites represented 20 countries (as listed in Exhibit A–1). The unit of analysis—the case—was a project, usually referred to as a version or release cycle by software organizations.

Headquarters and degree of US influence. Most companies were US-headquartered (75%). The exception cases to US-headquartered firms were companies headquartered in Finland, France, Israel, and the Netherlands. The vast majority of projects (95%) had at least one US development team. Of the US-headquartered firms, 33% of the projects were managed primarily from outside the United States.

Number of sites per team. In order to qualify as one of the cases, the threshold requirement was that there be at least two sites collaborating across an international border. In fact, in 55% of the cases, there were development sites in at least three nations. Additionally,

Belarus

Belgium

Brazil

Britain

Bulgaria

Canada

China

Finland

France

Germany

India

Israel

Japan

Latvia

Netherlands

Norway

Russia

Sweden

Switzerland

United States

Exhibit A–1   Countries with Sites in the Study's Data Set.

most of the US firms had multiple sites within the United States, although not all were involved in the specific project in focus.

Project/Product Type. Seventy-five percent of the cases were of packaged software development projects (also known as software products). The other cases were either information systems (IS) or embedded software.

Company Size. Of the packaged software firms, four appeared in the top 10 of Software Magazine's Software 500, and 10 appeared in the top 100. Rankings make use of the July 1997 list, which was based on 1996 revenues. Note that the listing includes software divisions of hardware companies (e.g., IBM) as well as some professional service firms.

Timeframe. Data collection and interviews took place between 1995 and 1998 and covered projects completed during this period or just prior to it.

Unit of analysis. A case was one project, one release cycle, or one software development cycle for one product.

Identification of teams

There is no registry for global software teams. Hence, identification and contacts came from professional and personal networks, as well as from informational leads from the trade press and web sites. For the primary segment of the study, namely, packaged software organizations, companies were selected based on a diversity of company size and team/site location. For example, after a majority of the initial cases ended up having primary collaboration with an Indian site, special efforts were made to include collaborative efforts that took place in other countries in order to create a more diverse view. Firm size covered the range of small to largest—from a one million dollar firm to a few of the top five software organizations. Within each company, the project and the eventual interviewees were identified through iterative discussions with contacts at each firm. Long lead times—as much as a year and more—sometimes took place between initial contact and the actual research interview.

Anonymity. All firms were pledged anonymity in exchange for their cooperation. This is standard practice in research that is academic rather than journalistic. Hence, many of the anecdotes in this book do not use real names. Specifically, the following company names are aliases: Arizona Systems, Bordeaux Associates, Contemporary Sciences, Ivory Systems, Magnetix, NetParadise, Orchestral Technologies, PrestigeSoft, Rose Software, Sensory Systems, Sharp Applications, Strategisoft, VisiBusiness. Some anecdotes and descriptions of cases are disguised slightly to preserve anonymity.

Nonresponse. The danger in any kind of sample is that those you do *not* sample represent a very different story from those who were willing to spend their time with an interviewer. This is unlikely here because, in spite of the relatively small sample, the software companies represent a cross-section based on many dimensions. While not all doors opened, these cases were relatively few. Legitimately, software managers are extremely busy people. On occasion, I waited a year or more until they had some time to talk.

Data collection

Company data were collected via direct interviews with executives, managers, team leads, or members of the global software team either in person or by telephone. In order to insure triangulation and increase objectivity, a research goal for all the packaged software cases was to interview one key person from every country site. For example, for a team with sites in the United States and India, two respondents were interviewed, one from each site. When the project was based in three countries, three interviews were the goal. This triangulation was done in most, but not all, packaged software cases. In all there were 32 interviews totaling roughly 70 hours.

In-person interviews have several benefits over the typical social science alternatives of mail-based questionnaires: First, the data tend to be more reliable due to the ability to explain questions and answers. Second, interviews uncover and underline explanations that cannot be established by questionnaire methodology alone, which is important in new management domains such as this one.

Interviews were conducted with a five-page questionnaire, which was intended as an interview guide and not as a written, check-the-boxes type questionnaire. In social science lingo, this is a semi-structured survey approach. All interviews were recorded and then transcribed. Within a project, second and third interviewees were not asked all questions.

Respondent bias is a risk in this type of study. Respondents were often the managers who had their jobs on the line to make the global move succeed. Not surprisingly, most saw their projects as successful. When more than one global project was taking place at a company, the interview was steered toward the more ambitious and complex project/release cycle. This project selection probably forced more problems to surface, but it may not be representative of all cross-border projects. Separately, the multiple interview method, rather than a single interview per project, has two advantages: a) it removed some respondent bias from the data; b) the additional respondent(s) introduced new issues to the story that the first respondent may have omitted.

DIFFERENCES BETWEEN IS
& PACKAGED SOFTWARE
DEVELOPMENT TEAMS

The bulk of this book is about teams that develop packaged software, while Part IV is specifically about global Information Systems (IS) teams. Since they both develop software, why make this distinction at all? Do the differences between these two team types warrant this distinction?

The answer is that, yes, there are marked differences in how these two types of organization develop software.[211] Fundamentally, they operate in a different milieu. The first and most important dimension to consider is where the two types of development units reside inside the organization. Packaged software developers develop the *core* products of the company—in most respects their environment is that of an R&D organization. In contrast, IS development groups provide a *support* function. In the cultural lingo of Chapter 5, these two types operate in two different functional cultures (a functional culture consists of those norms associated with functional roles within the organization such as marketing, sales, finance, R&D, and manufacturing).

Because of these industry and organizational differences, packaged software development managers can get resources and move quickly on decisions; IS development managers operate in a cost-sensitive environment and implement their decisions through consensus building. Packaged software developers work in an industry with a strong entrepreneurial ethos; IS developers operate in a relatively more bureaucratic, stable environment. The packaged software team generally integrates design and development, while the IS team is likely to separate these two tasks into fairly distinct stages. Most packaged software development teams have very little to do with users and customers because they are shielded by marketing and other functions; IS developers work more closely with their users in requirements gathering and, later, in roll-out. Table B–1 summarizes these and other differences.

Seemingly, this account does not address the huge sector of embedded software development. Actually, embedded software teams resemble packaged software teams in many of the characteristics described above. Teams in either of these industries are product organizations rather than support organizations.

Table B–1   Generalized Differences Between IS and Packaged Software Development Teams

Packaged Software	Information Systems
Line positions	Support positions
Time to market pressures	Cost pressures
Success measures: profit, market share	Success measures: user satisfaction, user acceptance
User is distant and less involved	User is closer and more involved
Somewhat integrated design and development	Distinct design and development
Design control via coordination	Design control via consensus-building
Less likely to have matrix structure	Matrix managed and project focused
Developers involved in entire development cycle	Developers assigned to multiple projects
Entrepreneurial	Bureaucratic
More cohesive, motivated, jelled	Work together as needed
Share a vision of their product(s)	Rely on formal specifications & documents

GLOSSARY OF KEY TERMS

Architecture The structure, or structures, of the software system that comprise software components, the externally visible properties of those components, and the relationships among them.

Asynchronous communication Communication that is not interactive (not at the same time), such as e-mail, voice mail, discussion lists, etc. Contrast this with synchronous communication (same time) such as videoconferencing, telephone, and regular face to face conversations.

Body shop Agencies in industrialized nations, such as the United States, that import programmers from India, China, and elsewhere and hire them out as temporary workers to professional services firms, corporations, and software companies. In the United States, most of the largest of these body shop agencies are Indian-owned or have strong Indian connections. Not surprisingly, a majority of the body shop employees are from India.

Build A process of generating a complete version of the end product from the master list of source code files that have been submitted by the developers. The build does not always work smoothly because not all programs will compile properly. Once the build is complete, then all developers can work, evaluate, and test a reasonably stable version of the work-in-process. Some companies try to do a daily build; others settle for less frequent builds. The frequency of builds increases as the product nears completion.

Capability Maturity Model (CMM)   Introduced by the Software Engineering Institute at Carnegie-Mellon University (USA), it legitimized the notion of "process maturity" in software engineering. The CMM is made up of five increasing levels of maturity to describe an organization's software development capabilities.

CASE   Computer Aided Software Engineering tools used to aid programmers in coordinating their development activities, maintain quality, and apply consistent methodologies.

Coordination   The act of integrating each task and organizational unit so that it contributes to the overall objective.

Control   The process of adhering to goals or policies or standards.

Center for Global Applications (CGA)   A development center with long-term *ownership* of a system that is deemed to be global.

CT-SE (Collaborative Technology to support Software Engineering)   A potpourri of tools and functions used by designers and developers to support the software development effort. Examples include: Software Configuration Management, Project Management, Computer Aided Software Engineering. Since these are all group programs, they are labeled CT-SE in this book to distinguish them from generic, nontask specific collaborative technology such as e-mail.

Daily Build   See *Build.*

Designer   A generic term that is increasingly used to encompass those involved in design activities such as systems analysts.

Developer   A generic term that is increasingly replacing the term programmer since many programmers engage in many other tasks besides programming (coding).

Embedded software   A category of software found in cars, VCRs, specialized instruments, etc.

Expatriate   Someone on foreign assignment for at least one year.

GDSD study (Globally Dispersed Software Development)   The reference used in this book to a multi-year study led by the author.

Groupware   A term used to describe generic software suites that include many of the collaborative technology features packaged together: e-mail, document repositories, discussion lists, calendars, and workflow automation.

High context and low context cultures A cultural classification that defines how people communicate—how they view language. Language is neutral and explicit for low context cultures, and emotional and implicit for high context cultures. High context cultures, such as the Latins, the Arabs, and the East Asians, communicate a message in which most of the information is in the person, the surroundings, and the social perspective. Much of what is communicated is not said.

ISO 9000 A set of quality standards from the International Standards Organization.

Lateral communication Communication between team members across the organization rather than through the formal hierarchy.

Localization The act of modifying software to the needs of the local market: creating manuals, translating on-line help and menus, and sometimes making special release versions for large markets (such as China or Japan).

Location transparency Elimination of the perception of distance through technology.

Low context See *High context.*

Methodology A systematic approach to conducting at least one complete phase (e.g., design) of software production, consisting of a set of guidelines, activities, techniques, and tools, based on a particular philosophy of system development and the target system. Examples include: Information Engineering, Unified Modeling Language.

Offshore programming (or offshore development) Seeking foreign professional services for coding and other software tasks outside the home country.

Organizational memory See *Team memory.*

Outsourcing A contractual arrangement whereby a firm employs a contractor to be entirely responsible for some or all aspects of its information systems functions. Outsourcing received wide attention in the late 1980s when US-based Kodak was the first major firm to announce that most of its information systems tasks were to be outsourced.

Process maturity Software development that is conducted in a consistent fashion rather than ad hoc. That is, it is not based on the heroics of key individuals.

Process model A representation of the sequence of stages (e.g., design, build, test) through which a software product evolves. The term "methodology" is often used synonymously with "process model."

SCM See *Software Configuration Management.*

Site See *Team.*

Software Configuration Management (SCM) A software tool used to coordinate the work and assure quality when groups of programmers are dealing with thousands of objects (such as code). SCM core features include version control and check-in/check-out of programs.

Synchronous communication See *Asynchronous communication.*

Team Composed of developers and designers who develop the software product or system. The multiple ways in which the term *team* is used presented a problem in the context of this book. For consistency, a *team* consists of two or more (geographically dispersed) *sites.* This usage follows the definition of global software team in Chapter One. "A global software team is separated by a national boundary while actively collaborating on a common software/systems project." Clearly, an acceptable alternative usage of the term team is that a site consists of multiple teams—but that is one that is generally avoided in this book.

Team lead Short for "team leader." This is a common designation for the person leading the smallest unit of work in software organizations—a team lead commonly heads a team of two to ten developers.

Team memory A large, well-structured database of all team information: meeting notes, design memos, correspondence, project documents, discussions, etc. The database, or *repository,* as it is often referred to, is built from shared data and is accessible to any team member on an as-needed basis.

Virtual organization Entities from different organizations formed in a structure resembling a network that has a weak hierarchy and a weak center.

ENDNOTES

1. For more on the globalization of software, see: Jones, Capers. Globalization of software supply and demand. *IEEE Software* 11(6)(November 1994):17–24. Apte, Uday M. and Mason, Richard O. Global disaggregation of information-intensive services. *Management Science,* (July 1995), v41n7, 1250–62. Carmel, E. American hegemony in packaged software trade and the "culture of software." *The Information Society,* 13(1), (1997) 125–142. Barr, A. and Tessler, S. The globalization of software R&D: the search for talent. Position paper presented to the Council on Foreign Relations, (December 12, 1996). Available from the *Stanford Computer Industry Project,* Stanford University. Mowery, D.C. *The International Computer Software Industry: A Comparative Study of Industry Evolution and Structure* (1996) New York: Oxford Univ. Press. Ravichandran, R. and Ahmed, N. "Offshore Systems Development." *Information and Management* 24, (1993) 33–40.

2. Specifically the results from the GDSD study were: Seek specialized talent 53%; Acquisitions, 47%; Reduce development cost, 40%; Globalized presence, 40%; Reduce time to market, 13%; Customer proximity, 13%. Each project executive/manager could indicate more than one factor in responding to this issue and most did.

3. Embedded software is found in cars, VCRs, specialized instruments, etc.

4. Humphries, W. S. *Managing technical people: innovation, teamwork and the software process.* Reading, MA: Addison-Wesley, 1997.

5. For more on the software professional shortage, see *Business Week.* Forget the huddled masses: send nerds. (July 21, 1997) 110–116. Barr, A. and Tessler, S. The globalization of software R&D: the search for talent. Position paper presented to the Council on Foreign Relations, (December 12, 1996). Available from the *Stanford Computer Industry Project,* Stanford University.

6. ITAA report on the software labor shortage is available from http://www.itaa.org/.

7. *Ibid.* (The report was criticized for overestimating the demand for software positions by some.)

8. Rubin Systems reports available on the web at www.hrubin.com.

9. Frye, C. The Software 500. *Software Magazine* (June, 1998).

10. De Meyer, A. & Mizushima, A. Global R&D Management, *R & D Management,* vol. 19, no. 2, (1989) 135–146.

11. See von Hippel, E. *The Sources of Innovation* 2nd ed, New York: Oxford University Press, 1994, for the importance of working with lead customers. For a discussion specific to software see Keil, M. and Carmel, E. Customer-developer links in software development. *Communications of the ACM* (1995) 38(5) 33–44.

12. The GDSD study—for Globally Dispersed Software Development—is the basis for much data and many cases throughout the book. It is a study which I conducted in recent years. The study's research methodology is covered in Appendix A.

13. Niccolai, J. Success not a guarantee for remote projects. *Computerworld daily news flash* (on the web) (April 30, 1998).

14. Grenier Ray & George Metes. *Going Virtual: Moving your organization into the 21st century.* Upper Saddle River, NJ: Prentice Hall, 1995.

15. Galbraith, J.R. *Designing Organizations.* San Francisco: Jossey-Bass Publishers, 1995.

16. The table is based in part on Grenier Ray and George Metes. *Going Virtual: Moving your organization into the 21st century.* Upper Saddle River, NJ: Prentice Hall, 1995.

17. Carroll, P.B. 1991. How an IBM attempt to regain PC lead has slid into trouble. *Wall Street Journal,* (December 2, 1991) 1.

18. Industry estimates were based on: Frye, C. The Software 500. *Software Magazine* (June, 1998). Business Software Alliance *World Trends.* Washington DC: BSA. (1997). Leebeart, D. "News From the Frontiers," in Leebeart, D. (Ed), *The Future of Software,* Cambridge, MA: MIT Press, (1995), 1–28. Barr, A. and Tessler, S. The globalization of software R&D: the search for talent. Position paper presented to the Council on Foreign Relations, (December 12, 1996). Available from the *Stanford Computer Industry Project,* Stanford University. US global trade outlook 1995–2000. Washington D.C.: US Department of Commerce, 1995. Mowery, D.C. *The International Computer Software Industry: A Comparative Study of Industry Evolution and Structure.* New York: Oxford Univ Press, 1996.

19. Data were compiled by Mowery, D. C. *The International Computer Software Industry: A Comparative Study of Industry Evolution and Structure.* New York: Oxford Univ Press, 1996. Data were taken from the OECD and IDC.

20. Rubin, H.A. *Critical issues: the global software engineering and information technology competitiveness of the United States.* Report presented to the US Department of Commerce (March, 1997) available from Rubin Systems in Pound Ridge, New York; www.hrubin.com.

21. Hopkins, M. The antihero's guide to the new economy. *Inc.* (January 1998) 36–38.

22. Chiesa, V. Strategies for global R&D. *Research Technology Management* (September–October, 1996).

23. A comparison of software globalization with R&D globalization as well as manufacturing globalization appears in DuBois, F. & Carmel, E. Globalized Software Development: Roots in globalized R&D and global manufacturing. *Proceedings of Information Resources Management Association* (May, 1997) 54–60.

24. Suris, O. Behind the wheel. *Wall Street Journal* (November 18, 1996).

25. Recent statistics are from Lorenz, C. Global webs still spun from home. *Financial Times* (August 18, 1995). Background on global R&D is from: Ronstadt, R. *Research and Development abroad by US multinationals.* New York: Praeger Publications, (1977). De Meyer, A. & Mizushima, A. Global R&D Management, (1989) *R & D Management* vol. 19, no. 2, 135–146.

Pearson, A., Brockhoff, K., von Boehmer, A. Decision parameters in global R&D management. *R&D Management* (July 1993) v23n3, 249–262.

26. Exhibit 1–4 reflects the median percent for 10 projects (in 10 different companies). For illustration, in company A the two foreign sites consist of 39 developers and the one home site consists of 61 developers.

27. The names of two of the three cases are aliases.

28. At this writing, the IBM project is ongoing.

29. Yourdon, E. *The rise and resurrection of the American programmer.* Upper Saddle River, NJ: Yourdon Press, 1996.

30. Cusumano, M. A. and Selby, R. W. *Microsoft Secrets.* New York: The Free Press, 1995.

31. Rubin, H. A. *Critical issues: the global software engineering and information technology competitiveness of the United States.* Report presented to the US Department of Commerce, (March, 1997). Available from Rubin Systems in Pound Ridge, New York: www.hrubin.com.

32. De Meyer, A. & Mizushima, A. Global R&D Management, *R & D Management* vol. 19 no. 2, 135–146.

33. Melymuka, K, Conversation with Tom DeMarco. *Computerworld* (Dec. 4, 1995), 108.

34. Allen, Tom, *Managing the flow of technology,* Cambridge MA: MIT Press, 1977.

35. Americans are more likely than Europeans and Japanese to put every person in a separate office (versus shared space). There are strong opinions regarding the trade-offs of the quiet of private offices versus collaborative potential of shared space; see for example, DeMarco, T. and Lister, T. *Peopleware: productive projects and teams.* New York: Dorset House Publishing, 1987.

36. Rafii, F. How important is physical collocation to product development success. *Business Horizons* (January–February, 1995) 78–84.

37. Allen, T. *Ibid.*

38. Stalk, G. and Hout, T. M. *Competing against time.* New York: The Free Press, 1990.

39. Galbraith, J. R. *Designing Organizations,* San Francisco: Jossey-Bass Publishers, 1995.

40. Based on the IBM study of its Santa Teresa R&D facility, 50% of the time is spent working with one other person, 20% working with at least two other people, and only 30% working alone. See p. 62 of DeMarco, T. and Lister, T. *Peopleware: productive projects and teams.* New York: Dorset House Publishing, 1987.

41. Perry, D. E., Staudenmayer, N. A., and Votta, L. G. People, organizations and process improvement. *IEEE Software* (July 1994) 36–45.

42. Thompson, J. D. in *Organizations in action,* New York, NY: McGraw-Hill, 1967. (p. 55) also proposed general coordination mechanisms for each of the three forms of interdependence. Pooled interdependence can be coordinated by standardization, sequential interdependence can be coordinated by plan, and reciprocal interdependence needs to be coordinated by mutual adjustment.

43. Bartlett, C. A. and Ghoshal, S. *Managing across borders: the transnational solution.* Cambridge, MA: Harvard Business School Press, 1989.

44. The exhibit is based on Martinez, J. I. and Jarillo, J. C. The evolution of research on coordination mechanisms in multinational corporations. *Journal of International Business Studies* (Fall 1989) 489–514.

45. Perry, D. E., Staudenmayer, N. A., and Votta, L. G. People, Organizations and process improvement. *IEEE Software* (July 1994) 36–45.

46. Trevino, L. K., Daft, R. H., and Lengel, R. L. Media symbolism, media richness, and media choice in organizations. *Communication Research* (October, 1987) 14(5).

47. The media richness continuum was derived from the work of Daft, R. L. and Lengel, R. H. Information richness: a new approach to managerial behavior and organization design. In B. Staw and L. L. Cummings, (ed), *Research in organizational behavior* (vol 6), Greenwich, CT: JAI Press, 1984.

48. Apte, Uday M., Mason, Richard O. Global disaggregation of information-intensive services. *Management Science* (July 1995) v41n7, 1250–1262.

49. Leonard, D. A. Brands, P., Edmondson, A. Fenwick, J. Virtual teams: using communication technology to manage geographically dispersed development groups, in *Sense and Respond: Capturing Value in the Network Era*. S. P. Bradley and R. L. Nolan (eds.), Cambridge, MA: Harvard Business School Press, 1997.

50. The exhibit is from Hossan, G., Stoddard, D., Nolan, R., and Kao, J. Verifone, The transaction automation Company, Case 195–008. Cambridge, MA: Harvard Business School, 1994. Used with permission Harvard Business School Press.

51. Chidambaram, L., Lim, L. H., and Chan, H. C. The media coexistence approach: organizational and individual determinants of media choice in Singapore. *Proceedings of the Hawaii International Conference on Systems Sciences*, (January 1998).

52. Phillips, N. *Managing International Teams*. Bur Ridge, IL: Irwin Professional Publishing, 1994.

53. O'Hara-Devereaux, Mary and Johansen, Robert. *Globalwork: Bridging Distance, Culture and Time*. San Francisco, CA: Jossey-Bass, 1994.

54. Useful definitions of groups can be found in Hackman, J. R. *Groups that work and those that don't*. San Francisco, CA: Jossey-Bass, 1990.

55. Evaristo, R. and van Fenema. P. C. A typology of project management: emergence and evolution of new forms, *Rotterdam School of Business Management Report* (November, 1997) No 49(13).

56. Advantages and disadvantages of diverse teams is based on Adler, N. J. *International Dimensions of Organizational Behavior,* Southwestern College Publishing, 1997. An academic treatment of this question is in Jackson, S. E. May, K. E., and Whitney, K. Understanding the dynamics of diversity in decision-making teams, in Guzzo, R. A.., Salas, E., and Associates, *Team effectiveness and decision-making in organizations*. San Francisco, CA: Jossey-Bass, 1995. Their survey of various studies (a meta-analysis) suggests more positive results for diverse teams, but the overall findings are not conclusive.

57. Belbin, R. M, *Management teams: why they succeed or fail*. New York, NY: John Wiley & Sons, 1976

58. Phillips, N. *Managing International Teams*. Bur Ridge, IL: Irwin Professional Publishing, 1994.

59. DeMarco, T. and Lister, T. *Peopleware: productive projects and teams*. New York: Dorset House Publishing, 1987.

60. Adler, N. J. *International Dimensions of Organizational Behavior*. Cincinnati, OH: Southwestern College Publishing, 1997.

61. Handy, C. Trust and the virtual organization. *Harvard Business Review,* (1995) 73(3), 40–50.

62. The quote appears on page 234 of Diego Gambetta, *Trust: making and breaking cooperative relations*. Basil Blackwell, 1988.

63. Tuckman, B. (1965). Developmental sequence in small groups. *Psychological bulletin,* 63, 384–389

64. For a critique of the Tuckman model and other group development models, see Mc-Collom, M. Reevaluating group development: a critique of familiar models, in *Groups in Context*. Gillette, J. and McCollom, M., eds. Reading MA: Addison-Wesley, 1990.

65. Carmel, E. and Bird, B. Small is beautiful: a study of packaged software development teams. *Journal of High Technology Management Research* (Spring, 1997) 8(1), 129–148.

66. attributed to David Cutler, architect of Microsoft Windows-NT, in p. 146 of Zachary, Pascal. *Showstopper: the breakneck race to create Windows NT and the next generation at Microsoft*. New York, NY: The Free Press, 1994.

67. Schach, S.R. *Software Engineering*. Homewood, IL: Irwin, 1990.

68. Melymuka, K. With IT projects, small is beautiful. *Computerworld online news* (June 6, 1998).

69. Van Maanen, J. and Laurent, A. The flow of cultures: some notes on globalization and the multinational corporation." In Ghoshal, S. and Westney, D. E. *Organization, theory, and the multinational corporation*, New York, NY: St. Martin's Press, 1993.

70. Schneider, S. C. and Barsoux, J. *Managing Across Cultures*. London: Prentice Hall, 1997.

71. Schneider, S. C. and Barsoux, J. *Managing Across Cultures*. London: Prentice Hall, 1997.

72. The study was conducted by André Laurent and appeared in Adler, N. J. International Dimensions of Organizational Behavior, 2nd edition, Boston, MA: PWS-Kent Publishing, 1991.

73. Phillips, N. *Managing International Teams*. Bur Ridge, IL: Irwin Professional Publishing, 1994.

74. O'Hara-Devereaux, Mary and Johansen, Robert. *Globalwork: Bridging Distance, Culture and Time*. San Francisco, CA: Jossey-Bass, 1994.

75. The presentation of Hofstede and Hall is influenced by Rosenzweig, P. M. *National Culture and Management*. Teaching Note, (March 24), Boston, MA: Harvard Business School, 1994.

76. The five dimensions in Hofstede's work is based on a summary in Hofstede, G. Cultural constraints in management theories. *Academy of Management Executive* (1993) 7(1), 81–93; with some additional data from Hofstede, G. *Cultures and organizations: software of the mind*. London: McGraw Hill, 1991. The 1993 article uses some of Hofstede's own estimates where empirical data were not available.

77. Hampden-Turner, C. and Trompenaars, A. *The seven cultures of capitalism*. New York, NY: Currency Doubleday, 1993.

78. Rosenzweig, P. M. *National Culture and Management*. Teaching Note, (March 24), Boston, MA: Harvard Business School, 1994.

79. Hall, E. T. *The silent language*. New York, NY: Doubleday Books, 1959, Hall, E. T. *Beyond culture*. NY: Doubleday Books, 1976.

80. O'Hara-Devereaux, Mary and Johansen, Robert. *Globalwork: Bridging Distance, Culture and Time*. San Francisco, CA: Jossey-Bass, 1994.

81. Hampden-Turner, C. and Trompenaars, A. *The seven cultures of capitalism*. New York, NY: Currency Doubleday, 1993.

82. Shore and Venkatachalam conducted an interesting meta-study (a review of previous studies) of culture in the systems development process and applied it to the Hofstede model. Shore, B. and Venkatachalam, A. R. The role of national culture in systems analysis and design. *Journal of Global Information Management,* (Summer 1995) 3(3).

83. Constantine, L. *Constantine on Peopleware*. Englewood Cliffs, NJ: Yourdon Press. 1995.

84. De Meyer, A. & Mizushima, A. Global R&D Management, *R & D Management* (1989) vol. 19, no. 2, 135–146.

85. Couger, J. D., Adelsberger, H., Borovits, I, Zviran, M. and Motiwalla, J. Commonalties in motivating environments for programmer/analysts in Austria, Israel, Singapore, and the USA. *Information & Management* (1990) (18), 41–46.

86. Kumar, K. and Bjørn-Andersen, N. A cross-cultural comparison of IS designer values. *Communications of the ACM* (May 1990) 33(5), 528–538.

87. Foley Curley, K. Meyer, M. H. and Sorensen, E. V. A comparison of US, Japanese and Europeans software development practices and processes. *Journal of Global Information Management* (Summer 1996) 4(3), 18–26.

88. Azuma, M. and Mole, D. Software management practice and metrics in the European Community and Japan: some results of a survey. *Journal of Systems and Software* (1994) 26, 5–18.

89. Carmel, E. American hegemony in packaged software trade and the "culture of software." *The Information Society* (1997) 13(1), 125–142.

90. Hunter M. G. and Palvia, S. C. Information Systems Development: a conceptual model and comparison of methods used in Singapore, USA, and Europe. *Journal of Global Information Management* (Summer 1996) 4(3), 5–17.

91. Shore, B and Venkatachalam, A. R. The role of national culture in systems analysis and design. *Journal of Global Information Management* (Summer 1995) 3(3).

92. Nelson, R. R., Weiss, I. R., Yamazaki, K. Information Resources Management within Multinational corporations. *International Information Systems* (October 1992) 1(4), 56–83.

93. Fernandes, T. *Global Interface design: a guide to designing international user interfaces*. Boston, MA: Academic Press, 1995.

94. The GDSD study—for Globally Dispersed Software Development—is the basis for much data and many cases throughout the book. It is a study which I led in recent years. The study's research methodology is covered in Appendix A. Note that aliases are used for most of the organizations in the study and some identifying details are slightly disguised.

95. An interesting study of social usage of continuous video took place between two Xerox PARC research locations and was summarized in Bly, S. A., Harrison, S. R., and Irwin, S. Media spaces: bringing people together in a video, audio and computing environment. *Communications of the ACM* (January, 1993), 28–46.

96. Some commercial products heading in the direction of a team wall are SmartBoard from Smartech, TeamBoard from TeamBoard, and Softboard from Microfield.

97. Failla, A. Technologies for coordination in a software factory, in *Groupware and Teamwork* edited by C.U. Ciborra. New York, NY: John Wiley & Sons, 1996.

98. As Dorothy Leonard and colleagues point out, it is unfortunate that social scientists have studied mostly *single* collaborative technologies (e.g., e-mail or meetingware) and have yet to do systematic research of groups that use a whole portfolio of multiple technologies (ranging from video-conferencing to discussion lists to specialized project notification).

99. Perry, D. E., Staudenmayer, N. A., and Votta, L. G. People, Organizations and process improvement. *IEEE Software* (July 1994) 36–45.

100. The list of collaborative technology processes is based in part on Nunamaker, J. F., Briggs, B. O., Mittleman, D. D., Vogel, D. R. and Balthazard, P. A. 1997. Lessons from a dozen years of groups support systems research. *Journal of Management Information Systems*, (Winter 96–97) 13(3), 163–206.

101. One pilot effort of a team knowledge center took place at Andersen Consulting's CASCADE Virtual Project Site project, which began in 1995. Andersen tested technologies such as electronic yellow pages, electronic discussions, and rich documents with voice annotation. The pilot project was conducted with an actual Andersen systems development project that had two sites: in Chicago at Andersen's headquarters and in France.

102. 360° is also used for a performance review process whereby employees evaluate those under them, beside them, and above them. There is no relationship between this Human Resource Management technique and the one discussed in this book.

103. Zack, M. H. and Serino, M. Supporting teams with collaborative technology. Cambridge MA: The Lotus Institute, 1996. Available from www2.lotus.com.

104. The Microsoft Lexicon can be found on http://cinepad.com/mslex.htm.

105. Grantham, C. Carr, J., and Coleman, D. Groupware in hardware and software development environments, in Coleman, David, ed., *Groupware: collaborative strategies for corporate LANs and Intranets.* Upper Saddle River, NJ: Prentice Hall, 1997.

106. Perey, C. Desktop videoconferencing, in Coleman, David, ed., *Groupware: collaborative strategies for corporate LANs and Intranets.* Upper Saddle River, NJ: Prentice Hall, 1997.

107. In Leonard and colleagues' study of dispersed systems development, those teams that used *more* video- or teleconferencing had lower perceptions of their project success. The likely explanation for this paradox is that the projects that were in trouble made use of more conferencing technology to try to overcome problems.

108. Melymuka, K. What you heard is not what I said. *Computerworld* (July 13, 1998), 63.

109. In order to make collaborative technology culturally neutral (or culturally sensitive) Ishii, who is now with the Institute for the Study of Languages and Cultures of Asia and Africa at the Tokyo University of Foreign Studies, is working on culturally neutral groupware tools.

110. Discussion lists are frequently used for brainstorming, but brainstorming can be threatening to hierarchical cultures like the Chinese (O'Hara-Devereaux & Johansen, 1994).

111. Ishii Hiroshi. Cross-cultural communication and CSCW. *Global networks: Computers and international communication.* L. M. Harasim, ed. 143–151 (Chap. 8); Cambridge, MA: MIT Press, 1993.

112. *Collaborative Technology to support Software Engineering* is also known as concurrent software engineering.

113. Failla, A. Technologies for coordination in a software factory. *In Groupware and Teamwork.* C. U. Ciborra, ed. New York, NY: John Wiley, 1996.

114. Hawryskiewycz, I., Gorton, I., and Fung, L. Putting software development on the information highway. *American Programmer* (August 1995) 8–14. Gorton. I., Hawryszkiewycz, I. T. and Ragoonaden, K. Collaborative tools and processes to support software engineering shift work. *British Telecom Journal* (July 1997) 15(3), 189–198. Gorton, I., Hawryszkiewycz, I.T., Ragoonaden, K., Chung, C., Lu, S., Randhawa, G. Groupware Support Tools for Collaborative Software Engineering. *Proceedings of the 30th Hawaii International Conference on System Sciences* (1997). Hawryskiewycz, I., Gorton, I. Platforms for cooperative development. *American Programmer* (August 1996).

115. Grinter, R. E. Doing Software Development: Occasions for Automation and Formalisation, *European Conference on Computer Supported Cooperative Work.* Lancaster, UK: September, 1997, 7–11.

116. The list is partially based on the work of Hawryskiewycz and colleagues. *Ibid.*

117. Grinter, R. E. Doing Software Development: Occasions for Automation and Formalisation, *European Conference on Computer Supported Cooperative Work.* Lancaster, UK: September, 1997, 7–11.

118. Dewan, P and Riedl, J. Toward computer supported concurrent software engineering. *Computer* (January 1993).

119. Rani, Geetha. Managing Dispersed Development teams. *Proceedings of Software Development-East.* Available from San Francisco, CA: Miller Freeman Publications, 1994; Harding, Elizabeth. U.S. Companies Finding that CASE Travels Well in India. *Software Magazine* (Nov. 1991), 24–29.

120. Grantham, C., Carr, J., and Coleman, D. Groupware in hardware and software development environments, in Coleman, David, ed., *Groupware: collaborative strategies for corporate LANs and Intranets.* Upper Saddle River, NJ: Prentice Hall, 1997.

121. Pride in homegrown tools was also observed in Failla's study of IBM's software research center. Failla, A. Technologies for coordination in a software factory, in *Groupware and Teamwork.* C.U. Ciborra, ed. New York, NY: John Wiley & Sons, 1996.

122. Rothman, J. Managing global teams. *Software Development* (August 1998), 36–40.

123. O'Hara-Devereaux, Mary and Johansen, Robert. *Globalwork: Bridging Distance, Culture and Time.* San Francisco, CA: Jossey-Bass, 1994.

124. The study was conducted by US-based Pitney-Bowes and appeared in Deck, S. Too many messages can mean a failure to communicate. *Computerworld* (May 26, 1998) daily news flash (on the web).

125. Carmel, E. and Becker, S. A process model for packaged software development. *IEEE Transactions on Engineering Management.* (February, 1995) 41(5), 50–61.

126. Gibbs, W. W. Software's chronic crisis. *Scientific American* (September 1994) 271: 85–95.

127. Heroics are discussed in: Bach, James, "The challenge of 'good enough' software." *American Programmer* (October, 1995); and by Yourdon, E., *The rise and resurrection of the American programmer.* Upper Saddle River, NJ: Yourdon Press, 1996.

128. The Dynamic Systems Development Method can be found at www.dsdm.org.

129. Rani, Geetha. Managing Dispersed Development teams. *Proceedings of Software Development-East.* San Francisco, CA: Miller Freeman Publications, 1994.

130. Dedene, Guido and De Vreese, Jean-Pierre. Realities of Off-Shore Reengineering. *IEEE Software* (Jan. 1995) 35–45.

131. Rothman, J. Managing global teams. *Software Development* (August 1998) 36–40.

132. Not surprisingly in a study conducted by Leonard and colleagues in the large US-based consulting firm AMS, the virtual teams did have lower interdependence than did co-located teams. Leonard, D. A. Brands, P., Edmondson, A. Fenwick, J. Virtual teams: using communication technology to manage geographically dispersed development groups, in *Sense and Respond: Capturing Value in the Network Era,* S. P. Bradley and R. L. Nolan, ed. Cambridge, MA: Harvard Business School Press, 1997.

133. Constantine, L. *Constantine on Peopleware.* Englewood Cliffs, NJ: Yourdon Press. 1995.

134. Bass, Len, Clements P., and Kazman, R. *Software Architecture in Practice.* Reading, MA: Addison-Wesley, 1997.

135. This is partially based on a study of Meadows, who refers to phase based allocation as time allocation. Meadows, C. J. Globalizing software development. *Journal of Global Information Management* (1996) 4(1), 5–15. Other commonly used terms are "horizontal" versus "vertical" allocation.

136. Apte, Uday M. and Mason, Richard O. Global disaggregation of information-intensive services. *Management Science* (July 1995) 41(7), 1250–1262.

137. Rothman, J. Managing global teams. *Software Development* (August 1998) 36–40.

138. Larger companies typically have a marketing liaison working with the development team during the entire development cycle. Often titled "program manager," the liaison usually resides in the headquarters location close to other marketing functions.

139. Earley, Christopher. East meets West meets Mideast: Further explorations of collectivistic and individualistic work groups. *Academy of Management Journal* (April, 1993) 36(2), 319–348.

140. The team performance model has seven stages: Orientation; Trust Building; Goal/Role Clarification; Commitment; Implementation; High Performance; Renewal. It was developed by Drexler/Sibbet and it appears in O'Hara-Devereaux, Mary and Johansen, Robert. *Globalwork: Bridging Distance, Culture and Time*. San Francisco, CA: Jossey-Bass, 1994.

141. Meyerson, D., Weick, K. E., & Kramer, R. M. Swift trust and temporary groups, in R. M. Kramer and T. R. Tyler (ed.), *Trust in organizations: Frontiers of theory and research*. 166–195. Thousand Oaks, CA: Sage Publications, 1996.

142. Jarvenpaa, Sirkka L., and Leidner, Dorothy E. Communication and Trust in Global Virtual Teams. *Journal of Computer-Mediated Communication* (June, 1998), Vol 3, 4.

143. De Meyer, A. Tech talk: how managers are stimulating global R&D communication. *Sloan Management Review* (Spring 1991).

144. Adler, N. J. *International Dimensions of Organizational Behavior*. Cincinatti, Ohio: Southwestern College Publishing, 1997.

145. Leonard, D. A. Brands, P., Edmondson, A. Fenwick, J. Virtual teams: using communication technology to manage geographically dispersed development groups, in *Sense and Respond: Capturing Value in the Network Era*. S. P. Bradley and R.L. Nolan, eds. Cambridge, MA: Harvard Business School Press, 1997.

146. Based in part on De Meyer, A. Tech talk: how managers are stimulating global R&D communication. *Sloan Management Review* (Spring 1991).

147. DeMarco, T. and Lister, T. *Peopleware: productive projects and teams*. New York, NY: Dorset House Publishing, 1987.

148. Galbraith, J. R. *Designing Organizations*. San Francisco, CA: Jossey-Bass Publishers, 1995.

149. O'Hara-Devereaux, Mary and Johansen, Robert. *Globalwork: Bridging Distance, Culture and Time*. San Francisco, CA: Jossey-Bass, 1994.

150. Stern, Aimee. "Managing by Team is Not Always as Easy as it Looks." *New York Times* (July 18, 1993).

151. An alternative, more appropriate for larger organizations, is derived from IBM-Rome: A team "doctor" formally charged with improving team work takes part in meetings to help facilitate. Failal, A. Technologies for coordination in a software factory, in *Groupware and Teamwork*. C. U. Ciborra, ed. New York, NY: John Wiley & Sons, 1996

152. The compilation of communication protocols in Exhibit 13–5 is based in part on O'Hara-Devereaux, Mary and Johansen, Robert. *Globalwork: Bridging Distance, Culture and Time*. San Francisco, CA: Jossey-Bass, 1994.

153. The compilation of e-mail protocols in Exhibit 13–4 is based partially on Grenier, Ray and Metes, George. *Going Virtual: Moving your organization into the 21st century*. Upper Saddle River, NJ: Prentice Hall, 1995. O'Hara-Devereaux, Mary and Johansen, Robert. *Globalwork: Bridging Distance, Culture and Time*. San Francisco, CA: Jossey-Bass, 1994., Hohmann, L. *Journey of the software professional: a sociology of software development*. Upper Saddle River, NJ: Prentice Hall, 1997.

154. Ishii, Hiroshi. "Cross-Cultural Communication and CSCW," in L. M. Harasim, ed. *Global networks: Computers and international communication.* Cambridge, MA: MIT Press, 1993. Ch. 8, 143–151.

155. Adler, N. J. International Dimension of Organizational Behavior. Cincinnati, OH: Southwestern College Publishing, 1997.

156. Phillips, N. *Managing International Teams.* Bur Ridge, IL: Irwin Professional Publishing, 1994.

157. Leonard, D. A., Brands, P., Edmondson, A. Fenwick, J. Virtual teams: using communication technology to manage geographically dispersed development groups, in *Sense and Respond: Capturing Value in the Network Era,* S. P. Bradley and R. L. Nolan, eds. Cambridge, MA: Harvard Business School Press, 1997.

158. Zeira, Y. and Banai, M. Present and desired methods of selecting expatriate managers for international assignments. *Personnel review,* 13(3), 1984.

159. Tung, R. L. Expatriate assignments: enhancing success and minimizing failure. *Executive* (1987) 1(2), 117–126.

160. A study of distributed teams found that in those teams that were successful, the team members actually enjoyed working with their peers. Hofner Saphiere, D. M. Productive behaviors of global business teams, in *International Journal of Intercultural relations* (1996) 20(2).

161. Phillips, N. *Managing International Teams.* Bur Ridge, IL: Irwin Professional Publishing, 1994.

162. Carmel and Bird, *Ibid.*

163. A number of dispersed brainstorming tools have appeared, such as that of Facilitate.com.

164. Hohmann, L. *Journey of the software professional: a sociology of software development.* Upper Saddle River NJ: Prentice Hall, 1997.

165. Constantine, L. *Constantine on Peopleware.* Englewood Cliffs, NJ: Yourdon Press, 1995.

166. In a study of Xerox software development teams dispersed in two US locations, the technical communicator who made several usability suggestions from the remote site was ignored. Pieratti, D. D. How the process and organization can help or hinder adding value. *Technical Communication* (First Quarter, 1995) 61–68.

167. O'Hara-Devereaux, Mary and Johansen, Robert. *Globalwork: Bridging Distance, Culture and Time.* San Francisco, CA: Jossey-Bass, 1994.

168. Kumar, K. and Willcocks, L. P. Offshore Outsourcing. A country too far. *Management report,* number 298 Erasmus University, Rotterdam, Netherlands, November 1996.

169. At AMS the higher performing dispersed teams were those that valued learning—team members sought ways to improve group processes, discuss errors, and communicate with other groups in the company. Leonard, D. A., Brands, P., Edmondson, A. Fenwick, J. Virtual teams: using communication technology to manage geographically dispersed development groups, in *Sense and Respond: Capturing Value in the Network Era,* S. P. Bradley and R. L. Nolan, eds. Cambridge, MA: Harvard Business School Press, 1997.

170. Schneider, S. C. and Barsoux, J. *Managing Across Cultures.* London: Prentice Hall, 1997.

171. For a list of cultural training videos see Odenwald, S. B. *Global solutions for teams: moving from collision to collaboration.* Chicago, IL: Irwin Professional Publishing, 1996.

172. Curtis, B., Hefley, W. E., Miller, S. People Capability Maturity Model. *Software Engineering Institute,* MM-02, September, 1995. Available at www.sei.cmu.edu.

173. MSI, Management Strategies, Inc. *Tools for distributed teams.* White paper available from company web site at www.mgtstrat.com.

174. The structure is due in part to Zahisner's concept of team of teams in Zahniser, R. A. Building software in groups. *American Programmer* (July/August 1990) 50–56.

175. Schneider, S. C. and Barsoux, J. Managing Across Cultures. London: Prentice Hall, 1997.

176. At General Electric's medical systems division, two small teams were tasked with developing embedded software for an new ultrasound device. One was in Japan and the other in the United States and each reported to separate managers at each unit. The result: duplicate functionality. Stern, Aimee. "Managing by Team is Not Always as Easy as it Looks." *New York Times* (July 18, 1993).

177. The Eastern approach to team consensus building serves to attain "wa," or harmony in all human interactions.

178. The commitment model is based on Zahniser's framework of "breakaway projects," which is largely based on Digital's project structure encompassing 28 teams in ten nations. Zahniser, R. Breakthrough Project Management, *American Programmer* (June 1994) 13–17.

179. *Program manager* is a most unfortunate title that has stuck all over the industry due to its use at Microsoft. The Microsoft program manager is responsible for coordinating product development with marketing, documentation, testing, and product support. Other roles developed and refined at Microsoft and now commonly emulated all over: a project lead, who is acts in a project manager capacity but typically also writes code. A technical lead is the project's technical expert who is also responsible for all tech documentation.

180. Fisher, R. and W. Ury. *Getting to Yes: Negotiating Agreement Without Giving in,* 2nd ed., New York, NY: Penguin Books, 1991.

181. Odenwald posits a kind of cultural commando team that is ready to deal with cultural interventions for mediation and conflict resolution. She calls these commandos—a Cultural Process Team (CPT). The CPT has responsibility for assisting organizational teams at all levels. It plays a consultative role in a variety of functions: feedback when setting up the teams (such as selecting members and performing cultural assessments), conflict resolution, and operational support such as coaching and translation services. The CPT needs to have a member from each of the principal cultural groups. Odenwald, S. B. *Global solutions for teams: moving from collision to collaboration.* Chicago, IL: Irwin Professional Publishing, 1996.

182. Humphrey, W. S. Managing technical people: innovation, teamwork and the software process. Reading, MA: Addison-Wesley, 1997.

183. Humphrey, W. S. Managing technical people: innovation, teamwork and the software process., Reading, MA: Addison-Wesley, 1997.

184. Grenier Ray & George Metes. *Going Virtual: Moving your organization into the 21st century.* Upper Saddle River, NJ: Prentice Hall, 1995.

185. Some measures are from: Hawryskiewycz, I., Gorton, I., and Fung, L. Putting software development on the information highway. *American Programmer* (August 1995) 8–14; and from Perry, D. E., Staudenmayer, N. A., and Votta, L. G. People, Organizations and process improvement. *IEEE Software* (July 1994) 36–45.

186. Faila, A. Technologies for coordination in a software factory, in *Groupware and Teamwork.* C. U. Ciborra, ed. New York, NY: John Wiley & Sons, 1996.

187. Schneider, S. C. and Barsoux, J. *Managing Across Cultures*. London: Prentice Hall, 1997.

188. Simon, S. J. and Middleton, K. L. Asia's pending labor crunch: an analysis of human resources management best practices in IS departments. *Journal of Global Information Technology Management* (1998) 1(3), 9–26.

189. Bartlett, C. A. and Ghoshal, S. *Managing across borders: the transnational solution*. Cambridge: MA: Harvard Business School Press, 1989.

190. Schneider, S. C. and Barsoux, J. *Managing Across Cultures*. London: Prentice Hall, 1997.

191. Phillips, N. *Managing International Teams*. Bur Ridge, IL: Irwin Professional Publishing, 1994.

192. Jarvenpaa, S. and Tractinsky, N. Information Systems design decisions in a global versus domestic context. *Management Information Systems Quarterly* (December, 1995) 19(4): 507–534.

193. Leonard, D. A., Brands, P., Edmondson, A., Fenwick, J. Virtual teams: using communication technology to manage geographically dispersed development groups, in *Sense and Respond: Capturing Value in the Network Era*. S. P. Bradley and R. L. Nolan, eds. Cambridge, MA: Harvard Business School Press, 1997; and Odenwald, S. B. *Global solutions for teams: moving from collision to collaboration*. Chicago, IL: Irwin Professional Publishing, 1996.

194. Bartlett and Ghoshal have added enormously to understanding how global organizations are structured and transform themselves. However, they chose confusing terms for the four archetypes—multinational, global, international and transnational. Bartlett, C. A. and S. Ghoshal, *Managing across borders: the transnational solution*. Cambridge, MA.: Harvard Business School Press, 1989.

195. Globalization drivers are based in part on Ives, B. and S. Jarvenpaa, "Applications of Global Information Technology: Key Issues in management." *MIS Quarterly* (March 1991), 32–49.

196. Based in part on Karimi, J. and B. R. Konsynski, "Globalization and information management strategies." *Journal of MIS* (Spring 1991) 7(4), 7–26.

197. Roche, E., *Managing Information Technology in Multinational Corporations*. New York, NY: MacMillan, 1992.

198. Ives, B. and S. Jarvenpaa, "Applications of Global Information Technology: Key Issues in management." *MIS Quarterly* (March 1991) 32–49.

199. On standardization, also see Vitalari, N. and J. C. Wetherbe, "Emerging best practices in global systems development," in S. Palvia, P. Palvia and E. Roche (eds.), *Global Information Technology and Systems Management: key issues and trends*. Nashua, NH: Ivy League Publishing, 1996.

200. Laudon and Laudon use co-optation. Laudon, K. C. and J. P. Laudon, *Management Information Systems*. 4th ed., Upper Saddle River, NJ: Prentice Hall, 1996.

201. For more on outsourcing, see Lacity, Mary and R. Hirschheim, "The Information Systems Outsourcing Bandwagon," *Sloan Management Review* (Fall 1993) 73–86; and see Patane, Joseph and Jaak Jurison, "Is Global Outsourcing Diminishing the Prospects for American Programmers?" *Journal of Systems Management* (June 1994) (45:6), 2–11.

202. Apte, Uday M. and Richard O. Mason, "Global disaggregation of information-intensive services." *Management Science* (July 1995) 41(7), 1250–1262.

203. Apte. *Ibid.*

204. This item is partially based on a list compiled by James Harvey, program director at DHL's international global coordination center in Brussels, which appeared in Dalton, G., "Ready To Go Global?" *Information Week* (February 9, 1998).

205. The PSR methodology is based in part on Laudon, K. C. and Laudon, J. P.: Management Information Systems, 4th ed. (1996), as well as input from Bill DeLone of American University.

206. Multiple source assessment benefited from discussions with the Concours Group.

207. The team matrix and its associated discussion benefited from Vitalari, N. and J. C. Wetherbe, "Emerging best practices in global systems development," in S. Palvia, P. Palvia and E. Roche (eds.), *Global Information Technology and Systems Management: key issues and trends.* Nashua, NH: Ivy League Publishing, 1996.

208. Young, Derby. Team heat. *CIO Magazine* (September 1, 1998) 43–51.

209. The Seagate case study is from Palvia, S. and K. Lee, "Developing and implementing global information systems: lessons from Seagate technology," in Palvia, S., Palvia, P., and Roche, E. (eds.), *Global Information Technology and Systems Management: key issues and trends.* Nashua, NH: Ivy League Publishing, 1996.

210. Printed with permission. From Kumar, K. and L. P. Willcocks, "Offshore Outsourcing. A country too far," *Management report,* no. 298, Erasmus University, Rotterdam, Netherlands, November 1996.

211. Most of Appendix B is based on Carmel, E. and S. Sawyer, "Packaged software development teams: what makes them different?" *Information Technology & People* (1998) 11(1).

REFERENCES

Adler, N. J. *International Dimensions of Organizational Behavior.* Cincinnati, OH: Southwestern College Publishing, 1997.

Allen, Tom. *Managing the flow of technology.* Cambridge, MA: MIT Press, 1977.

Apte, Uday M. and Richard O. Mason, "Global disaggregation of information-intensive services," *Management Science* (July 1995) 41(7), 1250–1262.

Azuma, M. and D. Mole. "Software management practice and metrics in the European Community and Japan: some results of a survey," *Journal of Systems and Software* (1994) 26, 5–18.

Bach, James. "The challenge of 'good enough' software." *American Programmer* (October, 1995).

Barr, A. and S. Tessler. "The globalization of software R&D: the search for talent," position paper presented to the Council on Foreign Relations, December 12, 1996; available from the *Stanford Computer Industry Project.* Stanford, CA: Stanford University.

Bartlett, C. A. and S. Ghoshal. *Managing across borders: the transnational solution.* Cambridge, MA: Harvard Business School Press, 1989.

Bass, Len, Paul Clements and Rick Kazman. *Software Architecture in Practice.* Boston, MA: Addison-Wesley, 1997.

Belbin, R. M. *Management teams: why they succeed or fail.* New York, NY: John Wiley & Sons, 1976.

Bly, S. A., S. R. Harrison and S. Irwin, "Media spaces: bringing people together in a video, audio and computing environment." *Communications of the ACM* (January 1993) 28–46.

Business Software Alliance. *World Trends.* Washington, DC: BSA., 1997.

Business Week, "Forget the huddled masses: send nerds." *Business Week* (July 21, 1997) 110–116.

Carmel, E., "American hegemony in packaged software trade and the 'culture of software'." *The Information Society* (1997) 13(1), 125–142.

Carmel, E. and S. Becker, "A process model for packaged software development." *IEEE Transactions on Engineering Management* (February 1995) 41(5), 50–61.

Carmel, E. and B. Bird, "Small is beautiful: a study of packaged software development teams." *Journal of High Technology Management Research* (Spring 1997) 8(1), 129–148.

Carmel, E. and S. Sawyer, "Packaged software development teams: what makes them different?" *Information Technology & People* (1998) 11(1).

Chidambaram, L., L. H. Lim and H. C. Chan, "The media coexistence approach: organizational and individual determinants of media choice in Singapore." *Proceedings of the Hawaii International Conference on Systems Sciences* (January 1998).

Chiesa, V., "Strategies for global R&D." *Research Technology Management* (September–October, 1996).

Constantine, L. *Constantine on Peopleware*. Englewood Cliffs, NJ: Yourdon Press, 1995.

Couger, J. D., H. Adelsberger, I. Borovits, M. Zviran and J. Motiwalla, "Commonalties in motivating environments for programmer/analysts in Austria, Israel, Singapore, and the USA." *Information & Management* (1990) (18), 41–46.

Curtis, B., W. E. Hefley and S. Miller, "People Capability Maturity Model." *Software Engineering Institute* (September 1995) MM-02, available at www.sei.cmu.edu.

Cusumano, M. A. and R. W. Selby. *Microsoft Secrets.* New York, NY: The Free Press, 1995.

Cutkosky, M. R., J. M. Tennebaum and J. Glicksman. "Madefast: collaborative engineering over the internet." *Communications of the ACM* (September 1996) 39(9), 78–88.

Daft, R. L. and R. H. Lengel. "Information richness: a new approach to managerial behavior and organization design," in B. Staw and L.L. Cummings (eds.). *Research in organizational behavior*, vol. 6, Greenwich, CT: JAI Press, 1984.

Dalton, G. "Ready To Go Global?" *Information Week* (February 9, 1998).

De Meyer, A. and A. Mizushima. "Global R&D Management." *R & D Management* (1989) vol. 19, no. 2, 135–146.

De Meyer, A. "Tech talk: how managers are stimulating global R&D communication." *Sloan Management Review* (Spring 1991).

Dedene, Guido and Jean-Pierre De Vreese. "Realities of Off-Shore Reengineering." *IEEE Software* (January 1995) 35–45.

DeMarco, T. and T. Lister. *Peopleware: productive projects and teams.* New York, NY: Dorset House Publishing, 1987.

Dewan, P and J. Riedl. "Toward computer supported concurrent software engineering." *Computer* (January 1993).

DuBois, F. and E. Carmel. "Globalized Software Development: Roots in globalized R&D and global manufacturing." *Proceedings of Information Resources Management Association.* International Conference (May 1997) 54–60.

Earley, Christopher. "East meets West meets Mideast: Further explorations of collectivistic and individualistic work groups." *Academy of Management Journal* (April 1993) 36(2), 319–348.

Evaristo, R. and P. C. von Fenema. "A typology of project management: emergence and evolution of new forms." *Rotterdam School of Business Management Report* (November 1997) no. 49(13).

Failla, A. "Technologies for coordination in a software factory," in C. U. Ciborra, ed., *Groupware and Teamwork*. New York, NY: John Wiley & Sons, 1996.

Fernandes, T. *Global Interface design: a guide to designing international user interfaces*. Boston: Academic Press, 1995.

Fisher, R. and W. Ury. *Getting to Yes: Negotiating Agreement Without Giving in*, 2nd ed, New York, NY: Penguin Books, 1991.

Foley Curley, K., M. H. Meyer and E. V. Sorensen. "A comparison of US, Japanese and European software development practices and processes." *Journal of Global Information Management* (Summer 1996) 4(3), 18–26.

Frye, C. "The Software 500." *Software Magazine* (June 1998).

Galbraith, J. R. *Designing Organizations*. San Francisco, CA: Jossey-Bass Publishers, 1995.

Gambetta, Diego. *Trust: making and breaking cooperative relations*. New York, NY: Basil Blackwell. 1988.

Gibbs, W. W. "Software's chronic crisis." *Scientific American* (September 1994) (271), 85–95.

Gorton. I., I. T. Hawryszkiewycz and K. Ragoonaden. "Collaborative tools and processes to support software engineering shift work." *British Telecom Journal* (July 1997) 15(3), 189–198.

Gorton, I., I. T. Hawryszkiewycz, K. Ragoonaden, C. Chung, S. Lu and G. Randhawa. "Groupware Support Tools for Collaborative Software Engineering." *Proceedings of the 30th Hawaii International Conference on System Sciences* (1997).

Grantham, C., J. Carr and D. Coleman. "Groupware in hardware and software development environments," in David Coleman, ed. *Groupware: collaborative strategies for corporate LANs and Intranets*. Upper Saddle River, NJ: Prentice Hall, 1997.

Grenier, Ray and George Metes. *Going Virtual: Moving your organization into the 21st century*. Upper Saddle River, NJ: Prentice Hall, 1995.

Grinter, R. E. "Doing Software Development: Occasions for Automation and Formalisation." *European Conference on Computer Supported Cooperative Work*. Lancaster, United Kingdom (September 1997) 7–11.

Hackman, J. R. *Groups that work and those that don't*. San Francisco, CA: Jossey-Bass, 1990.

Hall, E. T. *Beyond culture*. New York, NY: Doubleday Books, 1976.

Hall, E. T. *The silent language*. New York, NY: Doubleday Books, 1959.

Hampden-Turner, C. and A. Trompenaars. *The seven cultures of capitalism*. New York, NY: Currency Doubleday, 1993.

Handy, C. "Trust and the virtual organization." *Harvard Business Review* (1995) 73 (3), 40–50.

Harding, Elizabeth. "U.S. Companies Finding that CASE Travels Well in India." *Software Magazine* (November 1991) 24–29.

Hawryskiewycz, I., I. Gorton and L. Fung. "Putting software development on the information highway." *American Programmer* (August 1995) 8–14.

Hawryskiewycz, I. and I. Gorton. "Platforms for cooperative development." *American Programmer* (August 1996).

Heeks, Richard. *India's Software Industry: State Policy, Liberalisation, and Industrial Development.* Thousand Oaks, CA: Sage Publications, 1996.

Hofner Saphiere, D. M. "Productive behaviors of global business teams." *International Journal of Intercultural Relations* (1996) 20(2).

Hofstede, G. *Cultures and organizations: software of the mind.* London: McGraw Hill, 1991.

Hofstede, G. "Cultural constraints in management theories." *Academy of Management Executive* (1993) 7(1), 81–93.

Hohmann, L. *Journey of the software professional: a sociology of software development.* Upper Saddle River, NJ: Prentice Hall, 1997.

Hopkins, M. "The antihero's guide to the new economy." *Inc.* (January 1998) 36–38.

Humphrey, W. S. *Managing technical people: innovation, teamwork and the software process.* Reading, MA: Addison-Wesley, 1997.

Hunter M. G. and S. C. Palvia. "Information Systems Development: a conceptual model and comparison of methods used in Singapore, USA, and Europe." *Journal of Global Information Management* (Summer 1996) 4(3), 5–17.

Ishii, Hiroshi. "Cross-Cultural Communication and CSCW" (Chapter 8) in L.M. Harasim, ed. *Global networks: Computers and international communication.* Cambridge, MA: MIT Press, 1993, 143–151.

ITAA. *Help Wanted 2: A Call for Collaborative Action for the New Millenium.* Available from the Information Technology Association of America, www.itaa.org, January, 1998.

Ives, B. and S. Jarvenpaa. "Applications of Global Information Technology: Key Issues in management." *MIS Quarterly* (March 1991) 32–49.

Jackson, S. E., K. E. May and K. Whitney. "Understanding the dynamics of diversity in decision-making teams," in R. A. Guzzo, E. Salas and I. Goldstein. *Team effectiveness and decision making in organization.* San Francisco, CA: Jossey Bass, 1995.

Jarvenpaa, S., L. and Dorothy E. Leidner. "Communication and Trust in Global Virtual Teams." *Journal of Computer-Mediated Communication* (June 1998) vol. 3, issue 4. This is an electronic journal available at http://jcmc.huji.ac.il/.

Jarvenpaa, S. and N. Tractinsky. "Information Systems design decisions in a global versus domestic context." *Management Information Systems Quarterly.* (December 1995) 19(4), 507–534.

Jones, Capers. "Globalization of software supply and demand." *IEEE Software* (November 1994) 11(6), 17–24.

Karimi, J. and B.R. Konsynski. "Globalization and information management strategies." *Journal of MIS* (Spring 1991) 7(4), 7–26.

Keil, M. and E. Carmel. "Customer-developer links in software development." *Communications of the ACM* (1995) 38(5), 33–44.

Kumar, K. and L. P. Willcocks, "Offshore Outsourcing. A country too far," *Management report* no. 298. Erasmus University, Rotterdam, Netherlands, (November 1996).

Kumar, K. and N. Bjørn-Andersen. "A cross-cultural comparison of IS designer values." *Communications of the ACM* (May 1990) 33(5), 528–538.

Lacity, Mary and R. Hirschheim. "The Information Systems Outsourcing Bandwagon." *Sloan Management Review* (Fall 1993) 73–86.

Laudon, K. C. and J. P. Laudon. *Management Information Systems,* 4th ed., Upper Saddle River, NJ: Prentice Hall (1996).

Leebeart, D., "News From the Frontiers," in D. Leebeart, ed. *The Future of Software.* 1–28. Cambridge, MA: MIT Press, 1995.

Leonard, D. A., P. Brands, A. Edmondson and J. Fenwick. "Virtual teams: using communication technology to manage geographically dispersed development groups," in S. P. Bradley and R. L. Nolan, eds. *Sense and Respond: Capturing Value in the Network Era.* Cambridge, MA: Harvard Business School Press, 1997.

Lorenz, C. "Global webs still spun from home." *Financial Times* (August 18, 1995).

Martinez, J. I. and J. C. Jarillo. "The evolution of research on coordination mechanisms in multinational corporations." *Journal of International Business Studies* (Fall 1989) 489–514.

McCollom, M. "Reevaluating group development: a critique of familiar models," in J. Gillette and M. McCollom, eds. *Groups in Context.* Reading, MA: Addison-Wesley Publishing, 1990.

Meadows, C. J. "Globalizing software development." *Journal of Global Information Management* (1996) 4(1), 5–15.

Melymuka, K. "What you heard is not what I said." *Computerworld* (July 13, 1998) 63.

Melymuka, K. "With IT projects, small is beautiful." *Computerworld online news* (June 6, 1998).

Melymuka, K. "Conversation with Tom DeMarco." *Computerworld* (December 4, 1995) 108–117.

Meyerson, D., K. E. Weick and R. M. Kramer. "Swift trust and temporary groups," in R. M. Kramer and T. R. Tyler, eds. *Trust in organizations: Frontiers of theory and research.* 166–195. Thousand Oaks, CA: Sage Publications, 1996.

Mowery, D.C. *The International Computer Software Industry: A Comparative Study of Industry Evolution and Structure.* New York, NY: Oxford University Press, 1996.

MSI, Management Strategies, Inc. Tools for distributed teams, white paper available from company web site at www.mgtstrat.com.

Nelson, R. R., I. R. Weiss and K. Yamazaki. "Information Resources Management within Multinational corporations." *International Information Systems* (October 1992) 1(4), 56–83.

Niccolai, J. "Success not a guarantee for remote projects." *Computerworld online news* (April 30, 1998).

Nunamaker, J. F., B. O. Briggs, D. D. Mittleman, D. R. Vogel and P. A. Balthazard. "Lessons from a dozen years of groups support systems research." *Journal of Management Information Systems* (Winter 1996–1997) 13(3), 163–206.

O'Hara-Devereaux, Mary and Robert Johansen. *Globalwork: Bridging Distance, Culture and Time.* San Francisco, CA: Jossey-Bass, 1994.

Odenwald, S. B. *Global solutions for teams: moving from collision to collaboration.* Chicago, IL: Irwin Professional Publishing, 1996.

Palvia, S. and K. Lee. "Developing and implementing global information systems: lessons from Seagate technology," in S. Palvia, P. Palvia, and E. Roche, eds. *Global Information Technology and Systems Management: key issues and trends.* Nashua, NH: Ivy League Publishing, 1996.

Patane, Joseph and Jaak Jurison. "Is Global Outsourcing Diminishing the Prospects for American Programmers?" *Journal of Systems Management* (June 1994) (45:6), 2–11.

Pearson, A., K. Brockhoff and A. von Boehmer. "Decision parameters in global R&D management." *R&D Management* (July 1993) vol. 23, no. 3, 249–262.

Perey, C. "Desktop videoconferencing," in David Coleman, ed. *Groupware: collaborative strategies for corporate LANs and Intranets.* Upper Saddle River, NJ: Prentice Hall, 1997.

Perry, D. E., N. A. Staudenmayer and L. G. Votta. "People, Organizations and process improvement." *IEEE Software* (July 1994) 36–45.

Phillips, N. *Managing International Teams.* Bur Ridge, IL: Irwin Professional Publishing, 1994.

Pieratti, D. D. "How the process and organization can help or hinder adding value." *Technical Communication* (First Quarter 1995) 61–68.

Pressman, R. S. *Software Engineering,* 4th ed. New York, NY: McGraw Hill, 1996.

Rafii, Farshad. "How important is physical collocation to product development success." *Business Horizons.* (January–February 1995) 78–84.

Rani, Geetha. "Managing Dispersed Development Teams." *Proceedings of Software Development-East.* Available from San Francisco, CA: Miller Freeman Publications, 1994.

Ravichandran, Ramrathnam and Nazim Ahmed. "Offshore Systems Development." *Information and Management* (1993) 24, 33–40.

Roche, E. *Managing Information Technology in Multinational Corporations.* New York, NY: MacMillan, 1992.

Ronstadt, R. *Research and Development abroad by US multinationals.* New York, NY: Praeger Publications, 1997.

Rosenzweig, P.M. *National Culture and Management.* (Teaching note) Boston, MA: Harvard Business School, March 24, 1994.

Rothman, J. "Managing global teams." *Software Development.* (August 1998) 36–40.

Rubin, H. A. *Critical issues: the global software engineering and information technology competitiveness of the United States.* (March 1997) Report presented to the US Department of Commerce, available from Rubin Systems in Pound Ridge, New York; www.hrubin.com.

Schach, S. R. *Software Engineering.* Homewood, IL.: Irwin, 1990.

Schneider, S. C. and J. Barsoux. *Managing Across Cultures.* London: Prentice Hall, 1997.

Shore, B. and A. R. Venkatachalam. "The role of national culture in systems analysis and design." *Journal of Global Information Management* (Summer 1995) 3(3).

Simon, S. J. and K. L. Middleton. "Asia's pending labor crunch: an analysis of human resources management best practices in IS departments." *Journal of Global Information Technology Management* (1998) 1(3), 9–26.

Stalk, G. and Hout, T. M. *Competing Against Time*. New York: The Free Press, 1990.

Stern, Aimee. "Managing by Team is Not Always as Easy as it Looks." *New York Times* (July 18, 1993).

Suris, O. "Behind the wheel." *Wall Street Journal* (November 18, 1996).

Thompson, J. D. *Organizations in action*. New York, NY: McGraw Hill, 1967.

Trevino, L. K., R. H. Daft and R. L. Lengel. "Media symbolism, media richness, and media choice in organizations." *Communication Research* (October 1987) 14(5).

Tuckman, B. "Developmental sequence in small groups." *Psychological Bulletin* (1965) (63), 384–389.

Tung, R. L. "Expatriate assignments: enhancing success and minimizing failure." *Executive* (1987) 1(2), 117–126.

US global trade outlook 1995–2000. Washington DC: US Department of Commerce, 1995.

Van Maanen, J. and A. Laurent. "The flow of cultures: some notes on globalization and the multinational corporation," in S. Ghoshal and D. E. Westney, eds. *Organization, theory, and the multinational corporation*. New York, NY: St. Martin's Press, 1993.

Vitalari, N. and J. C. Wetherbe. "Emerging best practices in global systems development," in S. Palvia, P. Palvia and E. Roche, eds. *Global Information Technology and Systems Management: key issues and trends*. Nashua, NH: Ivy League Publishing, 1996.

Von Hippel, E. *The Sources of Innovation*, 2nd ed. New York, NY: Oxford University Press, 1994.

Young, Derby. "Team heat." *CIO Magazine* (September 1, 1998) 43–51.

Yourdon, E. *The rise and resurrection of the American programmer*. Upper Saddle River, NJ: Yourdon Press, 1996.

Zachary, Pascal. *Showstopper: the breakneck race to create Windows NT and the next generation at Microsoft*. New York, NY: The Free Press, 1994.

Zack, M. H. and M. Serino. *Supporting teams with collaborative technology*. Cambridge, MA: The Lotus Institute, 1996. Available from www2.lotus.com.

Zahniser, R. "Breakthrough Project Management." *American Programmer* (June 1994) 13–17.

Zahniser, R. A. "Building software in groups." *American Programmer* (July/August 1990) 50–56.

Zeira, Y. and M. Banai. "Present and desired methods of selecting expatriate managers for international assignments." *Personnel Review* (1984) 13(3).

INDEX

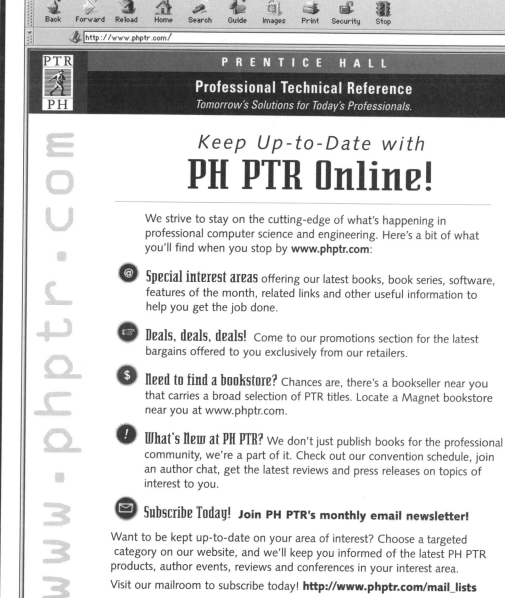